ATTACK POODLES

JAMES WOLCOTT

Attack Poodles

And Other Media Mutants:
The Looting of the News
in a Time of Terror

MIRAMAX BOOKS

TO GRAYDON CARTER

CONTENTS

AUTHOR'S NOTE   ix

The Poodle Parlor   1

Punditry for Dummies   63

Git Along, Li'l Doggies   101

The Year of Lying Dangerously   135

Fox Populi   163

Bungle in the Jungle   193

Peggy Noonan: Best in Show   231

The Miller's Tale   261

Hour of the Wolfhound   283

ACKNOWLEDGMENTS   313

OVER THE COURSE OF MY CAREER AS A WRITER, which began at the *Village Voice* in the early seventies when I was barely out of my teens, I've developed something of a reputation for being a troublemaker. Well, I should hope so! Since most of my favorite American writers and free swingers in print have been troublemakers and disturbers of domestic tranquility, from Ralph Waldo Emerson, Edgar Allan Poe, and H. L. Mencken to Edmund Wilson, Gore Vidal, Dwight Macdonald, Marvin Mudrick, Seymour Krim, Manny Farber, and Pauline Kael, I can't imagine wanting it any other way—that's where the fun is. Why become a writer if you're going to let caution be your guide and take in the world through everybody else's eyes? But I try to avoid being controversial for the sake of being controversial, taking a radical or perversely quirky stance on an issue that means little to me personally will get a guaranteed rise out of readers. You may be able to fool some readers one or twice by waving around your wooden sword like the last crusader, but the bad faith and shambolic rhetoric has a hollowing effect on your writing; it's the lousiest actors who shout the loudest. Don't fake what you don't feel is an adage I try to live and write by, because the pieces that mean the most to me will mean the most to the reader as long as the emotions behind the arguments are true.

So it's not a coincidence that the pieces I've cared about the most in recent years are the ones that have received the largest outpouring from readers. In all my years of writing I've never experienced the rush-roar of positive feedback that I did from my columns for *Vanity Fair* on how the news media folded in two before the overweening presence of President George W. Bush. Oh, a few letter writers accused me of being a whining liberal crybaby hysteric. But most were happy to have someone hop up and down in print and ratify what they'd been feeling: the sense that turning on the TV now was like tuning in to the invasion of the body snatchers. The country they had grown up in was being held captive, under anesthesia. Pod people had taken over the airwaves and the news pages. The anchors, reporters, and columnists looked like American earthlings, spoke our language, and wore our native garb, yet conducted themselves as if carrying out instructions implanted aboard an alien vessel. All the replicants asked of us was passive compliance. Our chief duty under the shadow of terrorism was to do nothing different until further instruction. Earlier generations in times of war were asked to accept sacrifice and material cutbacks. Post–September 11, we were encouraged to head to the malls with credit cards in both hands and go kung fu shopping: a good citizen was a good consumer. Although I've been a political news junkie since a teenager, hooking school to attend anti-Vietnam rallies and hearing the battle hymn of Norman Mailer's *The Armies of the Night* (the book that made me want to become a writer), I've never been a doctrinaire lefty or righty. I've written happily for both liberal and conservative publications, and I was quite content doing what I primarily do, pop-culture criticism. I wasn't looking for a cause. But I can't bear bullies, and I can't stand cowardly deceivers; and in the Bush administration and the conservative media, we have the worst of both combined. We can't wait around for them to fall of their own dead weight, because it'll be us they fall on. When I began writing about the Bush imperium, it seemed near impossible to topple, much less chop down to size. The president's popularity was so high that cable news channels ran polls asking viewers, "Is Bush unbeatable?" But the idiot wind that blows from the Grand Coulee Dam to the Capitol finally caught up with the House of Bush, and whatever happens in 2004, the political atmosphere is alive again, dramatically charged. Bush and his confederates in the media may actually face what they fear the most: a fair fight. And wouldn't that be the most fun of all?

—March 14, 2004

The Poodle Parlor

SOMETIMES YOU HAVE TO HEAR AND SEE THINGS in the flesh to get the full, insidious effect. In November 2002 I accompanied my wife, Laura Jacobs, to a Newswomen's Club dinner at the W Hotel, where she was accepting an award for her *Vanity Fair* profile of the fashion designer Mainbocher. Dinner was preceded by a cocktail reception where the decibel level quickly reached that of a submarine drill in *Run Silent, Run Deep*. Then everybody was ding-dinged into the banquet room.

The keynote speaker for the awards ceremony was Judith Miller, the Pulitzer Prize–winning national security correspondent for the *New York Times* and the author of *Germs: Biological Weapons and America's Secret War*. On television, Miller is a sprightly organism, with her Girl Scout bangs, chipmunk cheeks, and bubbly laugh, but this evening she sounded starched and valedictorian. Some valedictory. Invoking the horrors of September 11, a morning that permanently resides in the dark back room of every New Yorker's mind, she warned of possible worse inflictions to come—the mass scything threatened by biochemical terrorism. Holding up her hand and spacing her thumb and index finger apart just so, she told the audience as they buttered their dinner rolls that a vial of toxic material *this small* could wipe out everyone in the room. That put a slight damper on things, as allusions to anthrax and smallpox tend to do. Miller had had her own anthrax scare in the autumn of 2001, which added to the dramatic impact. In her own baccalaureate manner, Miller was emulating the fat boy in *The Pickwick Papers* who says, "I wants to make your flesh creep."

I could have happily beaned her with a dinner roll. Not only because her keynote address lacked a proper sense of occasion, casting a preachy pall over an event intended to acknowledge and celebrate outstanding journalism. And not only because she seemed to take prim glee in lifting our eyes to the dangerous world out there, unspooling the possible scenarios by which we were going to *die hopeless, horrible deaths.* Flapping on the floor like poisoned fish.

No, what really got up my snoot about Miller's doomsday preview was that she didn't sound like a journalist, she sounded like a jingoist, as if sowing anxiety were her second job, and she had forgotten what her first job was. Her scare talk was the same cheap melodrama being foisted that winter by the Bush administration and its media consorts to mau-mau the country into going to war against Saddam Hussein and strip Iraq of Weapons of Mass Destruction. By November 2002, it was evident to anyone not on glue that the United States was determined to oust Hussein by force; the United Nations' Scheherazade dance of diplomacy as troops massed in Kuwait, Qatar, and Bahrain was nothing more than a diaphanous divertissement. The Bush administration wanted this war, wanted it until it made their eyes water, and that night it was evident to me that the national security correspondent of the *New York Times* wanted it too. I knew from reading the papers, watching TV like a maniac, and pinballing across the Internet that the press had unplugged and warehoused its bullshit detectors after September 11, becoming an accessory to the Bush agenda, its amplifier. But it was one thing to observe such cheerleader behavior on screen and in print, and another to see it up close and in person—"vis-à-vis," as Tennessee Williams used to drawl. Judith Miller personified a media elite that wasn't standing up to the government but standing alongside the government, practically rubbing shoulders.

Well, they got the war they wanted, and the next time I saw Miller, it was on a *Charlie Rose* panel the Monday after Saddam

Hussein had been scraped out of his spider hole. Her forehead should have been flat on the table, her head hung in shame. "If reporters who live by their sources were obliged to die by their sources, *New York Times* reporter Judith Miller would be stinking up her family tomb right now," Jack Shafer had written in *Slate*. "In the 18-month run-up to the war on Iraq, Miller grew incredibly close to numerous Iraqi sources, both named and anonymous, who gave her detailed interviews about Saddam Hussein's weapons of mass destruction. Yet...none of the sensational allegations about chemical, biological, or nuclear weapons given to Miller have panned out, despite the furious crisscrossing of Iraq by U.S. weapons hunters." On January 28, 2004, veteran weapons inspector David Kay testified before the Senate Armed Services Committee that, to his own surprise and embarrassment, his investigation had determined that Iraq had no stockpiles of chemical and biological weapons of mass destruction prior to the invasion. None had been found, none were likely to be found. "We were almost all wrong—and I certainly include myself here," he told the stunned committee. Kay also cast doubt on the claim made by Colin Powell and others in the Bush administration that the aluminum tubes found in Iraq were part of a covert nuclear program. Ahmed Chalabi and other Iraqi exiles had fed Miller, the Bush administration, and the world a load of birdseed; every hot tip turned out to be a dry hole, with Chalabi later accused of leaking classified intelligence to Iran, a club member of the Axis of Evil. Compared to Judith Miller, wrote radical journalist Alexander Cockburn in his *Counterpunch* site, Jayson Blair was a little stinker. "[The] *Times* thumped its breast in contrition and self-abasement for minor, unimportant works of the imagination by its young black reporter.... [It] has remained more or less silent about the exposé of its star reporter, but Miller's shameless propagandizing, abetted by her editors, will stand as one of the most disgraceful displays of tendentious reporting in the history of the U.S. press, and I include in this category the *Times*' terrible performance in the Wen Ho Lee affair."

Yet that night, appearing on PBS with Charlie, Miller was as bubbly as ever, having fun ridiculing some of the out-there comments Hussein's eldest daughter, Raghad, had made about her father's arrest. (Raghad claimed that her father had been drugged by the U.S. after his capture, which broadcast his medical examination worldwide to "break the spirit of Arabs.") Even though Miller's journalistic credibility lay in a heap of feathers, despite being played by her sources for a dope and a dupe, she carried on as if she were in the winner's circle. the *New York Times* finally, grudgingly addressed the furor over the paper's gullible regurgitation of the lies and exaggerations regarding Iraq's WMD programs. On May 26, it bestirred itself to deliver an editor's note semi-buried on page A-10 that admitted that its pre-war reporting "was not as rigorous as it should have been," the understatement of the young century. This was no institutional profile in courage. The editor's note was inserted pre-emptively to blunt the impact of an upcoming autopsy of the paper's failings by its ombudsman, Dan Okrent. It sprinkled the blame evenly and thinly acreoss the editorial machinery, the fragrant name of Judith Miller chivalrously omitted, even though her byline graced the majority of the bogus scoops. Media critics were unappeased, continuing to challenge Miller's privileged status and chummy sources, only to be told to buzz off. Bill Keeler, the editor of the *Times*, grouched to *Editors and Publishers*, "It's a little galling to watch her pursued by some of these armchair media ethicists who have never ventured into a war zone or earned the right to carry Judy's laptop." Everything but the hounds snappin' at her rear end, to quote Thelma Ritter in *All About Eve*. Miller had her own explanation as to why she was being hunted by effete ethicists. Disengaging herself from reality, she told *Salon*, "You know what, I was proved fucking right. That's what happened. People who disagreed with me were saying, 'There she goes again.' But I was proved fucking right." It's impossible to *embarrass* these people. And by these people, I mean those members of the press who have converted TV studios, radio booths, and newsprint into their personal show rings.

The attack poodles.

I hasten to explain that the phrase "attack poodles" should not be misconstrued as an insult to those of the canine breed, whose beauty, intelligence, and athleticism make them among the most noble of companions. (John Steinbeck's *Travels with Charley* remains an endearing testimony to the fidelity of man and poodle.) It's their human mutations that are the menace. I first encountered the term in the British press in 2002 to describe the fierce "New Labour" loyalists and party whips trained to spring at the foes of Prime Minister Tony Blair, himself derided as Bush's lap dog. For example, a renegade member of Parliament who ran afoul of Labour chief whip, Hilary Armstrong charged that Blair was setting out "one of his attack poodles [to] get me into some sort of kangaroo court," a zoological mixed metaphor that would never dishonor the mellifluous lips of Tony Blair. As Prime Minister Blair nail-pounded his policies and beliefs into the boozy consciousness of the British public with a discipline, reiteration, and fruity eloquence that was the envy of American mumblers (as British playwright David Hare put it neatly, "America provides the firepower; we provide the bullshit"), the attack poodles served as his bodyguards of spin.

Our attack poodles could eat their attack poodles like cheese-puffs. We breed them bigger, meatier, and fluffier over here. They need that extra muscle and gloss for the versatile roles they play. American attack poodles are more than bodyguards of spin, though spin they do. Attack poodles advance the narra-tive of the political power struggle; they supply the "beats" in the storyline, the weekly soap opera crisis. They are the right-wing hacks and liberalish enablers with obedience-school diplomas. If the master narrative is "Liberals, weak on defense," the storyline being pushed that week might be "John Kerry's Purple Hearts—did he really deserve them?"— a diversion intended to leave doubt that even this authentic war hero is all he's cracked up to be. (A feckless fop named Jay Nordlinger, who does a column for National Review Online, even had the tiny balls to jeer, "As for 'decorated Vietnam vet-eran': Is there one who's not? Just wondering.") Attack poodles alter the vocabulary, so that those opposed to abortion become hallowed as "pro-life" (those who favor a woman's right to choose being, implicitly, pro-death), tax cuts become "tax-relief," and every enemy from the highest terrorist planner to the lowest guerrilla fighter is villainized as a comic book "evildoer." Attack poodles are apostles of war, and we are never not at war. We fight wars abroad, wars at home, endless wars of words that baptize actions. Attack poodles are brainy sensationalists. They don't care about the greater good, harmony among nations, the spirit of bipartisanship. That's a bore. That doesn't move the football down the field. Whatever issue they're fronting, attack poodles care about one thing and one thing only. *Their side must win.* Even if in the end it means everybody loses. As witness Iraq.

In Britain, attack poodles are mostly confined to ministerial halls and party events. In America, attack poodles enjoy the run of a much bigger dog park: the mass media. Their eager eyes and wet noses propel them into exciting careers in talk radio, newspapers, magazines, books, public speaking, and—the place where all doggies go if they're especially good at being bad—cable news. Some were bred and groomed in Beltway finishing schools and modeling academies, getting their barking orders at think tanks and foundations funded by right-wing zealot Richard Mellon Scaife (in the nineties, some of these Ann Coulteresque blondies struttin' their bony bootay in righteous ire were nicknamed the "Scaifettes"). Others levitated their way up from prosperity with the dream of helping those even more fortunate than themselves. Still others converged on hotel lobbies in Manhattan and Washington from foreign lands to lend their accents and ethnicities to needy panel discussions and seminars. (This helps efface the impression that attack poodles consist exclusively of homegrown Wonder Bread honkies.) But whatever asteroid they came in on, attack poodles nurture a fanatical purposefulness that sets them apart from diddly-dabblers such as, say, Tucker Carlson, a *Crossfire* cohost whose on-air philosophy, as revealed in his enjoyably inconsequential memoir *Politicians, Partisans, and Parasites*, is, "I care...just not too much." This lesson, he says, he imbibed from CNN's ageless Larry King, who took the lad aside in a Polonius moment and imparted his wisdom on the key to longevity in television: "The trick is to care, but not too much. Give a shit—but not really."

"Not too much" and "not really" aren't nearly enough for genuine attack poodles, who have no patience for dilettantes who practice careerist semidetachment. They are on a sacred, fervent, postmillennial mission. These hardcore bow-wows have got mountains to climb, enemies to crush, cameras to hog. Antitax, anti-abortion, anti–gun control, antifeminism, anti-environment, antimultilateralist, antigay (they'll countenance male homosexuality if it consents to be tasteful, discreet, and not try to lead Boy Scout hikes), and anti–political correctness (well, there they have a point), attack poodles are fighting for an American empire of iron-fisted affluence. Their ideal America is a cross between a resort community and an armed compound, a manicured blend of Rush Limbaugh's Palm Beach mansion and a Roman garrison.

Liberals have their attack poodles, but they're fewer in number, less disciplined, and more likely to stray. Take Susan Estrich, for instance. (Take her and leave her somewhere.) A feminist law professor, Estrich is the author of *Real Rape*, *Getting Away with Murder*, and *Making the Case for Yourself: A Diet Book for Smart Women* (dumb women presumably being left to unwedge their own heads out of the ice-cream carton). After serving as the national campaign manager for that model of futility known as the 1988 Michael Dukakis presidential campaign, she evolved into a columnist and cable news analyst, giving a broader audience the benefit of her screeching, and acting as one of Gary Condit's hanging judges during the summer of Chandra Levy. Estrich has achieved noisiest notoriety as a Fox News contributor, her hiring another tribute to the gangland genius of chairman Roger Ailes. In Estrich, he had found the perfect liberal fright mask for Fox's conservative pantomime, a self-caricature so grimacing, cheese-grating, and dry-heaving in her delivery that Democrats shudder any time she defends their side, which is rarer and rarer. Estrich is now a liberal in label-tag only, the sellout type who urges other liberals to put aside their thorny grievances and take a page from conservatives if they wish to excel, like a yenta who keeps nagging, "Why can't you be more like your cousin Morty?"

Another subset of nominal liberals consists of journalists who pride themselves on being counterintuitive—super subtle onion-peelers of spin. Infatuated with the Swiss precision of their minds, counterintuitives specialize in giving the conventional wisdom a playful flip. Nothing hits them on a visceral level; it's all gamesmanship and advanced calculus. Commitment—*caring* about something—would make them uncool and require climbing down from the catbird seat. They practice a contrarianism that isn't the product of their own idiosyncratic personality (as it was with H. L. Mencken and Murray Kempton), but rather is a navigational device. They're always positioning themselves, trying to find the cleverest carom to play.

The schoolyard leader of the counterintuitives is *Slate* blogger Mickey Kaus, a once serious journalist (he and I were colleagues at *Harper's* in that luminous interregnum in the early eighties when Michael Kinsley was editor) who has cutened up into quite a dimply little cheap-shot artist. Although he still calls himself a liberal, beginning sentences "As a liberal, I...," his bacon slabs of loathing are all on the liberal side. The format of his weblog resembles an old showbiz column by Earl Wilson or Walter Winchell, a cluster of short takes...separated by three dots...where he constantly niggles at liberal targets such as Paul Krugman, Al Gore, Robert Reich...carrying on a head-spinning Gollum-like dialogue with himself. One of his more creative feats of upside-down reasoning was ripping Hillary Clinton's 2003 trip to Baghdad as a cynical "stunt" while giving Bush's Thanksgiving turkey-drop the benefit of the doubt, even though Clinton also visited Afghanistan as part of her tour, spent more time on the ground in Iraq than the president, met with more people, and actually *listened*. Facts were immaterial. Using his special X-ray vision to peer into Hillary's sallow soul, Kaus detected telltale shadows of phoniness and opportunism, slicing and dicing her every utterance from the worst possible angle until he convinced himself of what he believed to be true about her all along—that she's the queen of calculation, a platinum phony. Kaus loves proving things to his own satisfaction, his idea of a good time.

The mental autoeroticism of the Mickster, as some of his fans insist on calling him, infects his imitators, who spend a lot of time polishing their egos and who tend to tout the same CVs. Harvard. The *Washington Monthly*. The *New Republic*.

Slate. The Hair Club for Men. Their primary loyalty is to each other, to the conceit of being part of a charmed circle cleverer than the common run of hacks. When journalist, *New Republic* blogger, and Panglossian environmentalist Gregg Easterbrook, irate over Quentin Tarantino's ultra-violent *Kill Bill*, condemned Jewish movie executives, such as Disney's Michael Eisner and Miramax's Harvey Weinstein, "who worship money above all else" for profiting from human suffering (the sort of comment that can be easily misinterpreted), colleagues formed a line to distance themselves from his remarks and yet plead for clemency. Kaus, who knew Easterbrook from The *Washington Monthly*, wrote, "He's not remotely an anti-Semite, as his colleagues from the *New Republic* have attested, nor have I ever heard him express a bigoted thought in the 24 years I've known him." Similar testimonials were served up by Jack Shafer at *Slate* and *Newsweek*'s Jonathan Alter. There's nothing wrong with defending a journalist friend. I'd defend mine if I had any. But Easterbrook's pals extended him a leniency that they seldom offer to any public figure, unless they have counterintuitive points to score. To the journalistic fraternity (a boys' club, no matter how many women belong), Easterbrook was One of Us, and We know We never mean wrong.

The author and activist Saul Alinsky, who died in 1972, was

too crustily shrewd to be conned by Wee Willie Winkies like Estrich or sophists like Kaus. He had come across many such types in his organizing days and recognized that their unwillingness to take a strong stand on one side meant that they were always in the damned way. "These Do-Nothings," he wrote in *Rules for Radicals* (1971), the guidebook that is to grassroots organizing what Sun-Tzu's *The Art of War* is to military and business strategy, "profess a commitment to social change for ideals of justice, equality, and opportunity, and then abstain from and discourage all effective action for change. They are known by their brand, 'I agree with your ends but not your means.' They function as blankets whenever possible smothering sparks of dissension that promise to flare up into the fire of action." Sweet reason and scoring points on technicalities don't get it done, Alinsky argued. "Change means movement. Movement means friction." For too many overpsychologized, college-educated liberals, friction makes them uneasy, brings up all their anger issues. They're more comfortable forming a committee or commission.

Attack poodles value friction. They thrive on it. For them, means drive the ends, and antagonism dramatizes the issues and intensifies the responses. Poodles rely on the divisiveness of wedge issues to sharpen what may otherwise be fuzzy differences between conservatives and liberals, and to keep liberals on the defensive. It doesn't take much to get their dudgeon high and their dandruff scattered. They can generate friction in a vacuum, chewing the carpet over everything from the latest hip-hop video they hear tell is offensive (not that they've actually seen it) to John Kerry's use of the "F" word in *Rolling Stone*, which Dennis Prager, a sanctimonious pundit and amateur theologian, declared as the sort of latrine language which could imperil "the preservation of our civilization." In the second American Civil War, another round. On matters great and small, attack poodles on the right seldom break ranks except to pause and lick themselves. A streak of independence is a grave disqualifier when it comes to earning the diamond collar of a division-champion attack poodle. Pivoting on your ideological compatriots and deviating from the party line can get you projected into the phantom zone, as David Brock—a self-described road warrior of the right and the author of *Blinded by the Right*—discovered when he mellowed toward Hillary Clinton. Before long a leper's bell tinkled whenever Brock darkened the door of a conservative séance, where he sustained multiple snubbings seldom seen outside the drawing rooms of Edith Wharton novels. By not doing Hillary as dirty-nasty as he had done Anita Hill, he had let down the side, tilted to the enemy. To prevent these snubbings from breaking out into open snideness, hostesses began to bar him from the cotillion, disinviting him for his own good. One of these considerate hearts treated him to the classic kiss-off: "Given what's happened, I don't think you'd be comfortable at the party."

The attack poodles present wouldn't be comfortable either. A clannish breed, poodles prefer their own company, the sweet smell of each other's butts. They preen like prima donnas, refusing to share the mirror, but pounce as one whenever they hear the whistle, forming a warm, squirming fur pile. Once they spit you out of the pile, it's time to find another career course and start collecting a new set of shrunken heads.

A true understanding of the species requires a close look at what makes them growl and how they perform their favorite tricks. Let us venture into the poodle parlor and meet some of the alpha males and Malibu Barbies of opinion journalism, punditry, and other occult arts. Some are more famous than others, some are smarter, some are definitely saner. But all have done their bit to heighten hysteria, hobgoblinize their adversaries, and persuade Americans that force is the first, best, and manliest option in a world gone mad.

Rush Limbaugh. The Republicans have no more loyal four-legged friend than Limbaugh, who trots ahead without a leash. He's so tethered to conservative orthodoxy that he doesn't need one. Here is a man who treasures his creature comforts and would never endanger them by biting the hand that strokes him. Conservatism has kept him in hair tonic and stinky cigars since he began liberal-bashing at radio station KFBK, in Sacramento, in 1984, and he would no more wander off the reservation now and flirt with other political creeds than he would take up the blues harmonica to understand the black man's soul. He has been an invaluable gasbag for the Bushes, seldom heard to utter a discouraging word against Poppy and son. I recall hearing Limbaugh on the air in 1992, taking it personally when it became undeniable that Bush the father was facing defeat to Bill Clinton. Rush sulked as if the American people were about to pull the lever against him too. And after all he had done for them—trying to stuff some sense into their pumpkin heads!

Rush's flame of devotion blazes even brighter for Bush the son. If the unthinkable were to happen and George W. fails to get reelected, Limbaugh might have to board himself up in the attic to baby his frustration until martial law is imposed and the election results overturned. Rush conducts his daily three-hour filibuster on lunchtime radio (interspersed with fawning questions and salutations from "dittoheads") in the jovial, off-hand manner of an old-time DJ spinning platters, but his king-sized addiction to painkillers reveals that beneath the ho-ho humor, he is one tightly wound ball of compulsion, holed up inside a protective bubble. Never again will he risk the trauma of that day in 1990 when gay activists from ACT UP took over Pat Sajak's talk show as the gay-unfriendly Limbaugh was filling in as guest host, heckling him and creating such a ruckus that the entire audience had to be ushered out…leaving a deflated Rush to peter out in an empty studio. A CBS executive said of the incident, "He came out full of bluster and left a very shaken man. I had never seen a man sweat as much in my life." Henceforth Rush would never allow himself to be humiliated in situations beyond his control and be left sitting in his own puddle. He would construct his personal airspace to guarantee absolute sovereignty. When he hosted his own syndicated TV talk show, produced by Roger Ailes, the studio audience consisted entirely of dittoheads who appreciated his sophisticated humor, such as alluding to "the White House dog" as a photo of the teenage Chelsea Clinton was flashed on the screen.

This is his psychological affinity to George W. Bush. Both of them are bubble boys, sealing themselves off from anything that might pinprick their preconceptions, expose them to antagonists, or interrupt them while they're watching the ballgame. They're never wrong, and they're never sorry. Even the slightest admission of mistakenhood has to be dragged out of them by mule team. Just as Rush refuses to invite liberal guests on his radio show or engage them elsewhere in real, open debate, Bush avoids press conferences, doesn't read newspapers or magazines, and brushes off demonstrations—from which the Secret Service keeps him a sanitary distance anyway, claiming he doesn't listen to "focus groups." Bush has everything digested for him, like a baby chick swallowing momma bird's regurgitation. Power, money, and success have allowed both to contrive a self-reinforcing loop wherein everything they say is repeated back to them with heel-clicking assent. You think they'd get sick of the sound of their own echo, but that's the amazing thing about bubble boys—they never do.

Armstrong Williams. White conservatives who get into mischief have no stauncher friend than this African-American poodle, a radio host, columnist, and conservative Republican who's willing to bail their pasty behinds out of the briar patch, protecting them from the angry brothers. Williams absolved

The Poodle Parlor

Limbaugh of any racist intent after Rush brought his ESPN career as a football commentator to a skidding stop by proposing that Philadelphia Eagles quarterback Donovan McNabb was a protected mediocrity, overrated by affirmative-action types "desirous" of a black QB making good. To Williams, Rush was the one who had been wronged by the subsequent furor, the victim of a racial double standard. "If Limbaugh had been blessed with dark skin like me, there is little doubt that he would still be working for ESPN." The white man just can't get a break in this society.

A former legislative aide to the late Senator Strom Thurmond, Williams is long experienced in excusing and forgiving the failings of the massa. For years, he confessed in a column published in December 2003, he stayed mum about Thurmond's most hypocritical and sensational indiscretion—that the former segregationist had sired a child with a black woman, a young maid in the family household. Williams and his former boss were being honored at a Washington Urban League ceremony when Thurmond coyly let drop backstage, "You know, I have deep roots in the black community...deep roots." Williams, who had heard the rumors of Thurmond's dalliances, asked if they were true. "'I've had a fulfilling life,' cackled Thurmond, winking salaciously." Oh, the places his pecker had been.

If Williams was repulsed hearing this ancient, wizened former race-baiter brag about his "deep roots" (didn't that wink make him ill inside?), he failed to record it in his column.

When not nobly doing damage control for the oppressors of his people, Williams sticks to the standard conservative tally sheet. He urges a "restoration of morality." He makes an enlightened call to bring back the firing squad for traitors, letting them bleed to death should no bullet reach the heart. He promotes a bootstrap philosophy of minority advancement, something he shares with black conservatives such as radio hosts Larry Elder (who calls himself "The Sage from South Central") and Ken Hamblin (who battles liberalism as "The Black Avenger"), who oppose racial preferments or any kind of special compensation for past wrongs. Williams opposes gay adoption, worrying that it would undermine "gender stability" and place vulnerable lives in the tattooed arms of those pushing aberrant lifestyles, and railed against the ghettoizing of gay students, bisexuals, cross-dressers, and other teenage fans of *Rent* at Harvey Milk High School in New York City. Not one to mince words (you'll never catch him mincing), Williams titled the column "Homo High."

Matt Drudge. The *Drudge Report* is the toxic dump site of Republican oppo research, a tabloidy Web site whose daily roundup of news attracts millions of hits a day. It's also where the mainstream media go to dip their buckets. In 1997 Drudge posted a report from anonymous Republican sources that journalist and White House aide Sidney Blumenthal had a record of spousal abuse—i.e., was a wife beater. According to Blumenthal the charge was recklessly false and Drudge issued a retraction, but just having the rumor out there long enough to be picked up on all the talk radio and cable news shows was enough to help foster the legend of "Sid Vicious," as he was nicknamed by the right. In 2002 Drudge splashed an exclusive on his Web site about John Kerry's expensive haircuts, which was bandied about by Judy Woodruff on CNN as if it were actual news. Then, in February of 2004 he pulled another dead rabbit out of his fedora, a world-exclusive report that news organizations were probing rumors of an affair between Kerry and an intern. All it took was the word "intern" to set off a chain of associations—thong, dress, semen stain, cigar—and get the attack poodles sprinting through the gutter. The story was immediately dumped on the front pages of the London *Times* and *Sun,* both papers owned by Rupert Murdoch, and on Murdoch's Fox News Susan Estrich wondered if Kerry might have "a Clinton problem." The story died when both Kerry and his accused squeeze Alexandra Polier denied the allegation, and reporters looking into the story found there was nothing to report. But it was a messy death, with a woman's name and reputation dragged through the muck by attack poodles craving another Monica moment. In the short-attention-span theater of cable news, a messy falsehood swamps the tedious truth. Playing detective on her own case, Alexandra Polier investigated "How I Got Smeared" for *New York* magazine, confronting the rumormongers who did her dirt. She concludes, "I am struck by the pitiful state of political reporting, which is dominated by the unholy alliance of opposition research and its latest tool, the Internet." A tool that can be used as a whip.

Robert Novak. A Washington fixture, which does no honor to Washington nor to fixtures. For decades Novak shared a syndicated political column with his partner Rowland Evans— "Errors and No-facts," as they were known along the boulevard. Even before Evans retired from the partnership (he died in 2001), Novak had carved out his nasty identity as name-caller, Red-baiter, and defender of anti-Communist tyrants, earning himself the nickname "Prince of Darkness" long before Richard Perle obtruded on the scene. Over the course of forty years Novak has published hundreds of thousands of words and not one cadenza of them will be remembered for grace, eloquence, wisdom, or elevation. In 2004 Novak accused Native Americans of participating in election fraud, allowing a recent senate contest in South Dakota to be "stolen by stuffing ballot boxes on Indian reservations." He published the name of undercover CIA operative Valerie Plame, being either complicit in or a useful tool for an act of retaliation against Plame for the aspersions her husband, the former ambassador Joseph Wilson, had cast on the veracity of Bush's claim in his State of the Union address that Saddam Hussein had tried to procure uranium from Niger. (Wilson's book, *The Politics of Truth*, patches together the whole shabby story.) Novak reportedly revealed the contents of private memos on Democratic computer files that had been illegally hacked by Republican staffers and leaked to him. Novak aims low at his targets and often hits even lower, then hides behind the skirts of his "sources." Were he to fall into a ditch, the ditch would spit him out again, in disgust. Yet his journalistic peers in the capital hold him in fond esteem as a lovable curmudgeon, teasing him about his wealth and his devotion to capital gains tax cuts, and venerating him as a heckuva reporter, a true patriot, and a devoted sports fan.

Ann Coulter. Eyes. Teeth. Legs on top of legs. Arrayed in unholy alliance. Coulter's flaxen hair has been compared to an Afghan hound's, but make no mistake: she is the centerfold queen of attack poodles. Reviewers assailed her defense of Joe McCarthy in *Treason*, which set an indoor record for historical illiteracy and inaccuracy (the watchdog *Spinsanity* groaned beneath the weight of her "utter falsehoods and egregious factual misrepresentations," saying that this book was revealed to be "not just inflammatory but blatantly irrational"), and talk show host and comic Bill Maher has accused her point-blank of taking liberties with the truth—"You just make shit up!" It can be fascinating to watch her make shit up on the spot, to see how that wicked little lie factory works. On *Hardball*, she claimed that the movie *Patton* was intended to lampoon the general and make an anti-military statement, only to backfire when audiences ended up loving the general's patriotic swagger. "That is why George C. Scott turned down his Academy Award," she explained. Unfortunately, host Chris Matthews was old enough to remember the original controversy, and corrected her on the air: Scott declined to go to the Oscars because he abhorred pitting one actor against another and considered the whole evening a meat parade. Coulter did her customary blinking and head-shaking, but she was caught dead wrong trying to make an ideological point. "Facts mean nothing to you, Ann," Matthews told her. They never have. But such nitpicking presumes a rational world where rules of fairness, accuracy, and fundamental decency apply, which the rising arc of Coulter's career repudiates. She is the Paris Hilton of postmodern politics, an elongated zero, a white-hot sex symbol symbolizing nothing.

Monica Crowley. A poodle princess, jostling with the likes of Laura Ingraham and columnist/radio personality Debbie Schlussel (what monster-truck rally did they find her at?) in the runner-up category. A onetime amanuensis to the retired Richard Nixon, Crowley recorded his sour-pickle insights on American politicos and foreign leaders in a pair of readable, affectionate memoirs, *Nixon in Winter* and *Nixon Off the Record* (affection for the former president being so scarce a mercy that it lent the books a forlorn poignancy). Since Nixon's death, she has abandoned the skeptical, polyhedral acuity that Nixon trained on domestic power games and geopolitics, forgetting everything she learned from him, assuming she ever truly learned it (perhaps she was too busy working the buttons on her tape recorder to actually listen). His haggard ghost would be appalled by the simplistic yapper his former Boswellian confidante has become on talk radio and Fox News. Crowley is not as sound-biteable as Coulter (her incisors aren't as keen), but she compensates with volubility, a cascade of zero-calorie cant. It's hard to pin down someone who doesn't stop talking: Even Crowley's flagrant episode of plagiarism—passages in an op-ed piece she wrote for the *Wall Street Journal* were purloined from an article in *Commentary* by historian Paul Johnson—failed to chip her enamel and pause her ascent. Victory among attack poodles belongs not to the true and brave but to the careless and brazen.

Bill O'Reilly. The question posed by the title of O'Reilly's latest book, *Who's Looking Out for You?* answers itself: He is. He's a big guy defending the little guy against other big guys. He's the tribune of the people and never lets the people forget it. This ripsnorter has made himself a pillar of cable news, yet he complains like Rodney Dangerfield that he's somebody who gets no respect, no respect at all. No matter how many best-selling books he compiles, no matter how high his ratings climb and how often he makes headlines, a sense of grievance gnaws on his corncob. He craves the approval of the very elites he excoriates.

The Poodle Parlor

His opening monologues on Fox News's *The O'Reilly Factor* are
like stomach rumbles set to words—arias of acid indigestion,
and his interviews often resemble police interrogations that have
turned ugly. He pretends to be independent, beholden to no
party or faction, but it's left-wingers on whose limbs his jaws
most tightly fasten. Like so many conservatives who dress up as
independents when they go into town, he bays about individual
liberty and the overencroachments of the State, yet froths at the
mouth over the American Civil Liberties Union, calling it "the
most fascist organization I have seen in decades," the Aryan
Brotherhood apparently having eluded his notice. To O'Reilly,
ACLU lawyers are Nazi swine with briefcases: "They're intellectual fascists. And they use the courts as their Panzer divisions." Unstopped, these First Amendment freaks are rampag-
ing through America as if it were Poland, 1939. Attack poodles
such as O'Reilly pride themselves on being hardheaded realists
(they're hardheaded, all right), but in fact they lead the richest of
fantasy lives, any resemblance to reality being strictly accidental.

Joe Scarborough. Don Imus has compared him to the develop-
mentally challenged boy playing the banjo in *Deliverance*. And
Imus is a fan. A former Republican congressman, Scarborough

was brought in by MSNBC in the hopes of replicating Bill O'Reilly's success. He pillories the same enemies of freedom and decency that O'Reilly does (Hollywood liberals, French diplomats, Ivy League intellectuals, porn merchants, foul-mouthed rappers) and points his finger at the camera on behalf of the little guy, but there is no replicating a plus-sized sourpuss like O'Reilly. True hostility must come from within, and enough affability leaks out of Scarborough to sap his effectiveness as an attack poodle. But when he tackles a tough, complicated problem, it's like watching someone who's all thumbs finger paint, and the mess Scarborough makes of (say) gay marriage or the Iraqi insurgency has a certain lurid curiosity. Put him down as one of our minor, promising primitives.

Peggy Noonan. The dashboard saint of Republican piety, giving off a phosphorescent glow. As a speechwriter, she was a miracle worker for President Reagan. As a political spiritualist (she sees dead people, and they're all Democrats), she's content to contemplate the miracles wrought by President Bush and Mel Gibson. And yet she can never be truly content as long as Hillary Clinton's pantsuits stalk the land, pursuing the presidency. It's the one rain cloud in the diorama of her mind. Don't be fooled by Noonan's Donna Reed demureness on camera. She is the attack poodle par excellence, a smear mistress with a smiley face.

David Frum. A lapdog looking for a lap, the larger the better. A Canadian import, Frum is the author of two conservative tracts, *What's Right* and *Dead Right*, books that impressed even liberal journalists such as Joshua Micah Marshall with their learning and insightfulness. In 2000 Frum decided to take a holiday from being insightful, junk all that nuanced jazz, and become a presidential speechwriter loading buckshot for George Bush. Perhaps no speechwriter in the annals of the profession has done as much destruction to rational discourse and international comity as this little wiggler, whom history will rue as the author of the infamous phrase "Axis of Evil" in Bush's 2002 State of the Union address. Not exactly a lapidary contribution to Ciceronian rhetoric, but no matter, it became the hottest sensation since Reagan's "Evil Empire." Frum's wife, conservative antifeminist author Danielle Crittenden, was so toothy with delight that she e-mailed friends outing her husband as the secret elf whose words had the whole world cowering. The e-mail was leaked to *Slate*, and not since Laura

Petrie made Rob sound like the unsung genius behind *The Alan Brady Show* has there been such a to-do. When Frum announced soon after that he was leaving the White House to resume a career in journalism, columnist Robert Novak implied that Frum had been sent packing over his wife's indiscretion, which Frum and unnamed White House sources denied. But the perception remained that Frum had been penalized for tooting his kazoo and upstaging the boss.

Attack poodles refuse to lie low and let a little adversity get them down. The cardboard boxes containing Frum's personal effects had barely left the premises before he was batting out a book as fast as Kerouac on bennies about his tiny spell inside the White House. In keeping with Frum's earlier titles, the book was called *The Right Man*. Frum's Bush is the right man because, unlike Bill Clinton, he's a real man, not some Li'l Abner chasing every Daisy Mae. Frum does rhetorical deep knee bends on the page to persuade us of Bush's no-crap authenticity: "There is a Holden Caulfield streak to Bush's personality: a deep distaste for the necessary insincerities of political life....Yet troubled though he was, Holden articulated the feelings and captured the sympathy of a nation and a generation—and so, in those ten days in September, did George W. Bush." Spare us. Bush's pieties would have made

Holden puke. Salinger's hero would have lumped him in with all those other letter-sweater handsomes giving each other Indian burns after varsity practice.

Yet for all its jaw-jutting, heroic-rendezvous-with-destiny, and pinch-me-I'm-dreaming effusions, *The Right Man* presents an often unflattering likeness of the commander in chief. Frum's Bush is not the genial backslapper of the campaign trail shown in Alexandra Pelosi's ditzy documentary *Journeys with George* but an autocratic control freak who keeps his temper in a tight jar. "Bush was a man of fierce anger. When he felt that he had been betrayed or ill-used, his face would go hard, his voice would go cold, and his words would be scathing." The Bush II White House is run with a hierarchical rigor with Bush himself as CEO dictator. "The Bush staff rose to their feet with a snap that would have impressed a Prussian field marshal. When Bush was in a kidding mood, he would direct the staff like an orchestra conductor: He would press his hands palms down to direct them to sit and then, when they had taken their seats, raise his hands palms up to order them to rise again. Only then would they get the final palms-down." Bush has his own poodles beautifully trained.

The Bushies, with their code of omertà, were rumored to be none too thrilled with Frum's loose tattle about Bush being testy. A red face didn't go with his blue suits. As if to atone for having lapsed into candor, however well-cushioned, Frum has been overcompensating ever since in his diary for *National Review Online*. If he were any more of a suck-up, he'd have to have his tongue recoated. He praised Bush's stumblebum press conference on the eve of war against Iraq ("Good press conference! Bush looked good and sounded calm"—this about a performance that even Bushmaniac Andrew Sullivan found dehydrated and dour); and interpreted the news of Saddam Hussein's capture as a sign of divine intervention—"It's becoming increasingly difficult to doubt that God wants President Bush re-elected." Frum's latest ode to international thuggery is a collaboration with neoconservative policy architect Richard Perle, a foreign policy polemic modestly titled *An End to Evil*, which would have us do unto Syria, Iran, Korea, and Saudi Arabia what we done dood to Iraq. The best capsule review of this evil-removal program was provided by blogger Steve Gilliard in three lovely words: "These people crazy."

Dennis Miller. The newest poodle on the promenade. After 9/11, he lifted his leg against liberal Democrats and Hollywood lefties and was eventually rewarded with his own weeknight wee-wee pad on CNBC. A comic scallywag turned courtier, Miller serves two kings: Arnold Schwarzenegger, whom he supported in the California recall election and who was the first guest on his CNBC premiere; and George Bush, whom he admires for dropping those bombs like nobody's business, baby. He says the kind of snappy things they would say if English were their first language.

Andrew Sullivan. Essayist, ex-editor of the *New Republic*, author (*Virtually Normal, Love Undetectable*), conflicted Catholic (is there any other kind?), transplanted Brit, and superstar blogger, Sullivan emotes his ideas like Susan Hayward aching for an Oscar. He wheels his sorrows to the end of Lonely Street and back again, peddling each installment of the religious-political-sexual soap opera of the soul that is *Sullivan Agonistes*. He suffers under a spotlight and drinks in the attention, wrestling with a spiritual dilemma (should I pick up my pew cushion and leave the Church?) on the op-ed page of the *New York Times*, then posting a link on his Web site the following week for fans who may have missed his "anguished" statement. Each article he writes has become an Andygram. Intellectual rigor has dribbled away from Sullivan's writing as he's gotten older and rounder, replaced by a rubbery agility to twist himself into knots and reverse previously held positions while stoutly contending that he's maintaining moral consistency. He is consistent only in his pet hates, rapping Susan Sontag, Noam Chomsky, Howell Raines, the BBC, Jimmy Carter, and Paul Krugman like a repressed nun with a ruler.

But he also loves to love, and his loves are more lavish than his loathings. A hero-worshipper on the lookout for a new adulation, he carries his heart around like a housewarming gift and would leave it on the doorstep of 1600 Pennsylvania Avenue if he could. After September 11, Sullivan fell hard for George Bush, becoming a slave to passion, power, and purple prose. "There is a very bearable lightness [to] Bush," Sullivan lyricized in his regular column for the *Sunday Times* of London, regaling the paper's no doubt dubious readers with a few of Bush's hijinks, such as putting his hand on a bald man's head like a faith healer. Some pharisees might mistake Bush's frat-boy antics as evidence of a frivolous nature. "But he can only be so playful because he is so anchored. He is connected to faith but he is also connected to a profound love of his country and its destiny.... [L]ightness begets seriousness, detachment begets engagement, and a natural conservatism begets a determined and adventurous war."

It do? I would have thought that a natural conservatism would keep us out of adventurous war, conduct only wars of national necessity, and leave all that begetting to the Old Testament. It's the foolish dreamer who craves adventurous war, and in dreams begin responsibilities. Sullivan flubbed his. He refused to admit reality, taking refuge in playing Stratego above his competence level. As American casualties mounted in Iraq, truck bombs exploded at embassies, and the tempo of violence quickened, he saw through the dire headlines to discern faint outlines of an ingenious master plan. The first gleaning of the crafty game afoot came to Sullivan during a conversation with someone "close to the inner circles" of the Bush administration who expressed sanguinity at the prospect of jihadists hitchhiking in from neighboring countries to join the trigger spree. "If the terrorists leave us alone in Iraq, fine," Deep Throat told Sullivan. "But if they come and get us, even better." Why better? Because luring terrorists into the kill box would make it easier for the United States to wipe them out in concentrated numbers rather than root them out all over the map. After his briefing, a relieved and reassured Sullivan trumpeted this counterterrorist scheme in print as the "flypaper strategy," each pickup in hostilities trapping more flies on the adhesive strip until the country was pest-free. A metaphor that became a morale booster for war hawks such as Web logger Glenn "Instapundit" Reynolds, Christopher Hitchens (who preferred to picture occupied Iraq as a Roach Motel—terrorists check in, but they don't check out), and publisher and lame-o presidential candidate Steve Forbes, who smirked on Fox News, saying that Iraq would prove to be "Al Qaeda's Waterloo." Like an infomercial product, the flypaper strategy came with a special bonus. "The extra beauty of this strategy is that it creates a target for Islamist terrorists that is not Israel," Sullivan wrote. Yeah, that's the beauty part. The flypaper strategy was totally the product of magical thinking, enabling Sullivan to put bad news into the gingerbread oven and serve it up as comfort food.

But some bad news, even Sullivan couldn't swallow. He had talked himself into believing that Bush couldn't throw the weight of the presidency against gay marriage, not if he were the upright spirit that Sullivan believed him to be. Sullivan anxiously reassured himself and his readers that Bush's easygoing personal relations with gays bespoke a man who nursed no personal animus and prejudice against homosexuals, and wouldn't violate the grain of his compassionate nature. If it was too much to expect the president to defy the religious fundamentalists in his party and unequivocally support gay marriage, it wasn't too dear to hope that he might lend his tacit support by stepping aside and letting the states decide. Bush's decision to support an amendment to the Constitution that defined marriage as solely between a man and woman smashed that vain dream. Sullivan went to the White House, took back his broken heart, and now writes about Bush with the sadness of a lover betrayed. But Sullivan can never stay mad for long, and will find a way to forgive his beloved, having plowed too much passion into their one-sided relationship to call it quits.

Thomas Friedman. Hallowed be his name in the highest quarters. Nobody's poodle but his own, Friedman is experienced, knowledgeable, passionate, and indefatigable. If he were any more indefatigable, he could chase down his own line drives. The best-selling author, Pulitzer Prize–winning reporter, and *New York Times* columnist has emerged and emulsified as the media's answer man on the Mideast, its shadow secretary of state. (He's a celebrity in Isreal, where, according to *New York Times* editorial page editor Gail Collins, he's mobbed "like Britney Spears at a shopping mall.") When he appears on *Charlie Rose, Imus in the Morning, Meet the Press, Face the Nation*, or *News Hour with Jim Lehrer* after one of his fact-finding missions to the region, he's interviewed with a deference reserved for red-carpet dignitaries. His counsel is sought as if he were the wise Solomon who could bring all the different parties together at the bargaining table, if only they weren't such meshuggeners. He's a mood ring reflecting the condition of the Mideast, of the entire world. When he's ebullient, progress is being made. When he's overcast, it's backward into the abyss. Unlike so many foreign policy experts Friedman isn't a dry fig on camera, jargonizing in a Kissingerian monotone. He physicalizes his frustrations and imperatives, squirming in his seat and judo-chopping his hands as if trying to hack through two hairy millennia of religious-ethnic-nationalistic prejudice, superstition, and pride. He's perfect for TV because he looks and sounds like a regular guy on a coffee break, laying out complex dynamics in accessible pop language, as when he compared George Bush's barging into Iraq with Jack Nicholson's sticking his head through the door in *The Shining* and announcing, "Herrrrrrre's Johnny!" True, it made the president look like an ax-wielding psycho, which wasn't Friedman's intention, but it's *vivid*, and that's what counts.

Individually, Friedman's columns and appearances have a hammering certitude and lumpy consistency. It's when you string those columns and appearances together that he's chasing his own tail trying to pin down what he thinks, whirling like a tornado without ever coming to a sensible stop. Changing his mind so fast and so often, he always seems to be in motion, in play, susceptible to every influence; that's part of his magnetism to those magnetized by him. He's come up with as many explanations for invading Iraq as the administration, glomming on to whichever one seems most plausible at the moment. He admitted that, yes, it was partly about oil, then in other columns he hails it as a bold stroke to introduce democracy into the Arab world, then in another he puts on his tough-guy hat and explains the facts of life to us: "The real reason for this war, which was never stated, was that after 9/11 America needed to hit someone in the Arab-Muslim world." Needed? "Smashing Saudi Arabia or Syria would have been fine." Fine? "But we hit Saddam for one simple reason: because we could."

Raw power used to teach intransigents not to cross the United States has always excited Friedman more than seems, well, seemly. His most vein-popping outburst came during the NATO war in the Balkans in 1999, when Friedman complained of NATO's being too squeamish in selecting targets. He wanted Serbia put on notice and, sounding like the late General Curtis LeMay, the inspiration for *Dr. Strangelove*'s General Jack D. Ripper, threatened: "We will set your country back by pulverizing you. You want 1950? We can do 1950. You want 1389? We can do 1389 too." Friedman was just being practical, after all. "Twelve days of surgical bombing was never going to turn Serbia around. Let's see what twelve weeks of less than surgical bombing does. Give war a chance."

A slur on the memory of John Lennon, "Give war a chance" has become Friedman's theme song. He reprised it after September 11, when the United States decided to depose the Taliban regime in Afghanistan. "Let's all take a deep breath and repeat after me: Give war a chance. This is Afghanistan we're talking about. Check the map. It's far away." I checked the map. It's far away. Friedman not only believes in giving war a chance, but also the benefit of the doubt, a kiss on the forehead, and his blessing. He is the lyric poet of constructive destruction, bombing the old and sweeping away the debris to make room for the vibrant new. Unlike so many attack poodles, Friedman acknowledges that the United States has a responsibility to stick around and glue back some of the pieces. He compares a country like Iraq to a Pottery Barn vase—you break it, you own it. (According to Bob Woodward's *Plan of Attack*, Colin Powell made the same comparison to Iraq in discussions with President Bush. Pottery Barn denies that it has such a policy, but a catchy phrase is a catchy phrase.) He later amended this, saying that since Iraq was broken before we got there (something to which a decade of U.S.-British bombing and UN sanctions might have con-tributed—"Blow up a different power station in Iraq every week, so no one knows when the lights will go off or who's in charge," Friedman had advised back in 1999), we not only have to replace the vase, we have to build the kiln that makes the vase. Intent on remaking the world from his own ceramic recipes, he identifies his own positions so closely with the instruments of the state that, as the Iraqi invasion unfolded, he began referring to himself in the third person on *Charlie Rose* and elsewhere, specifying what would have been done differ-ently had this been "Tom's war." The first time he said it I thought I had misheard. No one, not even a *Times* writer, could be that narcissistic. But the phrase kept ticking off his tongue... Tom's war, Tom's war, Tom's war. If Iraq hasn't been a war worthy of Tom's designer label, he can still dream. There will be other wars, other countries to pulverize, other Pottery Barns to invade.

David Brooks. Like Paul Gigot before him, Brooks assumes the guise of Responsible Conservative on PBS's *News Hour with Jim Lehrer*, a role that requires respectfully disagreeing with the liberal viewpoint without raising one's voice loud enough to wake the nanny. But unlike Gigot, who would sound so civil across the table from Mark Shields or Tom Oliphant, only to sprout fangs in his column for the editorial page of the *Wall Street Journal*, Brooks, a former star at the *Weekly Standard*, doesn't turn into a wolf man once he loosens his tie. He writes as he speaks, pianissimo. His modest demeanor, subtle modulations, offhand versatility, and Tom Wolfe–ish knack for coining catchphrases that capture social trends and archetypes in a Polaroid snap (Bobos, Patio Man) have made him the journalism establishment's favorite diplomat from the ranks of Brooks Brothers conservatives, the second coming of George Will—as if the first weren't bad enough. His acceptance became complete when he was chosen to ornament the op-ed page of the *New York Times*, whose only other avowed conservative is a dinosaur bone from the Nixon era, William Safire.

Attack poodles who fretted that Brooks might inhibit himself at the Gray Lady—seeking the approval of his new peers by conforming to the liberal's ideal of a responsible conservative as a chinless erudite—have been relieved by his performance at the scratching post. To be an attack poodle is to defend and identify with the top-dog mentality, and behind those collegiate glasses Brooks aces every exam, establishing himself as the thinking man's Republican triumphalist. When not casting a wry look at winsome topics such as Internet dating or *Lucky* magazine (he should give his wry looks a rest), Brooks earns his biscuits by hanging tag phrases such as "Pelosi Democrats" on the whiny opposition party—an update of former United Nations ambassador Jeanne Kirkpatrick's sneer at "San Francisco Democrats," code for faggy peaceniks. (Nancy Pelosi, the minority leader in the House, represents San Francisco's 8th District.) On *Face the Nation*, he diagnosed Democrats as afflicted with distemper. "I spoke to a House Democrat who said to me, 'You know, I don't hate George Bush, but I regard him the way I would regard a guy who molested my granddaughter.' Now if that's not hatred, I don't know what hatred is." If that isn't hooey, I don't know what hooey is. I don't believe any House Democrat would talk with such raw indiscretion to a reporter, particularly to a conservative columnist. It's a dirt bomb disguised as an unsourced anecdote. He also implied in a column that anyone who criticized neoconservatives was a covert anti-Semite, another low blow.

Fighting dirty is one of the pillars of Brooks's foreign-policy platform. Popeye says we need to take off the mittens and quit mucking around with an enemy that doesn't play by the rules. Brooks has no compunction supporting ruthlessness abroad, but he has concerns about the repercussions at home. You know how queasy women and emasculated men can get at the sight of fisticuffs. "What will happen to the national mood when the news programs start broadcasting images of the brutal measures our own troops will have to adopt? Inevitably, there will be atrocities that will cause many good-hearted people to defect from the cause." And it will be up to the Bush administration, he continued, to tighten our chin straps and remind us that this ain't no disco, this ain't no foolin' around. I don't consider myself Pat Boone at the country fair, but even I never thought I'd see the *New York Times* publishing an op-ed column prepping Americans to accept "brutal measures" and brace ourselves for war crimes. When war advocates ask us to put atrocities in a wider framework, they're propagating their own form of moral relativism, a moral relativism for rugged realists—for those who think tough. And Brooks isn't the only poodle dog of war on the *Times* op-ed page prepared to send in the assassins. Meet...

Max Boot. He has the soft cheeks of a baby-faced killer and a byline that spells danger. The aptly named Boot is a man of words and a man of action trying to elbow a place in the front line of the march to empire. From the halls of Montezuma to the shores of Tripoli, Boot, a senior fellow at the Council on Foreign Relations and the author of *The Savage Wars of Peace*, salutes the past, present, and future of American imperialism. He wants it to come out of the closet, stand tall, and be proud of what it's done. Sure, he concedes, there are a few ink blots in America's family album, such as the "mistreatment of the Indians"—"mistreatment" being a rather genteel word to describe America's pioneer effort in ethnic cleansing—but our overall record is pretty impressive. In article after article he promotes the use of force to snuff out scattered insurrections and extend our sphere of influence until none dare defy us. It is America's fate and duty to be the world's Robocop. A tour of Europe in 2003 convinced Boot that the Old World was okay for sightseeing and savory delights ("Did I mention the handcrafted chocolates I found at a little shop in Brussels's Grand Sablon square?" he fluted in the *Weekly Standard*), but forget counting on its leadership class. They're soggy strudel when it comes to safeguarding civilization. To complacent Europeans, life is still a cabaret, old chum. It's up to us children of Valley Forge to be the eradicators of evil, even though, like Brooks, Boot frets that Americans have gotten too soft for sacrifice, too reluctant to mix it up with the enemy. In a column for the *Wall Street Journal* written during the war in Afghanistan, he was distressed that our troops had suffered too *few* casualties over-throwing the Taliban. "This is not a war being won with American blood and guts," he complained, sounding like Nick Fury, Agent of S.H.I.E.L.D.

Unlike most of his fellow interventionists, Boot is willing to get involved and lend a hand, as long as it's holding a gun. In an article for the *Weekly Standard* in September 2003, he described his role as a writer-commando as an embed with the marines in Iraq, where he watched over a prisoner during a raid, prompting a letter to the editor from a New Zealand reader who asked, "How can I believe anything written by Max Boot, a journalist who armed himself with a 9mm pistol and actively helped U.S. troops by guarding a suspected Iraqi suspect? No wonder people now read U.S. media reports with the same skepticism with which they once read *Pravda*." Excellent point, but the Kiwi neglected to mention that Boot's stay also afforded him the chance to contact his feminine side. "I felt like the Queen of England waving regally at Iraqis as we drove by in our three-Humvee convoy," he beamed, reporting that he returned home buoyed by what he saw, optimistic for Iraq's future. And no wonder. "Boot knows no Arabic and his report is sunny because he has no idea what he is talking about," Mideast expert Juan Cole deduced.

The Poodle Parlor

Boot's sunny afterglow didn't last. Two months later, Boot confessed on the op-ed page of the *New York Times* that the view through the binoculars was getting ugly. Liberated Iraq was deteriorating into occupied anarchy. Confronting donkey carts of death with conventional methods was a guaranteed no-gainer. Boot's formula for turnaround success was to adopt some of the counterinsurgency tactics from the Vietnam war, such as the Phoenix program, where units of CIA-supported South Vietnamese infiltrated the Vietcong infrastructure, killing as many as twenty-six thousand suspected VC. Yes, there were "excesses," as CIA chief William Colby has conceded. The brutal counterinsurgency tactics were often ineffective and frequently backfired, innocent villagers were tortured on the flimsy word of feuding neighbors, thousands of other innocents were murdered, and America ended up losing Vietnam and the respect of much of the world, but, hey, it's worth a try. Boot's prescriptions are signs of the brutalism that's leaked into the bloodstream of attack-poodle journalism in undetectable amounts until the unacceptable becomes the norm.

Jonah Goldberg, John Podhoretz, and *Mark Steyn.* The Tweedle-dum, Tweedledee, and Tweedledon't of conservative harlequinades, they jolly up the brutalism that Boot models down the catwalk in a full metal jacket. They take turns playing Falstaff, quaffing ale and trying to convince themselves that Bush is Prince Hal. Goldberg is a contributor to *National Review Online*, syndicated columnist, guest commentator on CNN, and a man without substance. He seems to write his pieces on a TV tray while consuming endless reruns of *Star Trek* and *The Simpsons*; it was he, as he so often reminds us, who popularized the putdown of the French as "cheese-eating surrender monkeys," a phrase he copped with attribution from a *Simpsons* episode. He and his dog Cosmo have become lovable cartoon characters themselves on NRO, where Goldberg regales easily regaled readers about the fun "Cosmo the Wonderdog" has playing in the snow and splashing in the bath. He even wrote a column in which Cosmo interviewed North Korean dictator Kim Jong Il, enabling Goldberg to get in a crack about how Koreans eat dogs. No one will ever accuse his humor of being too hip for the room. You can see his punch lines coming a block away, keeping his political opinions company before they hit their predictable targets.

New York Post columnist John Podhoretz is even more of a pop culture omnivore than Goldberg and an even less effective sit-down comic, squeaking whenever he tries to get sarcastic (in some columns, sarcastic is all he gets). As pundits, Goldberg and

Podhoretz are so similar in cheerfully hawkish outlook that they're like two sundae scoops, Goldberg taking special glee in the image of the United States belting around piss-poor Third World countries for disrespecting the Bada Bing. Part of Goldberg and Podhoretz's kinship is that both are second-generation sucklings at the snub-nosed bullet tit of neoconservatism. Goldberg is the son of Lucianne Goldberg, the chain-smoking crone and self-styled "agent provocateur" who convinced Linda Tripp to turn rat on Monica Lewinsky. Podhoretz is the son of Norman Podhoretz and Midge Decter, "that wonderful, wacky couple" (to quote Gore Vidal) who helped make *Commentary* what it is today, a sarcophagus. Neoconservatism promotes nepotism, and like so many children of neocons, Podhoretz has served in a Republican administration. He was a White House staffer and special assistant to drug czar William Bennett during the first Bush administration, hanging around all of five months. (He later went back to interview other midlevel White House staffers for his first book, *Hell of a Ride*.) Neither Goldberg nor Podhoretz seems to have gone through a rebellious stage against the dronings of their elders; their writings are a jokey recitation of hoary hand-me-downs from babyhood. This is why, for all their hectic activity, they remain stunted in place, like two poodles curled up at Mommy and Daddy's feet.

The only truly adept comedian of this trio, Mark Steyn is also the one most capable of unwedging himself from the sofa and venturing into sunlight, if only to reenter the dark. Though not as prolific as Joyce Carol Oates (the only author with octopus arms), the unstoppable Steyn still piles up a pretty impressive word tonnage, covering theater for the *New Criterion*, movies for the *Spectator* of London, and politics for the *Spectator*, the *National Post*, the *Telegraph* of London, the *Wall Street Journal*, and his own blog. Like Goldberg and Podhoretz, Steyn is a zany xenophobe who encourages Uncle Sam to pimp-slap punk-ass countries. For Steyn, Iraq's smackdown was just a preliminary bout. He did a column for the *Spectator* urging the United States to train the guns of Navarone next on the regimes of five noxious countries comprising a pentagon of evil (Syria, Iran, Sudan, Saudi Arabia, North Korea), as if he were already bored with Iraq and wanted to stick a new cartridge into his Game Boy. Loss of life, destruction of other cultures, dousing Islamic rage with additional lighter fluid, turning the U.S. military into mercenaries for corporate interests: such practical considerations never enter into Steyn's toy world. To him and his fellow attack poodles, casualties of war are as flies to wanton gods, killed for their own good if only they were alive to appreciate it.

The Poodle Parlor

The living always get the last word, and Steyn gets his with relish. Like Boot, he has been forced to listen to the patronizing prattle of Europeans who think that America is becoming a barroom brawler. "Not long ago," he wrote in a theater review, "I found myself sitting next to a cool Nordic blonde who turned out to be the Swedish Foreign Minister, Anna Lindh. Ms. Lindh wanted to know why the Americans present were so 'hung up' on war and terror. Why, it was absurd and prevented any normal conversation on the real issues facing the world—welfare, health care, etc. We agreed to disagree. I flew on to Iraq and had a grand old time in the Sunni Triangle. Ms. Lindh flew back to Stockholm and was stabbed to death in a department store by an anti-Euro fanatic." I guess that showed her.

Alan Keyes and *Michael Savage*. Poor little poodles that have gone astray. Both won and lost their own MSNBC talk shows, but there the resemblance ends. Keyes, a former Republican presidential contender, is a pipe organ of an orator; his rhetoric is bathed in a multihued radiance, as if he were preachifying beneath a stained-glass window. Savage, a self-appointed ambassador from Lower Slobbovia, personifies an earthy wisdom gleaned from the scrawlings on bathroom walls. Their shows offered a choice between two kinds of crap, smooth or chunky, and MSNBC viewers preferred neither. But attack poodles have a Rasputin gene, they're impossible to squelch, and both rejects are on the comeback trail, Keyes with TV appearances on *The O'Reilly Factor* and lectures at conservative conferences, Savage with his latest assemblage of pan drippings in print, *The Enemy Within: Saving America from the Liberal Assault on Our Schools, Faith, and Military*. Conservative punditry is the vaudeville circuit that never died, and even the most tired acts are given a second and third chance to claw their way back to national prominence and make fools of themselves all over again. That is why it is never safe to breathe a sigh of relief when an attack poodle falls off the ledge. Look at William Bennett, former drug czar and no-nonsense morality cop—did he let the revelations about his monstrous gambling addiction knock him out of the box? Heck, no. The hypocrite is now hosting his own daily radio talk show, as unsubdued as ever.

Cal Thomas. A goodly Christian and a badly writer, this author, columnist, and Fox News contributor dresses, speaks, and dispenses fireside wisdom like a grumpy gramp in a cardigan sweater. The kids wander out of the room . . . he scarcely notices...he just loves to hear himself harrumph. The impressive thing is that Thomas makes a living scolding sinners who are oblivious to his existence. He's no stage-prowling evangelist, sweating up a Jimmy Swaggart lather as he lays into the seven deadlies to a packed house of Jesus-seekers. As with other diagnosticians of America's moral-social decay (William Bennett, Michael Medved, the still bitter Robert Bork), Thomas's core readership consists of upright, uptight prudes who pride themselves on already being morally superior. Moralists love hearing moralizers moralize. It's what warms up their cocoa. But on the high road to salvation, one must sometimes detour to the dirt road of demagoguery, something Thomas does only when necessary, like once every few columns. He raised a dyed eyebrow at Howard Dean, a Congregationalist, for having a Jewish wife, implying there was something slimy in a mixed-religion marriage.

Thomas is another attack poodle who Nazifies his nemeses. Like Kaus, he took umbrage—umbrage being a regular part of every old coot's diet—at Hillary Clinton's Thanksgiving trip to Iraq. "While praising the troops, Sen. Clinton questioned the administration's postwar policy, a distinction I find inconsistent. The Nazi leadership believed the troops at Auschwitz also did a 'good job.' The policy and the performance go together, don't they?" A casual reader could be forgiven for coming away from that passage thinking that Thomas was comparing U.S. soldiers to concentration camp guards and the Bush policy team to the Nazi high command. His screwball logic lends itself easily to misinterpretation. Thomas is so determined to put the worst possible spin on everything Hillary Clinton says and does that he gets tangled up in his pajamas and loads his pipe with pencil shavings. If Hillary isn't stopped politically in 2008, he grimly prophesizes, "[T]his country will face a threat unlike any it has ever known," the Civil War, Hitler, Stalin, the Great Depression, the Cuban missile crisis, and September 11 presumably being warm-up acts for the she-devil in slacks. By 2008, some of the kids that Thomas scolds for their slutty clothes and wild jitterbugging will have grown to have kids of their own, who will also wander out of the room, keeping alive a grand tradition.

AS THIS PARTIAL ROSTER of tongue waggers illustrates, attack poodles come in many different sizes, skin colors, age groups, and brainwave patterns. Some have undeniable intellects, others show lazy motion in the windmills of their minds.

The Poodle Parlor

Some are students of history, others twinkle in an eternal present, the past little more than a barren backdrop dominated by a
few Big Names (Lincoln, Stalin, Churchill, Hitler, Reagan).
Some are capable of self-reflection (glimmers of doubt, recog-
nitions of error), others never rotate their glassy eyes inward.
Individually, attack poodles pull the sleds of their own careers,
no more obnoxious than any other species of media hustler. It's
when they all dash in the same direction, in hot group pursuit,
that they endanger others and debase the culture. Attack poodles are the posse in the politics of personal destruction, leaving red stains in the snow once they catch their latest victim.
They went after Anita Hill as if she were a runaway slave. The
2004 film *The Hunting of the President*—based on the book by
Joe Conason and Gene Lyons, and codirected (with Nickolas
Perry) by Harry Thomason, veteran sitcom producer and
longtime Clinton friend—is as much a nature documentary as
it is a journalistic investigation, reconstructing how attack poodles were sicced upon Bill and Hillary Clinton and any parcel
of warm flesh around them. Attack poodles travestied Al Gore
in the 2000 elections, minimizing Bush's absenteeism in the
National Guard, rinky-dink record as Texas governor, and
vacant portfolio in foreign relations to harp upon factoids such
as Gore-claims-to-have-invented-the-Internet and that whole

bogus kafuffle over Naomi Wolf advising the candidate to adopt "earth tones" in his wardrobe. (Google "Al Gore" and "earth tones" and more than five-thousand entries are excavated.) The factoids metastasized into the body politic, and by election day Gore lurched to the finish line as a lying loon insecure in his own masculine identity, and still managed to top Bush in the popular tally by a half-million votes. The same mauling was meted out to Howard Dean, after the Democratic frontrunner stumbled. "In forty years of observing presidential contests," wrote William Greider in the *Nation* (February 19, 2004), "I cannot remember another major candidate brutalized so intensely by the media, with the possible exception of George Wallace." And they did so gleefully. "Privately, they chortle over their accomplishment," Greider wrote. John Kerry might be next. In December 2002, Mickey Kaus queried, "What *is* it that makes so many people, myself included, intensely dislike Sen. John Kerry?" He finds Kerry "pompous," "humorless," "narcissistically theatrical," but, gee, there must be more to it than that. To solve this psychological mystery, Kaus offered a copy of Kerry's book *The New War* to whichever *Slate* reader "most precisely describes the root of Kerry's loathsomeness." After Kerry's candidacy got off to a clumsy start, Kaus gleefully announced a new competition, the Kerry Withdrawal Contest, where readers could bet on when this pompous, humorless narcissist, who "faces not just defeat but utter humiliation in the New Hampshire primary," would acknowledge that no one wanted to look at his furrowed brow any longer and quit the race. Spectacularly wrong in his predictions, Kaus has only doubled, tripled, quadrupled his attacks. If the Gore pattern holds, attack poodles will draw first blood with Kerry, leaving the pundits and analysts to finish the job, and Maureen Dowd to paint clown lips on the corpse.

It can be fun going after a lone figure—it gets the juices going, sinking into someone's flesh with the rest of the gang. But there is a broader agenda driving the attack poodles' flying wedge, and a larger threat. The strategic purpose of the wedge is to spearhead the movement toward an unassailable authoritarian one-party dominance of the United States akin to Berlusconi's Italy, Putin's Russia, Blair's Britain. Turn America into one giant red state—Bush Country forevermore. Writing in the *American Progressive*, editor, columnist, and economist Robert Kuttner laid out the scope of this conservative dream scheme. "The most predictable public-policy result of extended one-party rule would be the completion of the Bush/radical-right project: the dismantling of social investment, regulation, progressive taxation, separation of church and state, racial justice, and trade unionism." Which would include the privatization of Social Security, and shrinking future benefits to offset the tax cuts for the wealthy. The preconditions for radical-right hegemony are in place: Republicans control the presidency, the House, and the Senate; once they pack the judiciary with Scalia clones, they will have castrated every institutional check on their prerogatives and will be emboldened to gerrymander even more Democrats out of their districts. Republicans raise more money than Democrats, stroll K Street cheek by jowl with lobbyists, and are saturating the tax system with sweeteners for the super-rich. The interlocking interests of the media, the military, corporate giants, and the political ruling class are integrating into a Borg mentality where "resistance is futile." Liberalism will be demonized, stigmatized, and uprooted from the past until the only acceptable Democrat is one distinguishable from a Republican only by slender degree, slight tonality. (Joe Lieberman at his most Perry Como, he'll do.) Attack poodles are expert in sounding the false alarms of foreign threats, having first egged us on into Iraq with the hysteria over WMDs and then snorting to go after Syria, Iran, Saudi Arabia, North Korea, and the vineyards of France until the Iraqi resistance put a crimp in those plans. Next they'll be agitating for the militarization of space to protect us from the Chinese menace they'll begin to exaggerate when the terrorist threat level starts to flag.

To understand the deeper game unfolding, it is important to know how the game is played by poodles and pundits. A quick course, then, in...

Punditry for Dummies

NOTHING PUTS MORE OF A DINK in a writer's day than actually having to drop anchor and write. Civilians think a writer's workday consists of taking sips of coffee in a bathrobe while the rest of the world reports for work; and, sure, that's a large part of it. But from the bathrober's perspective, it seldom feels like the fun of playing hooky. Usually it's like being stuck in perpetual summer school, confined indoors doing assignments while everyone else is out running and playing. The writer stares unseeingly out the jail window and thinks: Life, it'd be fun to try it sometime, once I'm off deadline. Sigh. All the time-honored delay tactics and creative rituals handed down through generations of hacks—from the coffeehouse wits of eighteenth-century London to the Josh Freelantzovitzes of our own day, communing with their laptops in the window seats at Starbucks—only postpone the inevitable anticlimax of finally having to set aside the newspaper, mute the TV, scratch where it itches, and coax a few usable paragraphs out of one's inner blah. Then break for lunch, and repeat in the afternoon.

Nonfiction writers have discovered a lucrative way to sweeten this Sisyphean grind. It's called *punditry*, taken from the Hindi term for learned man, one of etymology's wittier ironies, and it can be the first-class ticket out of the tedium of trying to make every word on the page sing out like Louise. Once a writer parlays a byline into a TV ID-tag, the quality craftwork of journalism—constructing paragraphs as if they were fine cabinets, filigreeing the sentences with a cursive touch here, a bass note there—becomes a Victorian duty that no longer need weigh one down. Being granted a license to blab on TV licenses the writer to blab in print, since it all becomes part of the same shtick. Conveying a loftier persona on the page will only confuse your new fans! They *want* you to write like you sound. With so many print journalists opening branch offices in the blogosphere, the old Walter Lippmann formalities have gone the way of starched collars and whale-bone corsets. Punditry's golden rule: Chat is king.

Yeah, maybe punditry *looks* easy, doubters will scoff. Because it is! Do you think beanie heads such as Margaret Carlson (*GQ* and CNN's *The Capital Gang*) and Tucker Carlson (CNN's *Crossfire*) could do it if it weren't? Moreover, job prospects have never been riper. Everyone grouches about tracking polls, photo ops, spinmeisters, and "Sabbath gasbags" (Calvin Trillin's phrase for the Sunday morning talk show panelists) to equally futile effect. We're never going back to Easter Island statues seated behind the reporter's desk quizzing Adlai Stevenson on *Meet the Press*. The expansion of cable news coverage of the latest political or celebrity craze—what Frank Rich has christened the "mediathon"—requires a full roster of rotating faces, some fresh, others old-reliable. (The cable channels often show pundits chockablock in a *Brady Bunch* grid.) But if instant analysis seems like an E-Z Pass lane to fame, highway-robbery speaking fees, and unctuous phone calls from senior officials close to the president, beware. The spiral staircase of punditry is strewn with the skeletal remains of writers who couldn't quite make the climb to the top. In the mid-nineties, Ruth Conniff of the *Progressive* surfaced on CNN talk shows: so young, so idealistic, so blessed with flowing auburn hair. And where is she now? Where did she go? (Lassie, come home!) And where is *Washington Times* columnist and author Mona Charen (*Useful Idiots*), a once familiar sourpuss? Her conservative parking spot seems to have been reassigned to Kate O'Beirne of the *National Review* (a regular on CNN's *The Capital Gang*), leaving Charen in limbo. Michael Kramer, the *Daily News* columnist and former *McLaughlin Group* regular whose pride was tested each time McLaughlin made a Rogaine reference at his expense—MIA. Steve Roberts, husband of Cokie and once reliable chair-warmer on PBS's *Washington Week in Review*—another ponderer seldom seen in these parts any more. And they used to be big; big. They may still *publish*, but who has time to read? Punditry is a foster child of show business, a Friars Club for know-it-alls, and has to be approached as a performing art requiring drive, agility, and constant upkeep.

To assist my brothers and sisters in their remorseless ascent, I have devised a twelve-point program that will help prospective attack poodles not only check into the hospitality suite of celebrity journalism, but stay there.

I. ABANDON YOUR IDEALS

They're only holding you back. You'll feel so much better, so much lighter, once you let them go. There was a time when your role model might have been Bobby Kennedy in rolled-up shirtsleeves wading into a sea of outstretched hands in Harlem; Barry Goldwater squaring his granite jaw and confronting the

Communist menace in words of one syllable. Enshrine these idols on your den wall for inspirational value, but don't let them misty-color your mind. To be a successful pundit is to forgo quixotic crusades for a hard-boiled cynicism and sarcasm worthy of a film noir detective in some fancy gin joint. Henceforth, you must patronize politicians (aside from a few tennis buddies and leaky sources) as used-car salesmen, dismiss civil servants as faceless bureaucrats, and portray social reformers as faded laundry left drooping on the line.

Consider Chris Matthews, host of MSNBC's *Hardball*, and Lawrence O'Donnell, Jr., former host of MSNBC's *Saturday Final* and a panelist on *The McLaughlin Group*: Matthews worked for former Speaker of the House Tip O'Neill, O'Donnell for New York Senator Daniel Patrick Moynihan, yet you'll seldom hear them Springsteening the glory days of Democratic liberalism, mourning the loss of sweeping initiatives and national mission. They see through their former allies and cronies, saving their fire-breathing scorn for liberals who pad their ambition in soft, pandering baby fat. Their favorite target is Bill Clinton, who symbolizes the damp underbelly of the Kennedy legacy of public flair and private debauchery. They beat up on him like a couple of rogue cops while he was in office, and still rag on him whenever they can. (One liberal pundit who has kept the faith is Doris Kearns Goodwin, wrapping her rooting interest for a return to New Deal/Great Society big government rollout in warm anecdotage. Her media prominence flickered considerably after she admitted to plagiarizing another historian's work, and she overingratiates herself when she's on the air now, as if hoping everyone still likes her.) On the Republican side, Tony Blankley, Newt Gingrich's former mouthpiece, editorial page editor at the *Washington Times*, and a panelist on the *McLaughlin Group*, can barely recite the conservative mantra of less regulation, lower taxes without his lips betraying a smile. He dresses like a dapper riverboat gambler, as if to signal to the audience, "Don't fool yourself, folks— it's all a game."

2. DRESS THE PART

Tony Blankley can get away with a Jackie Gleason ensemble. You, buster, probably can't. Robert Novak's banker's vest marks him as a traditional Republican unwilling to part with his money, a Scrooge McDuck whose own tummy is the pot of gold. The casual Gap ad denim attire that once clad Andrew Sullivan telegraphed a nonconformist image consonant with his gay-Catholic-conservative-chunky-hunky identity, but in recent years he has serioused-up his wardrobe for the camera by drabbing it down. The last time I saw him on a pundit panel he was wearing a dark jacket and red tie, looking as if he had just paid his respects at the pet cemetery. He needs to go back into the dressing room and tinker. One popular accessory is the bow tie. The preeminent bow tie pundit is, of course, George Will (ABC's *This Week with George Stephanopoulos*), on whom this puckish accessory achieves an odd sobriety. It seems to fasten his gravitas in place. On Thomas Oliphant (PBS's *News Hour with Jim Lehrer*) and Tucker Carlson, it reverts to its more traditional role of twerp neckwear. For most male pundits, standard business attire is the safest bet.

Margaret Carlson employs Susie Student eyeglasses for that sorority look, but most female pundits choose a Park Avenue wardrobe and coif that might be called Hillary lite (such as Peggy Noonan, who Hillaryizes herself with a more pastel palette). The balancing act for women is to look attractively telegenic without coming off as too man-eater, which will only arouse the resentment of other women and impure thoughts in the horny hosts, a mistake made by former *New Republic* reporter Ruth Shalit, who appeared on *Politically Incorrect with Bill Maher* in do-me shoes and baby doll makeup. Her use of the word "fellate" startled even the rakish host, who knows several *Playboy* playmates on a first-name basis. Ann Coulter can get away with her skimpy attire because her bone-thin figure is "sexy" in ironic quotes, the *Basic Instinct* ride of her miniskirts and *Fatal Attraction* death stare a caricature of a nutso femme fatale. The sparky Laura Ingraham, who posed on the cover of the *New York Times Magazine* in a leopard-print miniskirt, has since lowered her wattage and adopted a tamer junior-law-partner getup that makes her political cheap shots sound like feisty advocacy. Perhaps the most ingenious counterintuitive political fashion statement is made by the editor of the *Nation*, Katrina vanden Heuvel, whose leather coats and bloodred lipstick defy the cliché that all lefties are wan dreamers subsisting on tofu, soy milk, and acid flashbacks. She needs to dress like a dominatrix to get a word in edgewise with *Hardball*'s Matthews, who's irritably impatient with women of the feminist persuasion. Liberal or conservative, the female pundit should find a look that works for her and remain faithful to it, making semiannual adjustments. It may be a treat watching what outfit Vanna wears next on *Wheel of Fortune*, but a female pundit who turns herself into a fashion saga risks coming across as too blithe spirited and superficial to unpack The Issues. A stable identity is a must. Similarly...

3. PICK A SIDE,

THEN STICK WITH IT THROUGH THICK AND THICKER

Crucial to the career prospects of an attack poodle is deciding which team to play for. Committing to conservatism based on a close reading of Edmund Burke, Russell Kirk, and the criticism of T. S. Eliot has become as quaint as enlisting in liberalism after enlightened exposure to John Stuart Mill and Arthur Schlesinger, Jr.'s *The Age of Roosevelt*. Leave the august quotations to George Will, who's cornered that market. Unless you've undergone strict Jesuit training and can argue a monkey out of a banana, having too much intellectual integrity will only slow you down and hamper your ability to defend Tom DeLay without gagging.

Today, one's political loyalty is mostly a matter of personal taste and brand preference, like choosing Coke over Pepsi, Leno over Letterman, boxers over briefs. Once your political label is adopted, however, it's stitched to your hide. Idiosyncratic political commentators who tackle issues from unorthodox angles, such as the brilliant Kevin Phillips, who went from crafting Nixon's Southern strategy to being the pin-striped populist of the books *Arrogant Capital, Boiling Point,* and *American Dynasty: Aristocracy, Fortune, and the Politics of Deceit in the*

House of Bush (catchy title), alienating many of his former fans and supporters. One measles patch of conservatives created the Kevin Phillips Award for such turncoats, "so named for a Republican who makes a living 'helping the other team'" (David Brock, *Blinded by the Right*). More important, idiosyncrats such as Phillips perplex talk show programmers trying to book a simple Punch-and-Judy act. They want guests to lock antlers, not rub antennae. Oh, a privileged few float above the vulgar, partisan fray, such as presidential adviser David Gergen—whose Marcus Welby bedside manner is beyond reproach—and the *Washington Post*'s David Broder, the dean of Washington correspondents, who calms the turbulent waters during periods of uncertainty and unrest. There is no crisis he can't barbiturate, no issue he can't stuff with cotton. Your task as pundit is not to hold complex problems up to a prism or to allay the anxiety of a troubled republic—Gergen and Broder have got that covered. *Your* job is to dig a foxhole on one side of the liberal-conservative divide, fix bayonets, and fight like a freedom-loving fool, giving no ground to the guy or gal you were chatting with in the green room only moments before.

4. LET IGNORANCE LEND A HELPING HAND

"I can speak to almost anything with a lot of authority," Fred Barnes is quoted as saying in Eric Alterman's book *Sound and Fury: The Making of the Punditocracy*. Speaking with airy authority on everything from global warming to the medical-ethical dilemmas of stem cell research is vital to establishing a pundit's aura of offhand infallibility. A pundit is someone who, unburdened with too much knowledge, reticence, and modesty, knows exactly how many twists on the tap Alan Greenspan should take to re-liquefy the faltering economy, how many troops are required for counterinsurgency in Iraq, what Hillary's latest hairstyle signifies for the 2008 presidential race, and how much jail time Martha Stewart should serve. You'll never hear an attack poodle shake his curls and confess, "Man, the Mideast, what a mess—I haven't a friggin' *clue* what to do about the Palestinians." Nor will you ever hear an admission of indifference. Hence the sentences "I don't know" and "I don't care" should never depart your collagen lips. Of course you don't know; of course you don't care! Having a conscience about such matters will only clog up your mental sinus passages, making it harder to speak before you think and impeding the free flow of blather. Think on your own time, as one of my bosses used to say, before she fired me. Remember, most of the audience knows less than you do. Hard to believe, but true. They haven't a clue who John Bolton or Elliott Abrams are, never mind what they do and why they're evil.*

A cautionary note: Be careful if you're asked to peruse the morning papers on C-SPAN's *Washington Journal*. Those call-in segments can knock you right off your rocking horse. Along with the usual cranks who sound as if they have a Confederate rifle cradled in their lap, the oldsters who keep forgetting to turn down the TV once they get on the air ("Ma'am, you're hearing the echo of your own voice, please turn down the set.... I'm afraid we're going to have to move on to our Democratic line"), and the spoilsports trying to pick a quarrel with the sainted Brian Lamb by accusing C-SPAN of political bias, there's often a troublemaker who actually *knows* something

---

* John Bolton is undersecretary of state for arms control and international security under George W. Bush, a title that does not do justice to his bellicose role and influence. A longtime opponent of arms control treaties and the United Nations, this unilateralist hawk keeps tabs on Colin Powell and other moderates in the State Department. He has made headlines with his baiting of North Korea. Elliott Abrams, a neoconservative hawk who served under President Reagan and pleaded guilty for lying to Congress about Iran-contra, was retrieved from the darkness and appointed to a top post in W.'s National Security Council.

about the topic being discussed. He or she may ambush you with an intelligent question, putting you and your debonair ignorance at a disadvantage. Keep your cool. Nod and keep nodding as if nothing they're saying is news to you. Then magnanimously suggest that many experts disagree with the caller's assessment without specifying who those experts are (since you just made them up) and, if the caller is persistent, graciously agree to disagree. At that point the host usually takes the next call, cueing you to take a thoughtful sip of coffee from the free C-SPAN mug you'll be taking home as a souvenir.

5. ONCE YOU STAKE OUT A POSITION, FEEL FREE TO ABANDON IT

Dramatic flip-flops can be fatal to the solvency of a political career ("Read my lips: No new taxes"), but are a vital component in every pundit's acrobatic repertoire, along with the whoopee cartwheel and the indignant whipback. Logical inconsistencies—championing states' rights until some states seek to legalize gay marriage, ridiculing "tax-and-spend" Democrats while defending the deficit-bloating spending binges of Bush II—can be tucked into the larger consistency of sticking to the ideological game plan. Twenty-twenty hindsight and a dose of amnesia allow even the most myopic opinion-maker to smooth out contradictory positions into the clean horizon of history. In an interview with *Salon* in 2003, Chris Matthews asserted that he "knew" George Bush had "won" the third presidential debate because he cinched the personality contest. "I knew Bush won because people liked him more," he told *Salon*'s Joan Walsh. "People just didn't like Gore. But all the journalists thought Gore won big, he cleaned the guy's clock." Yet as detective Bob Somerby unraveled on his *Daily Howler* Web site, Matthews himself had been one of those journalists who thought Gore may have won big and cleaned clock. "Clearly Gore outperformed Bush," he told CNBC's Ron Insana the night after the debate, describing Bush's performance as "lethargic." Matthews manages to outrace his contradictory statements by blustering so many excitable things so fast and so often that pinning down the discrepancies is like trying to grab a gust of wind by the tail. He isn't a cynical dissembler. He seems to suffer from some pundit variant of short-term memory loss. Each day on earth erases the days before. He says what he believes and believes what he says, and has the liberating advantage of always working from a blank sheet.

Others just don't give a damn. Consider the trapeze

artistry of conservative columnist Robert Novak on the war against Iraq. Novak is one of the few Washington pundits in less than total thrall to Israel and sympathetic to Arab interests. During the run-up to the war in Iraq, he belittled the administration's claims that Iraq was an imminent threat to America and its neighbors, saying such alarmist hysteria was a national security cover for the neoconservatives' power push to redraw the Mideast map to benefit Israel's security interests. By putting down a giant combat boot in Iraq, the U.S. would be doing Israel's dirty work for it. For a man of the right like Novak, speaking up against the war made for a lonesome quack. However, once the bombing stopped, the looting began, and the insurgency started, prewar Novak spun through a revolving door and emerged as his postwar Bizarro-world double. On CNN's *The Capital Gang*, Bizarro Bob excoriated the Democrats for "playing politics" with the nondiscovery of WMDs, the overhyped threat warnings, the bloodshed and chaos unleashed on the streets of Baghdad, and the U.S. casualty toll (politicians playing politics—my God, where will it all end?). In short, postwar Novak was ripping the Democrats a new aperture for making the same arguments prewar Novak had made! Fellow guest Al Hunt razzed him about this on *Capital Gang*, but of course there's no shaming or chagrining a cagey

Beltway operator like Novak. He's been at this forty years, out-lasted everybody, and knows that if the audience held a pundit's previous opinions against him (and they don't), none would 'scape whippin'.

Another nimble way to stay a step ahead of the last bone-head thing you said is to spew so many nonsensicals and hedge calls that it takes special filtration devices or software to keep track of all the misdisinformation. This is the ploy adopted with a combination of natural insouciance and frantic necessity by political adviser turned media spin doctor Dick Morris, who underwent career rehab after being caught paying to suck the toes of a woman not his wife ("shrimping," I believe this inno-cent pastime is called). A jolly roger with a mendacious pinch to the corners of his mouth, Morris fashions himself as Machi-avelli for the masses, providing an insider's perspective on the maneuverings of an electoral campaign. Problem is, Morris is no longer a savvy insider; he's just another outsider with a résumé, like all of those former baseball managers who end up in the broadcast booth. The longer Morris is out of the game, the wilder his calls go askew. He shanks every prediction into the trees. With all the juicy bacon of his being he assured us that Hillary Clinton would never run for Senate; once she decided to run, contended that she would pull out of the race;

then, when she stayed in the race, that she was doomed to defeat. This might come under the heading of "ongoing revision." In the more traditional practice of backward revision, Morris, as documented by Joe Conason on *Salon*, has told three different versions of the alleged incident in the Arkansas governor's mansion in 1990 when an angry Bill Clinton bear-hugged him to the kitchen floor. Each version of the tale becomes more lurid and violent than the last, like successive drafts of Sam Shepard's play *True West*. In the next retelling, he may have Clinton holding him down while Hillary kicks him senseless. No matter how sloppily Morris gets it wrong or rewrites the record, he manages to keep obtruding on the screen, as unstoppable as the bobbing white blob-balloon in the British cult series *The Prisoner*.

6. BURY YOUR NOSE IN DON IMUS

The view isn't pretty, but it'll pay off down the line.

The successful poodle understands that punditry begins at dawn, with a quick on-line skim of the buzz-worthiest Web sites (Drudge, Andrew Sullivan, *Salon*, *Slate*, ABC's *The Note*, Jim Romenesko's *Media News*, Joshua Micah Marshall's *Talking*

Points Memo, DailyKos), and a serious dip into the *New York Times* op-ed page to soak yourself in the media-elite mind-set as articulated by Thomas Friedman, Maureen Dowd, David Brooks, Nicholas Kristof, and the Voltairean Paul Krugman. Then it's time to toast the Pop-Tarts and tune into *Imus in the Morning*, a syndicated radio show simulcast on MSNBC, the breakfast club of the punditry. Although Imus has shed audience share in recent years, his bony grip on the Northeast Corridor illuminati has never been stronger. The I-man stamp of grumpy approval ("Bernie, see if you can get that lying weasel Paul Begala on the phone") means that the pundit has well and truly arrived. Tim Russert, Jeff Greenfield, Laura Ingraham, Jonathan Alter, Howard Fineman, Frank Rich, Chris Matthews, Christopher Hitchens, Mike Barnicle, Bob Schieffer, and Bill O'Reilly—all take their spin at the mike as members of the Imus all-star squad. To make it on the Imus show, however, his people must call you. Calling him first would be an impertinence. If you run into him at the gym, don't take the opportunity to say hello and to tell him how much you like his show; he might have a fit and fall off the treadmill. Being pushy will only earn you Imus's leather-tongued wrath. While waiting for your summons to the majors, familiarize yourself with every tedious aspect of his big-shot life. His bossy wife, Deirdre. His

Damien son, Wyatt. His ramshackle brother, Fred, who always sounds as if he just fell out of the hayloft. Become conversant in favorite I-man topics such as Joseph Abboud ties and custom-made cowboy boots; listen to the Flatlanders, read Kinky Friedman mysteries, catch Rob Bartlett and the Bartlettes at the Civic Auditorium in Bunghole, Arkansas. Prepare yourself, Grasshopper, for the trial ahead, always keeping in mind the message of hope delivered by Johnny Carson, who, after a particularly obsequious salaam from sidekick Ed McMahon, turned to the camera and, rising on his toes, pronounced: "Sucking up *does* work."

The danger of dealing with Imus is sucking up to excess, theoretically far-fetched as this sounds. An Imus rookie must be a *dignified* toady, making exaggerated bows to his exalted status ("Yes, Your Lordship, Delbert McClinton's new CD makes me think of old Hank"), extracting from his incoherent, repetitious ramblings a pithy nugget of wisdom or comedy, and accepting his teasing as part of the hazing process. If you have a few pounds to spare, try not to snap back when he describes you to the listening audience as "porker," "fat loser," "lard wagon," "thigh-scraper," or "Monica Lewinsky with a penis, and we're not too sure about the penis part." Go along with the gag. Once you've passed the Imus initiation, you can breathe easy, but don't get too chummy. Work in the fawning references to Deirdre, Wyatt, and the Imus Ranch in New Mexico slowly, judiciously, raising yourself from a prostrate position by imperceptible degrees. A sudden swagger will only provoke Imus to pop open a can of salsa-flavored whup-ass. I-man veterans such as CNN's Jeff Greenfield, sports radio host Mike Francesca, and sportswriter and novelist Mike Lupica may enjoy the privilege of flinging darts at Imus's expense, targeting his irascible temper and turkey neck, but insult humor from a relative newcomer is a chancy proposition. Err on the side of caution and, above all, never presume to call him "Don," an honor reserved for bigfoot media equals (Russert, Tom Brokaw) and longtime pals (Lupica). The deference you pay will yield lifelong dividends. Because once you're inducted into the Imus fraternity, you're set. The Cosa Nostra couldn't be tighter.

Consider the case of columnist Mike Barnicle. Accused of plagiarizing George Carlin and fictionalizing sources, this stale-beer man-of-the-people Mike Royko pretender (without Royko's wicked iconoclasm) was kicked to the curb by the *Boston Globe* and might have joined fellow miscreants Janet Cooke, Stephen Glass, and Jayson Blair in journalism's skunk collection. But braced by Imus, Tim Russert, and Chris

Matthews, who rallied around and kept putting him on the air despite the whistling holes in his reputation, Barnicle managed to win back his pundit's badge and repair his blowhard pride. No one suggests Barnicle should have been punished forevermore, but because of his connections he was granted a swift pardon few others would have received, and now we're stuck with him and his heart-on-the-sleeve, hole-in-the-head schmaltzifying. He has peeled off his disgrace like a store-bought tattoo and rebounded big-time, writing a column in New York's Sunday *Daily News*, pinch-hitting for Matthews as host of MSNBC's *Hardball,* and being hired to write a twice-weekly column for the *Boston Herald.* So take heart: Pundits are loyal to their own kind. Once you make the cut and earn your Imus spurs, you're in, baby!

7. MASTER THE SNAPPY PATTER OF POP CULTURE

If, as the joke goes, politics is show business for ugly people, knowledge of showbiz is a poodle imperative.

Many of the eulogies for Lars-Erik Nelson, the *Daily News* columnist and *New York Review of Books* contributor, whose death in November 2000 left an unfillable gap of candor, intelligence, and integrity, quoted a complaint he had lodged against his colleagues in the press—that what they were practicing these days wasn't political analysis but "theater criticism." They were graduates of the Copacabana School of advanced punditry. Shrewd handicappers like Jack Germond, whose insights are still redolent of smoke-filled rooms and sloshed beer, have become a diminishing breed. In the past a prospective pundit could pass inspection by mouthing a rosary of old-school political hand-me-downs. The New Hampshire primary: "retail politics." Social Security: "the third rail of American politics." International diplomacy: "high-stakes poker." Etc. Today's pundit, raised in front of the TV and computer screen, doesn't have the luxury of dismissing political theatrics as so much mascara and Method acting. His or her audience have only a faint flicker of what's in the Constitution, in what century the Civil War was fought, who our allies were in World War Two, who any of their elected officials are. Politics for them is about personalities, and for pundits this means putting an *Entertainment Weekly* face on every political player. It is not enough to trot out the same tired lines from *Casablanca* ("The Republicans were shocked, *shocked*, to discover pork in the appropriations bill") and the standard allusions to *The Wizard of Oz* (Karl Rove as the man behind the curtain). Unless you're the parents of teenagers and can suss out the latest trends and pop-star Twinkies through osmosis, keeping tabs on current pop culture fluff is hard work, requiring constant scanning, a cement butt, and the ability to turn attention deficit to your advantage.

Lucky for you, there's a neat shortcut. Let Maureen Dowd be your Love Boat guide. She and Frank Rich are the ones most responsible for pursuing politics through the multiplex, and their receptors for mainstream pop culture continue to pick up every particle wave. Unlike most boomers upholstered in comfortable middle age, their spider sense still tingles at the thrill of the new. Rich heard the underground rumbles of the Howard Dean Web surge and recognized it as an evolutionary spurt in political campaigning (rapid cellular self-reproduction through meet-up events and blogsites, unsupervised power diffusion—leaderless leadership) while Washington pundits were sniffing as if someone had let in the peasants. Yet even for lightning-reflex pros at the top of their game, there are pitfalls. Consider the Dowd column on George Bush that began, "President-elect (?) Mini-Me has not yet started gnawing on his cat, as the 'Austin Powers' Mini-Me did to the hairless Mr. Bigglesworth"—a wisecrack cited that week by Al Hunt on *The Capital Gang*, much to Robert Novak's unamusement. As that

Dowdian riff demonstrates, pop-cult patter dates fast. Much of it will be indecipherable to future readers, for whom the intricacies of *Buffy the Vampire Slayer* and *Alias* will hold little charm. Drop a cute reference to Christina Aguilera when all the kids have decided she's skanky and, like, totally over, and you'll look like the doofus you are. I saw a panel in which some pundit was trying to tout a controversial court nominee as the Seabiscuit of the confirmation process. "I believe he got a shaky start out of the gate but will break away during the home stretch." His fellow panelists seemed embarrassed for him, as well they ought. Not only was the analogy hinky, but *Seabiscuit* wasn't a box-office blockbuster, and citing a nonhit leaves one looking uncool. Don't herniate yourself to show how with-it you are either. Saying that John Kerry's wife, heiress Teresa Heinz, brings "major bling-bling" to the Democratic race embarrasses us all.

8. PRACTICE PSYCHIATRY ON STRANGERS

To an attack poodle, opponents aren't just wrong, they're bonkers too. Completely delusional—unable to distinguish reality from their kaleidoscope dreams, spouting gibberish like

Dutch Schultz on his deathbed, and having no impulsivity control whatsoever! The chief resident of the Beltway psychiatric clinic is *Washington Post* columnist, Fox News all-star, and unrepentant war hawk Charles Krauthammer, who finds one Democratic candidate after another certifiable. After Al Gore contended in December 2002 that Limbaugh–Fox News conservatism was a subsidiary of the Republican Party, something that struck many observers as glaringly self-evident, Krauthammer was ready to reserve him a rubber room. "I'm a psychiatrist," he said on Fox News. "I don't usually practice on camera. But this is the edge of looniness, this idea that there's a vast conspiracy, it sits in a building, it emanates, it has these tentacles, is really at the edge. He could use a little help." When Howard Dean made the same point, saying he thought it would be advantageous to break up media monopolies, the candidate went over the edge into a vertigo pinwheel drop, according to Krauthammer. In a column for the *Washington Post* called "The Delusional Dean," he diagnosed the former governor of Vermont as a victim of acute paranoia suffering from Bush Derangement Syndrome. What Krauthammer omitted from his psychic reading—as Bob Somerby revealed on *Daily Howler*—was the fact that in one of the damning quotes he used against Dean, Dean had been *joking*. Asked by

Chris Matthews on *Hardball* if Rupert Murdoch's media empire should be broken up, Dean responded, "On ideological grounds, absolutely yes," and the transcript indicates audience laughter, followed by Matthews's asking for a serious answer and Dean then providing one. Krauthammer elided the transcript to remove any trace of facetiousness, tampering with the evidence to give the impression Dean was a red-eyed fanatic. Krauthammer's thumbnail sketches of Democratic candidates as studies in abnormal psychology always illustrate a partisan purpose, topped with a sneer. (He reviewed Gore's impassioned address about the Iraq debacle with the observation, "Well, it looks as if Al Gore has gone off his Lithium again.") To date, he hasn't taken a hacksaw to Kerry's cranium, but if the election looks close. . . .

Just because you don't have a diploma framed on the wall like Krauthammer doesn't mean you can't practice crackpot psychiatry too. Peggy Noonan, for example, has pronounced, "The good news about Mr. Kerry, and I mean this seriously, is he does not appear to be insane." (That sly "appear to be" is of course a tip-off that there still may be something ominous brewing in his unconscious, invisible to the naked eye.) One of our leading unlicensed pathologists is Krauthammer's frequent tablemate on Fox News panels, *Roll Call* editor Mort Kondracke. On successive broadcasts in the winter of 2003, I heard him question the shaky state of Gore's "mental stability" and say point-blank of billionaire liberal donor George Soros, "I think he's lost his mind." Concurring with Mort's lay finding was White House correspondent for the *National Review*, Byron York, who in a *Wall Street Journal* review of Soros's *The Bubble of American Supremacy*, found grave signs of deterioration in Soros's declaration that Bush's you're-either-with-us-or-ag'in-us attitude "reminds me of the Germans." As a Hungarian Jew who came of age under both Nazi and Communist oppression before escaping to the West (and, having accumulated his investment wealth, spent millions trying to actualize the ideal of Karl Popper's "open society"), Soros might appear on the surface to know whereof he speaks. But not to the untrained, unlicensed, unprofessional pundit, for whom personal history is immaterial to understanding the cauldrons of the psyche. As one such, York rendered a Freudian reading: "At any given time, there is some small sliver of the American population that believes the president—any president—is a Nazi. Those people are usually thought of as nut cases. Now they can count among their number one of the world's richest and most influential men."

As an amateur psychiatrist pundit, you need never deal with

the chewy substance or content of a political opponent's position ever again. The next time the name of Soros or Gore or Kerry comes up, just whip out your invisible butterfly net and mime swishing it over the lunatic's head, or pronounce sentence on their sick souls à la Tony Blankley, who said of Soros on Fox's *Hannity & Colmes*, "He's a self-admitted athiest...a Jew who figured out a way to survive the Holocaust." If Big Tony can get away with that, who knows what *you'll* be able to slide by?

9. LEARN TO MODULATE

Each pundit must soup him- or herself up into a rapid-response machine, capable of racing on the air at a moment's notice with only a thin coat of makeup between you and onrushing events. The necessity to think fast on your loafers doesn't include the necessity to speak LOUD. Check out Jeff Greenfield, for example. He's as mellow as Mel Torme, gliding from one network to another (PBS, CBS, ABC, CNN) with his aplomb intact. Al Franken, another laid-back frog. A pundit can raise his voice on occasion for spurious dramatic effect—as long as it doesn't become a persistent foghorn.

Take instruction from the decline of John McLaughlin. A

former speechwriter and special assistant to Presidents Nixon and Ford and a former editor and columnist for the *National Review*, McLaughlin launched *The McLaughlin Group*, a syndicated weekly political panel show, in 1982. From the outset his band of pundits buffaloed through the modest compunctions and courtesies that characterized stodgier public affairs shows such as *Washington Week in Review* and *Agronsky & Company* (whose verbal foot-dragging was hilariously lampooned by Michael Kinsley in the *New Republic*). McLaughlin turbocharged the genre, his panelists making no pretense of objectivity or nonpartisanship, yapping over each other with enough cross talk to supply dialogue for a Robert Altman double feature. The Group even took their act on the road, playing corporate events like a traveling company of *Pippin*. The show's recognition factor peaked when *Saturday Night Live* parodied the program circa 1990, with Dana Carvey imitating McLaughlin's stentorian boom and gavel-rapping verdicts (*"Wrong!"*), asking absurd round-robin questions ("On a scale of one to ten, one being zero, ten being metaphysical annihilation, how would you rate the chances of a comet smashing the earth and bringing about the return of the dinosaurs?"), and ringing innumerable bananafana changes on Kondracke's name ("Morton Salt, when-it-rains-it-pours, what say you? ... *Wrong!*").

McLaughlin basked in the popularity of *SNL*'s satire and other comedy tributes until his brain blistered. He seemed to believe that the skit's whopping success signified that audiences found his excesses endearing: he became even more of a caricature after Carvey's send-up, as if to prove that not only was he in on the joke, he could add his own special topping. He woodenly presided over the special two hundredth episode of the sitcom *Cheers*, trading badly scripted wisecracks at the bar with Carla and Norm. For a man already inflated with self-importance, priding himself as a mirth-maker was the folly of follies. *The McLaughlin Group* began to drown in its own deafening cry. McLaughlin's introductions became longer and fuller of thunderation, his choice of topics ever more capricious and strange; he imperiously played musical chairs with the panelists, antagonizing longtime regulars Bob Novak and Jack Germond until they defected. In Germond's entertaining memoir of his journalistic career, *Fat Man in a Middle Seat*, he recounts how McLaughlin assumed the airs of a self-appointed Caesar in the studio and on the road, hogging the fee money and sliding into a chauffeured limo while the others had to pile into a van. His top-heavy ego eventually took its toll. In recent years, ratings for *The McLaughlin Group* have sunk like a damaged submarine, McLaughlin himself a rusty relic, a dull roar. So take heed: Today's loudmouth is tomorrow's "Old Yeller."

10. INSULATE YOURSELF FROM THE "LITTLE PEOPLE"

After you've clawed your way to media stardom like Stephen Boyd in *The Oscar*, kicking Elke Sommer out of bed as if she were trailer trash, your vulnerable exposure to informed citizens and their pesky questions will diminish. They will become a camera-pan of blurred faces seen from inside the tinted glass of the limo taking you to the studio. This is not only how it is, this is how it must be. Sometimes, sadly, to make new friends you must leave old friends behind. To become an attack poodle means saying adieu to all the "little people" you used to know, those superfluous folks who aren't on TV and lead humdrum lives in the flyover zone between the coasts. From now on the average American belongs to a vast, vague abstraction known as the American people, who can be spoken of as if they thought and felt the same thing at the same time ("The American people are concerned about rising natural gas prices this winter"), yet can be neatly subdivided into cardboard-cutout cartoons such as soccer moms, NASCAR dads, Reagan Democrats, suburban bobos, and retired seniors on fixed incomes, all of whose domestic concerns can be filed into the patronizing category of "kitchen table topics." (Pundits love to picture families gathering around the kitchen table to discuss prescription drug benefits.) These residents of Munchkin Land and their humdrum problems need not trespass upon your personal growth path, since you'll seldom have to meet them in the flesh, except in airports or town meetings or other places where the caste system has broken down.

Once you've joined the journalistic in-crowd and done your first *Slate* diary, it's time to draw the curtain in the first-class compartment and take refuge in an activity that has become the prophylactic of choice among attack poodles: poll watching. Where an old-shoe reporter like Haynes Johnson used to take palm readings of the masses to support his hazy platitudes (in Kinsley's parody of *Agronsky & Company*, he was Haynes Underwear, solemnly pronouncing, "For me to pass among the American people at this fleeting yet crucial moment in history, touch an outstretched hand here, accepting a gentle kiss on the foot there, was as stirring and moving for me as a journalist as it was for them as the American people"), such dirty work can be shunned through the mediation of polls.

Punditry for Dummies

Every pundit must be as conversant with polls and pollsters as a market analyst is with support levels and significant tops, able to divine the deeper booga-booga of conflicting numbers issuing from Zogby, Gallup, the newspapers, and TV networks. "Well, as you know, Brit, Zogby polls taken on Friday nights skew Democratic because they're more likely to be home watching *Washington Week in Review* and counting food stamps." ("Skew"—key verb in the pundit vocabulary.) Simple guideline: Cite the polls that agree with you as reliable and dismiss the ones that don't as outliers. ("Outliers"—another fine fudge word.)

Polling data are the white noise of political discourse, a jamming device to make public opinion seem decisive and dynamic when it's usually glaciering along. Polls also allow pundits to wriggle out of the traps reality sets for even the most fluent apologists. No WMDs unearthed in Iraq? No problem! "Polls show that 61 percent of the American people believe the war was justified if we don't find them." No link found between Iraq and Al Qaeda? The uninformed American people beg to differ. "Polls show 49 percent of the American people believe there was some connection between Saddam Hussein and 9/11, so I don't foresee this being a campaign issue next fall." Think the American people are anxious about rising unemployment? Nahhhh. Mere socialist propaganda. Fox's Bill O'Reilly set a guest straight on that score by telling him the American people didn't care about 6 percent unemployment because "it's only a number." The unemployment rate was then 6.4 percent, but, hey, the American people care even less about some diddly decimal. O'Reilly keeps his eye on the big picture, fuzzy though it may be from his Olympian bar stool, and why not? He can afford to! According to *Business Week* (March 8, 2004), O'Reilly earns $4 million a year from his contract with Fox, and rakes in tens of millions more from his best-selling books, public speaking engagements, radio show, and personal merchandise sold on his Web site, such as the classy "The Spin Stops Here" doormat. *Business Week* estimates that his mouth is worth $60 million a year. Now that's a number an aspiring attack poodle can get behind!

With that in mind...

I I. ALWAYS HAVE YOUR PALM READY FOR A HANDOUT

The expertise you pretend to have on issues great and small will stand you in good stead as a corporate consultant. Hot air travels upward, and you should travel with it. All sorts of fat-cat executive boards are aching to shell out the shareholders' money for perfectly useless advice, and that adviser could be you! Before it went blazooie, Enron forked over hundreds of thousands of dollars to deserving journalists, such as *Weekly Standard* editor William Kristol's six-figure fee for serving on its advisory board. That must have been some *pretty good advice*. Others were fortunate enough to hop aboard a gravy train like Hollinger International, which under conservative newspaper baron Conrad Black paid its board of advisors a nice allowance of around $25,000 a year to attend a few meetings and lay a little wisdom on the assembled. Along with geopolitical luminaries such as Margaret Thatcher, Valéry Giscard d'Estaing, and Henry Kissinger, Hollinger's seraglio included William F. Buckley and George Will, both of whom praised Black in print and blurbed his Franklin Delano Roosevelt biography without ever divulging they were on the take. Confronted on this rather gaping oversight on their part, Buckley tried to peer through his monocle like a Regency dandy past such trifling matters while Will, feeling his Wheaties, basically told the writer to bugger off: "My business is my business. Got it?" This is not the gentlemanly George who deigns to educate us each Sunday on ABC's *This Week*, but when you question this pundit's inalienable right to pad his wallet for doing little more than showing up and looking presentable, you strike at the very foundation of capitalism, and that makes him mad enough to spit (though, given Will's dry composition, he would probably spit sawdust). The post-Enron crackdown on corporate corruption and the shareholder revolts at other high-profile companies are making it harder to score work-free moolah, but don't fall into the nostalgic trap of thinking the good times are gone, you're too late for the Mardi Gras. Under Bush II, the nation's capital has never been friendlier to corporate flacks with shareholder money to waste, and once you establish your portfolio as an attack poodle, they'll be happy to waste some of it on *you*. So work those cocktail parties like a call girl at a downtown convention and learn to pick up the scent of money burning expensive holes in lobbyists' pockets.

12. ALWAYS END WITH A HEARTY CHUCKLE

It can get feisty under the hot lights of the studio. Tense. Things are said, faces made. But poodle spats should never be taken personally. Ripping off your lapel mike and storming out of the studio may feel good and look macho, but it will tend to cut down on future invitations. Besides, you can only get away with that sort of Jack Paar gesture once. Do it more than once and you'll look like one of those hotheads who's always leaving the restaurant in a huff ("Grab your coat, Muriel, we're going—no busboy's going to talk to me that way!"). Someone like O'Reilly, who flounced off of Terry Gross's *Fresh Air* show on NPR, unable to withstand the "ordeal" (his word) of being tortured by the pixie host, is a professional hothead with his own empire; he doesn't need guest gigs. You do. So pretend that you and your fellow panelists belong to the same V.I.P. club. Practice collegiality; tease but don't antagonize. Feign envy of Bob Novak's reputed wealth, poke humor at George Will's distaste for the designated-hitter rule, gently taunt Tim Russert about his beloved Buffalo Bills. Such funning is easily and airily deflected. But bringing up Newt Gingrich's past infidelity or Bill Bennett's gambling losses the next time they're lambasting some Democrat's incontinent libido will only make *you* look like the meanie. These giants among men are your future colleagues, and you may want them to cover your poodle posterior someday.

So lighten up and learn to laugh with others. Nearly every broadcast of *Crossfire, The Capital Gang,* and *The McLaughlin Group* ends with everyone sharing a no-hard-feelings chuckle as the credits roll. Chuckling isn't as easy as it seems: to convey the shallows of phony bonhomie calls for a relaxed diaphragm and a nice twinkle. You don't want to twinkle as if a gnat just flew in your eye (note the constipated strain of Louis Rukeyser's Wall Street guests laughing gamely at Lou's lame puns). Guests with too much self-respect and passionate integrity to produce a fade-out chuckle aren't as welcome at the banquet hall as more congenial spirits. They're booked, but not asked to join the regular roundtable. And then someday they won't be asked back anymore even for one-shot appearances, and they'll start to rot away in their lonely apartments, cursing the darkness, surfing the Internet in search of a friend.

Do you want that someone someday to be you? Then take these rules to heart and start your attack poodle regimen today. Adjust your thong, hit that hairspray, and start pontificating!

Git Along, Li'l Doggies

IN ONE OF HIS FINER ADDISON DEWITT MOMENTS, film critic John Simon once batted aside the persistent rumor that a well-known West Coast colleague, notorious for the praise he spread like ballpark mustard over the most mediocre movies, had been "bought" by the Hollywood studios. Simon jested: "Why should they pay for something that they can have for free?"

The same rhetorical question arises regarding the geisha behavior of the Washington press corps during the presidency of George W. Bush. Elected with no mandate, Bush has comported himself as a Sun Belt pharaoh, the second in a dynastic succession (Jebahotep of Florida waits on deck). Bush condescends to the commoners in the press with crisp disdain, and reporters justify his disdain by acting as if they deserve no better, O master. The sorrow, dread, and uncertainty following September 11 robed Bush in the shaman role of healer-avenger-protector. The press, like the American people, rallied behind a backbone display of strength and determination, and Bush has maintained that posture, that dramatic musculature, emerging from the helicopter or entering a room as if wearing a pair of shoulder pads under his blue suit. That seems to work for him. Unfortunately for the republic, much of the press corps has also frozen rigid. Mark Hertsgaard's scathing account of the fawning coverage Ronald Reagan enjoyed during his presidency was titled *On Bended Knee*. After September 11, the other knee dropped and has remained rooted. A raucous, liberal Web site didn't hesitate to impugn these genuflectors as "media whores"—Media Whores Online, a site that proclaims it "set out to bring the media to their knees, but found they were already there." Yet this colorful jab may do an injustice. If the press has taken turns giving Bush, Dick Cheney, Condoleezza Rice, Colin Powell, and Donald Rumsfeld horseyback rides, it isn't because they're paid submissives. As Simon asks, why pay for what you can have for free? The press corps aren't prostitutes, they're pushovers. Floozies.

Even pushovers should show a sliver of pride. On March 6, 2003, President Bush held a rare press conference—only his eighth—to prepare the country for its nonrefundable war against Iraq (flash-forward: By January 1, 2004, Bush would have held only ten press conferences, compared to his father's sixty-one and Clinton's thirty-three during the same period in their respective terms). It was a solemn marionette piece of absurdist theater: commedia dell'arte, without the comedy or art. Members of the press were marched into the room two by two, like schoolchildren on a field trip to the planetarium or the local dairy. Departing from precedent, the president refused to entertain a random volley of questions; instead, he chose reporters from a prepared list, the resulting colloquy so stilted he couldn't resist blurting out at one juncture that the entire evening was "scripted." As Matt Taibbi wrote in *New York Press*, the White House press corps collaborated in this charade, behaving as if they were being operated by remote control. "In other words," he wrote, "not only were reporters going out of their way to make sure their softball questions were pre-approved, but they even went so far as to *act* on Bush's behalf, raising their hands and jockeying in their seats in order to better give the appearance of a spontaneous news conference." Reporters from powerful breakfast papers humbled themselves like subjects in the court of Siam, the *New York Times*'s David Sanger "meekly sitting his ass back down" (Taibbi) when Bush ignored his question. Bush ignored a lot of questions that enchanted evening, his eyes straying to his cue cards as his mind skirted the clouds.

Jaw agape, convinced that he was "witnessing, live, an historic political catastrophe," Taibbi was stunned when the pundits and reporters compounded their sleepwalk by ignoring the evidence of their eyes and ears afterward, lauding Bush for being steady, stalwart, and—the pet word of the postmortems—"somber." Apart from Taibbi and Tom Shales of the *Washington Post*, no one mustered the candor of Groucho Marx in *Duck Soup* when he told the courtroom, "Gentlemen, Chicolini here may talk like an idiot and look like an idiot, but don't let that fool you—he really is an idiot." The American press regards as recherché the cult of personality that once plastered the walls and billboards of Iraq with Stalinoid portraits of Saddam Hussein, while staying dim to the cult of personality that cowed most of them into a torpor. (Two notable exceptions: ABC's Terry Moran and NBC's David Gregory, the latter once scaling up Bush's bad side by addressing a question in French to French President Jacques Chirac at a joint press conference, which Bush found *très* pretentious—"The guy memorizes four words, and he plays like he's intercontinental.") And "cowed" is the word. Bush's cult of personality is based on a rawhide image of masculinity as carefully storyboarded and marketed as the old Marlboro Man cigarette campaign. Now that the Marlboro Man has coughed up a lung and Clint Eastwood has climbed out of the saddle, Bush has the heroic sunset all to himself, a bloodred dusk silhouetted with missile launchers and oil rigs. Killing and drilling, that's what's driven his presidency.

"Years of rash statements...had earned Reagan a reputation as a trigger-happy extremist," Hertsgaard wrote in *On Bended Knee*. "Defusing the President's cowboy image thus became a top and enduring priority for Reagan's men." Bush's advisers took the opposite tack, giving his cowboy image regular infusions of cactus juice. After two terms of Bill Clinton, a voluminous policy wonk and voluptuary who could sweet-talk any group or "widder woman" into saying yes, yes, yes (even Newt Gingrich left meetings with Clinton with eyes melted, lips apart), it was time for a tough but compassionate hombre who squinted hard, spoke plain, and shot true. A buckskin buckaroo whose wife was happy to tend the home fires and not stick her beak into healthcare policy. Frequent photo ops of Bush clearing brush on his Ponderosa ranch in Crawford, Texas ("With all the time the president has spent clearing brush," Dana Milbank puzzled in the *Washington Post*, "how is it possible that there is still any brush left...?"), coupled with his bounty hunter statement about bringing Osama bin Laden to frontier justice ("There's an old poster out West, as I recall, that said, 'Wanted: Dead or Alive'"), inspired countless editorial cartoons showing a bow-legged president under a ten-gallon hat at high noon. When it came to evil, he was hell-bent for leather, ready to convert enemies into buzzard bait. Bush's aging sidekick, Dick Cheney, told Tim Russert on *Meet the Press*, "The notion that the president is a cowboy . . . is a Westerner, I think that's not necessarily a bad idea. I think the fact of the matter is he cuts to the chase. He is very direct and I find that very refreshing." Very.

The city slickers in the press swallowed this rootin'-tootin' persona like large-mouthed bass. William Schneider, a once respected political scientist who has rolled downhill as an inane poll watcher for CNN, breaking down the numbers as if explaining the birds and bees to backward children, wrote in the *National Journal*: "Talk tough and carry a big stick, but act with prudence. It's Reagan diplomacy with a Bush twist—just right for an Ivy League cowboy." Journalism's most lyric poet of the Pecos is Howard Fineman, who yodels from the pages of *Newsweek* and on MSNBC, his smirk eerily mirroring Bush's. It's as if they share the same nasty secret of snotty self-esteem. Fineman has been foremost in fluffing Bush as a hero on horseback who casts a lean shadow. No sooner had the president's zombie press conference staggered to a close than Fineman could be heard caroling on *Hardball*, "If he's a cowboy he's the reluctant warrior, he's Shane…because he has to, to protect his family."

Not much of a poet, Fineman is an even poorer scholar of the sagebrush genre. Alan Ladd's reluctant and repentant gunslinger wasn't protecting his family; he was strapping on the holster to defend the family for whom he toiled as a hired hand. Shane also made it a point of honor never to be the first to draw. It was the bad guys and yella' bellies who went for their guns to get the jump on decent folk. Far from being the reluctant, conscience-torn gunslinger, Bush had itchy trigger fingers on *both* hands. According to *Time* magazine, he stuck his head into Condoleezza Rice's office in early 2002 as she was discussing sanctions and other diplomatic options against Iraq with three U.S. senators, and cut through the niceties. "Fuck Saddam," he said, "we're taking him out." *Time*: "The Senators laughed uncomfortably; Rice flashed a knowing smile." *Fuck Saddam, we're taking him out* isn't how Zane Grey heroes talk. It's how big shots boast; Donald Trump with an arsenal at his disposal.

President Bush is no more of an old cowhand from the Rio Grande (roping steers, farting by the campfire) than Ronald Reagan was. If anything, he's further removed from reality, even granting that in the media funhouse, reality itself has become fungible. Ronald Reagan, an actor who played cowboys in movies, reinvented himself as a politician and became a popular president. George Bush is a politician who pretends to be a cowboy in order to remind us of Reagan as a popular president. Reagan represented Hollywood. Bush represents a Hollywood afterbirth, the TV spin-off of the hit movie. His being a double copy—a Warholian fake of a fake—hasn't kept the poodles in the press from rolling out a red carpet for each gala event, especially the fuck-Saddam invasion of Iraq. "This is a president who likes his stories upbeat, his plotlines simple, and his villains clearly marked," wrote Tamara Lipper and the inescapable Howard Fineman in *Newsweek* on the eve of "Shock and Awe" in March of 2003. *Newsweek*'s fan letter promoted the president from the nation's actor-in-chief to an Orson Welles–sized auteur: star, screenwriter, producer, director. As real bullets were about to maim real bodies, Lipper-Fineman punned that the war plan was Bush's "shooting script." They whisked the reader inside the White House to witness a wholesome vignette. Read the following paragraph and amaze yourself at what passes for adult journalism in a major newsweekly:

> The president loves regular order, especially now. He's been traveling less, which means more time for breakfast and dinner with First Lady Laura. Karen Hughes, his

original "mother hen" adviser, is back to vet his
speeches. ("You look good in that tie," she told him
before his Oval Office speech. "It's very powerful.")
Ever the runner, Bush now is fighting age as well as war:
he's given up sweets so he can lose weight and improve
his treadmill pace. "You don't know what six pounds can
do to a running time," he told an aide.

Along with forgoing sweets, Bush was keeping the worry birds
at bay. "If Bush has doubts, they're not visible," *Newsweek*
intoned, and a front-page profile in *USA Today* let us know that
Bush didn't want any Doubting Thomases drooping around
him either. "He has a special epithet for members of his own
staff who worry aloud. He calls them 'hand-wringers.'" Jesus on
the cross gave way to doubt, but Bush is made of sterner stuff.

Instead of being worried that Bush himself wasn't worried
about waging full-scale war, not the eensiest bit, *Newsweek*,
USA Today, and others warmed themselves in front of his inner
fire. They took comfort in a president who didn't overcomplex-
ify, whose thoughts and intentions traveled in a straight line.
After Vietnam and other debacles, you'd think the press would
know better than to entrust everything to the unswerving will
and resolute brows of our leaders as they guide us once again

into the lagoon, but reporters and columnists are as susceptible as anyone else to decisive actors—Gordian knot-cutters. To paraphrase Randolph Bourne, the true prophet of our imperilment, it's a mistake to believe that intellectuals and other brain workers crave in politics the ambiguity, paradox, subtlety, and storied depths that they prize in art, law, and literature. "The intellect craves certitude," Bourne wrote. "It takes effort to keep it supple and pliable. In a time of danger and disaster we jump desperately for some dogma to cling to." Or some dogmatic leader to bear our brute load of anxieties. Bush, whose signature phrase "there is no doubt in my mind..." seems grooved across his forehead, embodies chiseled certitude. He gives the impression that even his prayers fly on wings of steel.

This is where sexual politics—or, if you're in a candlelight mood, gender presentation—enters the equation and becomes ammo for the attack poodles. For a president to be anything less than rock-hard dead-cert looks womanly, and the press corps strings up womanly men by their sock garters. (Wrung out with fatigue over the Iran hostage stalemate, Jimmy Carter was called an old maid by his detractors, and his postpresidential peace efforts are denigrated by hostile conservatives—i.e., the whole mob—as spinsterish meddling.) In the retro-hetero ethos of the media elite, policed by fashion queens and social arbiters such as Maureen Dowd and Chris Matthews, real men don't wear earth tones or argyle sweaters, or change their minds, or take guff from their wives (only one pair of balls allotted per marriage). Being a good listener, that's for girls too, and one of the things we learn from Ron Suskind's *The Price of Loyalty*, his inside look based on the experiences and documents of outspoken former secretary of the treasury Paul O'Neill, is that *nobody* in the Bush administration listens. Their skulls are soundproofed and burglar-alarmed against any possible break-in by opposing viewpoints or contradictory data that might mess with their made-up minds. Only after the postoccupation of Iraq went bloodily awry was this cocooning seen as a liability, in part because the attack poodles practice their own cocooning and high-altitude hermetics. Like the inner circle of the Bush cult, the elite media hardly listen to anybody except themselves.

The punditocracy has embraced the widening class divisions of the society at large, the disengagement between the have-mores and the have-less. With its skybox view of the bulky spectacle below, TV punditry has created its own class strata, complete with genetically modified political coverage that works itself down the food chain as beat reporters aspire to the higher pay and roomier accommodations of punditry. Despite their hearty football metaphors, their paeans to town meetings and other vestiges of once vibrant democracy, their verbal solidarity with the rough-hewn populace (on *Meet the Press* David Broder described the Howard Dean volunteers as if he had discovered a cave of leprechauns ["they're young, they're female, they're gay, and they're small"], contrasting them with the average pro-Gephardt big, beefy union supporter—"My kind of guy," burbled Russert), media mandarins hold themselves high, aloof, and huggably close to each other. They identify less with society's underdogs and more with the top dogs, being the top rovers in their own green pasture. Mingling with The People every quadrennial delivers its sassy moments at the diner, but it's the lobbyists, consultants, media executives, political aides, and millionaire senators and representatives they socialize with year-round, whose culture they share. Social anthropologists may someday yield fruitful results studying the tapes of Washington, D.C., cocktail parties that are broadcast on C-SPAN 2 when a politician or pundit brings out a new book, notating this slow-motion status ballet of supertanker egos and fixed grins, each party a Tom Wolfe novella.

In the gray-flannel past, judicious journalists such as Walter Lippmann and James Reston may have been compromised by proximity to power, honoring a gentleman's agreement with the politicians they covered (which didn't immunize Reston against getting a scalding earful from LBJ); but if they chewed too much cud in their columns, generating mushy platitudes, at least they weren't purveyors of vapid chitchat and winky one-liners. They were serious adults, a waning species in the punditocracy. The irony today is that we have a cadre of ass-kissers who don't even have access to the asses they kiss in print. As the innocuous details of Lipper-Fineman's *Newsweek* article typify, White House star reporters don't come any-where near hollering distance of the inner workings of Bush, Cheney, Rumsfeld, et al.; they're more like trick-or-treaters, filling their bags with colorful anecdotes doled out like candy by the help. They hoard and treasure these trifles, taking glee in knowing it's more than the poor kids down the block got. Tucked within *Newsweek's* bouquet to the president is a snap-shot of Bush's Heisman Trophy stance as he stiff-arms the beat reporters. "No fan of the media, he couldn't hide a smirk [can he ever?] as the White House pool was hustled into—and quickly out of—a cabinet meeting without being given the chance to ask a question." See ya, chumps!

As a further check on the access of White House corre-spondents, when impertinent questions do manage to pene-trate the force field, the questioner risks retaliation. Under the Nixon administration, the intimidation was systematic. Nosy reporters, negative commentators, newspaper editors, and TV producers would get royal chewings-out from White House skulkers. The worst offenders—journalists Daniel Schorr and Mary McGrory, black Congressmen Ron Dellums and John Conyers, actor Paul Newman, and that candelabra of teeth, actress Carol Channing—landed on a secret Oval Office "Enemies List," to be taken care of later, when the dark lords of misrule took total command. A Nixonian note was struck early in the Bush administration when Press Secretary Ari Fleischer warned a reporter that his question about Jenna Bush's under-age-drinking citation "had been noted in the building." Compared with the lashings of distemper that crawled out of the snake pit of Nixon's henchmen—E. Howard Hunt, G. Gordon Liddy, Chuck Colson (who, before dedicating himself to Jesus, boasted he would run over his own grandmother to win an election), and Attorney General John Mitchell (who voiced a vivid desire to put *Washington Post* owner Katherine Graham's "tit... in a wringer")—Fleischer's admonition was Nixon lite, about as fear-inducing as Mel Cooley trying to get the Alan Brady writers to quit horsing around on *The Dick Van Dyke Show*. After Fleischer left the White House to return to private life and piece together the shards of his self-respect, he was replaced by a more advanced cyborg, Scott McClellan, who repels pestering questions from reporters by repeating a rote answer until the Q & A turns into a tautological tango. After it was revealed that the reference to Iraq's attempt to purchase Nigerian uranium should never have been inserted into Bush's State of the Union address, reporters tried to get McClellan to unclam during a White House press briefing on July 17, 2003.

QUESTION: Regardless of whether or not there was pressure from the White House for that line, I'm wondering where does the buck stop in this White House? Does it stop at the CIA, or does it stop in the Oval Office?

SCOTT MCCLELLAN: Again, this issue has been discussed. You're talking about some of the comments that—some that are—

QUESTION: I'm not talking about anybody else's comments. I'm asking the question, is responsibility for what was in the President's own State of the Union ultimately with the President, or with somebody else?

SCOTT MCCLELLAN: This has been discussed.

QUESTION: So you won't say that the President is responsible for his own State of the Union speech?

SCOTT MCCLELLAN: It's been addressed.

The truth is that the Bush regime doesn't need to work the phones and nutcrack the press with Nixonian spite, because it's got many enforcers in the media eager to do the seal-clubbing for them. The contempt and disdain the Bushies have for the press is a trickle-down phenomenon, an acid drip that seeps from Bush through his staff, from the staff to their political allies in the capital, from their political allies to their media propagandists. Payback has been outsourced to a pack of attack poodles. Bush can hit the treadmill and address his doughy midsection, letting Rupert Murdoch's minions patrol the waterfront. These sluggers may have press badges but they function as political operatives, auxiliary police of opinion whose weapons are ridicule, insult, phony indignation, and ostracism. Those they can't silence they try to squash and shunt aside.

Consider the tale of Helen Thomas, outlaw geezer and dean of the press corps. Eighty-three years old, Helen Thomas has covered White House briefings and presidential press conferences since the sea-breeze days of President Kennedy. For forty-some years, Thomas was White House correspondent for U.P.I., resigning in 2000 when the news agency was sold to the Reverend Sun Myung Moon's Unification Church. Aged, frumpy, sometimes grumpy-looking, Thomas is a throwback in this telegenic age, an unglamorous reminder of a more civic, idealistic era. She has always been a true egalitarian. Nicholas F. Benton, a former White House correspondent for the *Falls Church News-Press*, recalls that lesser-known reporters like himself from smaller newspapers were relegated to the rear of the briefing room, "generally ignored and not infrequently the butt of rude jokes and behavior by the press corps 'elites.'" The one consistent mensch, he wrote, was Helen Thomas, "the consummate professional." Retired as a correspondent, Thomas writes a column for the Hearst syndicate, but has been allowed to retain her front-row seat at briefings as a matter of courtesy and tradition. If her Casey Stengel tenure has made her a familiar fixture, her persistent, frank questioning has made her a pest to presidents and their minders. (She and Sam Donaldson were Reagan's peskiest inquisitors.) None, however, has expressed his annoyance more nakedly than Bush the Son. In a previous press conference, shortly after Bush's announcement of faith-based initiatives, Thomas asked, "Mr. President, why do you refuse to respect the wall between the church and state? Why do you break it down?" When Bush tried to fob off some boilerplate answer about his respecting the separation between church and state, she retorted, "Well, you wouldn't have a religious office in the White House if you did.... You are a secular official.... And not a missionary." Unused to being challenged or contradicted, a vexed Bush unveiled a Method actor's battery of mannerisms. His performance was like an audition reel for Elia Kazan. The camera recorded Bush staring, twitching, pursing his lips, and at one point nearly crossing his eyes like Anthony Perkins doing his fly-on-the-nose bit in *Psycho*. When Thomas presumed to interrupt Bush's platitudinous, unresponsive word-dither, he said with a cobra smile, "I didn't get to finish my answer, in all due respect." (Bush doesn't cotton to back talk. In an October 28, 2003 press conference, he denied a radio journalist a follow-up question, saying, "Excuse me—particularly since you interrupted me, no." And to another impudent creature who asked a follow-up—"[C]an you promise a year from now that you will have reduced the number of troops in Iraq?" he replied, "The second question is a trick question, so I won't answer it.")

Thomas committed a greater act of blasphemy when she opined to an interviewer that George Bush qualified as the worst president in American history, a remark she partially recanted, saying it was too early to render a final verdict since there's always hope of "redemption." Too little, too late: her first, damning quote had been noted in the building, marked in her permanent record, and filed with the principal. When Bush convened his March 6 press conference, Thomas was not only denied her customary front-row seat and the privilege to ask the first question, she was never called upon, period. (Also black-balled was Mike Allen of the *Washington Post*, the second time in a row the *Post* had been bypassed for offending His Majesty. Previously it was Dana Milbank, he of the cheeky humor about Bush's brush-clearing, who experienced the blue-eyed chill.)

The president's petty snub was followed by an attack poodle gang-on whose purpose was to kick Thomas to the curb permanently, treating her as if she were a bag lady who had shuffled past security. The attack was led by loyalists at (where else?) Murdoch's Fox News and the *New York Post*, who dependably swarm into action at the first head nod from Republican capos. (Thomas had been targeted by a Republican National Committee group e-mailing.) A few days after the comatose March 6 press conference, Fox News White House correspondent James Rosen sided with the president against a fellow journalist with a gem of sophistry wrapped in a lace hankie of prissiness. It was a real Eddie Haskell performance. Noting that the president sped through twenty-one questions in under an hour (men of few words and fewer thoughts need not dally), Rosen ruminated: "Most Americans would be happy to let their president speak for three minutes in response to any question they asked. One can only imagine how many fewer questions would have been asked had he picked on Helen Thomas." Yes, one can only imagine. Why, the press conference might have stretched to *an entire hour*, keeping the leader of the free world up past his beddy-bye.

Fox's always testy Brit Hume (who smiles as if he'd just caught a bullet between his teeth) was more *ad hominem*, comparing Thomas to "the nutty aunt in the attic" and claiming that the chief reason Ari Fleischer called on her in White House briefings was that her questions are so "outrageous and so over the top" that it created a sympathetic backlash in favor of the administration. (Hume is an old hand at disciplining his fellow journalists. Nicholas F. Benton recalls that when Hume replaced Sam Donaldson in 1989 as chief White House correspondent for ABC News after the election of W.'s father, he whipped his colleagues into line. "For the next four years, Hume functioned as the policeman of the press corps. Humorless and imposing, the tall Hume would frequently stand at the front of the room and glare back at reporters he deemed out of line, barking, growling, demeaning, and ridiculing as called for by circumstances." Under Hume's baleful watch, White House press conferences became tepid affairs after the raucous Donaldson era.) In his *New York Post* column, written between shvitzes, John Podhoretz boasted about slagging Thomas—

"the ancient White House pseudo-reporter"—as a has-been who ought to be carted off "to an old-age home." *New York Post* colleague Michelle Malkin, beating a tight deadline before her next pedicure, climbed in with her own column to chide, "Shame, shame, shame on Helen Thomas."

Why such a major fuss over such a minor nuisance? If Helen Thomas was really the useful foil Hume contends she is, why not just plop her in the front row of Bush's next recital and let him tee off on her?—deflect her mosquito attack with a Reaganesque sigh, an indulgent tilt of the head, and a pithy, rehearsed catchphrase that would bury her in a roomful of chuckles? I'll tell you why. Because to a bully it feels better to punish someone than to finesse them. At the radical core of modern conservatism burns a resentful lust to knuckle down on any deviator. Either sing with the choir or zip your lips and accept the consequences. It's the vigilantism of the victory party, and each victory increases the saliva flow.

Helen Thomas wasn't the only octogenarian geezer to be attack poodled. Broadcast legend Walter Cronkite (b. 1916), who departed the anchor chair of the *CBS Evening News* in 1981, had the temerity to make a speech at Drew University in March 2003 deploring the arrogance of the Bush administration's foreign policy and urging a more conciliatory, multilateral approach. Well, you simply don't get away espousing that kind of common sense without it sticking up someone's nose, not when Bill O'Reilly is pounding the beat, twirling his nightstick. In his weekly column, written between soulful examinations of his fan mail, the host of Fox News's *O'Reilly Factor* labeled Cronkite an "internationalist," a nasty term in Bushistan. "Call me a jingoist," wrote O'Reilly (okay, you're a jingoist), "but your family's security is more important to me than [German Chancellor] Gerhard Schroeder's political career." Nice touch, that "your family"—as if O'Reilly weren't concerned about his own family's security but is selflessly looking out for ours (unlike Cronkite, who doesn't care if we all croak). O'Reilly also didn't cotton to currying favor with the French. "The government of the United States must be proactive in protecting its citizens, and if the French don't like it, they can go eat snails." He wasn't simply content to excoriate Cronkite as a namby-pamby sauerkraut-lover and snail-eater, but sought to blacken his broadcasting legacy as worst he could.

Some background. On February 27, 1968, Cronkite announced to CBS viewers that the American military campaign in Vietnam was "mired in stalemate": "To say that we are closer to victory today is to believe, in the face of the evidence, the optimists who have been wrong in the past." Cronkite's dire prognosis was a kidney punch to President Johnson, who understood the cause was now lost: "If I've lost Cronkite," he was quoted as saying, "I've lost middle America." Not since Cronkite's CBS mentor and colleague Edward R. Murrow lifted Senator Joe McCarthy by the skunk tail for public inspection had one TV broadcast reflected such a fateful shift in the climate of public opinion. Or at least that's what we've all been taught.

Clearing his throat loud enough to scatter pigeons and practicing the sort of "revisionist history" that Bush and Cheney so eloquently deplore, O'Reilly begged to differ. With pristine hindsight, he argued that we shouldn't give "Uncle Walter" undue credit. "The truth is that Walter Cronkite stood by and said little while the Vietnam War raged out of control in the 1960s.... [His] conversion came very late in that deadly game." Once again O'Reilly's no-spin zone had spun out of orbit. First off, unlike Battlin' Bill, Cronkite was a nightly news anchor who seldom editorialized (that was Eric Sevareid's sententious task); his "conversion" came from leaving the anchor desk and returning to his reportorial roots, seeing with his own eyes in Vietnam that the war was unwinnable. The implication that by not speaking up sooner "in that deadly game" Cronkite was somehow craven and simply adding his own me-too is rich coming from O'Reilly. Where, pray tell, was *he* when the war was raging? On a student deferment, like so many of his fellow chickenhawks. He played football and worked for the school paper at Marist College, spent his junior year at the University of London in 1969–70, then returned to Marist to put on the protective cup and rejoin the grid squad. Which is not to say Vietnam didn't haunt him too. "In the early 90s," he wrote, "I decided to go to Vietnam myself to have a look around," thereby arriving in country a mere quarter century or so after Cronkite. By then things had quieted down considerably.

Mopping up domestic opposition is only part of the mission of the American media's Elite Republican Guard. Cunning enemies from afar, too, are trying to warp our minds and confuse Kmart shoppers with words and images quarantined by our own press. During the buildup to what some bloggers dubbed Dubya Dubya II, I spent hours bonded to the BBC World Service through the wonder of satellite radio. Uncluttered by mortgage refinance commercials, network promos, martial theme music, digital flags fluttering in slow motion, and the flying shrapnel of quick-cut montages to which most TV is addicted, BBC World Service was, is, a sonic beacon, its sprinting coverage fortified with commentary from reputable scholars, historians, and military analysts—know-somethings far more pungent and precise than the retired officers with their battle-map pointers employed by American networks. The increased penetration and upscale influence of BBC radio and TV news, carried here on a number of NPR and PBS stations, has been countered with fierce resistance by Andrew Sullivan, an attack poodle who needs no reintroduction.

Since W. became president of Bushistan, Sullivan has deputized himself to root out anyone who would undermine his war against terror. He has become as zealous and tireless as the late red-baiter Roy Cohn in sniffing out subversives wherever he finds them, which is usually wherever he directs his nose. Before the war in Afghanistan began, Sullivan warned of enemies within who would stop at no fancy metaphor or flaming-baton trick to distract America from the struggle to save civilization. He flung the highly charged term "fifth column" at suspected traitors, fellow travelers, and sly professors on the "decadent Left," "a paralyzing, pseudo-clever, morally nihilist" party of sophisticates that blames America first, last, and always. For such lurid overheating, Sullivan earned a wrist slap from *Slate*'s Timothy Noah. Sullivan backtracked a bit but was undeterred. He's always undeterred. Like Bush, he has an unshakeable belief in the rightness of whatever he's saying at the moment, even if it contradicts what he said last week, knowing history will vindicate what's in his heart.

To Yankee Doodle Andy, the BBC was the chief propaganda arm of the enemy without—the Tokyo Rose in the war against terror, giving comfort to fifth columnists in the States and confounding the forces of freedom everywhere. So antagonistic was the British news agency toward Bush and Blair that Sullivan redubbed it the Baghdad Broadcasting Corporation. On March 26, 2003, Sullivan posted on his blog:

> Remember one of the key elements, we're finding out, in this battle is the willingness of the Iraqi people to stand up to the Saddamite remnants.... What the BBC is able to do, by broadcasting directly to these people, is to keep the Iraqi people's morale as far down as possible, thereby helping to make the war more bloody, thereby helping discredit it in retrospect. If you assume that almost all these reporters and editors are anti-war, this BBC strategy makes sense. They're a military player. And they are objectively pro-Saddam.

Understand the import of what he's alleging. The former editor of the *New Republic* accused the BBC of slanting the war from the gloomiest angle in a deliberate ploy to prolong the conflict, boost the casualty toll, and undercut the coalition of the willing. "Objectively pro-Saddam" (how ironic seeing the sort of dishonest formulation Orwell deplored spouted by an avowed Orwell devotee like Sullivan), the BBC is accused of wanting more corpses in order to make the campaign to overthrow Saddam look bad. It's an ingenious judo flip of logic. In the wonderworld according to Sullivan, it's the doves who secretly lust for blood and chaos to justify their opposition to war, and the hawks who are the true apostles of peace.

Labeling the BBC as "a military player" was worse than loose talk. It was an invitation to treat BBC facilities and reporters as hostiles—to put them in the crosshairs. Sound melodramatic? Not when you consider how many journalists have died during the Iraq war (nineteen, of whom thirteen were killed in hostile actions), or that American jets fired missiles into Iraqi TV offices in Baghdad. A selection of prominent American journalists (such as NBC's Andrea Mitchell) approved of the raid, some wondering why it hadn't been done sooner, forgetting or not caring that it violated the Geneva Convention rules of conduct that the United States professes to care about when it suits our interests (i.e., when our soldiers are captured and videotaped). The Pentagon refused to release internal reports about the shooting and killing of two Reuters cameramen in

Iraq, and about the arrests of two other Reuters journalists. The targeting of Al Jazeera's offices in Baghdad, which resulted in the death of correspondent Tariq Ayoub, and the disputed attack on the Palestine Hotel, which took the lives of two journalists, raised far greater outrage in the international media than they did here. But why expect American journalists to stand up for foreign broadcasters when they don't stand up for themselves or their own colleagues at home? They don't stand up to anybody in authority. Have they forgotten how? Or have their knees locked?

IN LATE JULY 2003, a few months after the invasion of Iraq, Bush lowered the deflector shield to field a few questions in what was only the ninth press conference of his presidency. Here was opportunity for the press corps to upright itself and shed its weenie skin. As Rupert Cornwell, Washington correspondent for the London *Independent*, commented, "This ought to have been a tricky occasion for the President. His poll numbers are sagging, budget deficits are ballooning, jobs are vanishing, and American soldiers are dying almost daily in Iraq. And not one of Saddam's alleged weapons has turned up." But when it was over, Bush hadn't been even lightly toasted by the reporters present, whose disinclination to follow up on each other's questions made it impossible to pin him down on any particulars. Cornwell: "The main lesson to emerge from the 50-minute session...was how easily the chief executive evaded any serious damage—and how the reporters made it easy for him to do so."

It became easier each go-round. In January 2004 Bush held a mini press conference after meeting with the Polish president, Aleksander Kwasniewski. Again he was asked about the absence of WMDs in Iraq, again he justified the decision to uproot Saddam Hussein for blocking U.N. weapons inspections. "He chose defiance. It was his choice to make, and he did not let us in." It was the second time Bush had uttered this whopper, the first time in the presence of an understandably perplexed U.N. chief Kofi Annan, and on neither occasion did reporters' polygraph needles so much as twitch. As Campaign Desk, the watchdog Web site of *Columbia Journalism Review*, commented, "What's especially dismaying about [the] incident is that, although the entire White House press corps was in attendance, not a single reporter chose to ask Bush the obvious question: If Saddam refused to let weapons inspectors in, what were Hans Blix and UNMOVIC doing in Iraq last fall?" Perhaps, to be uncharitably charitable, the press corps was bored into stupefaction by Bush, so hypnotized by his mindless reiterations that they could no longer register the meaning of his words, only their staccato rhythm.

The most animation the Washington press corps has shown during his too long post-9/11 honeymoon was after a chosen few were invited to hop aboard Bush's 2003 Baghdad Thanksgiving Day magical mystery tour photo-op turkey drop. The thirteen journalists accompanying Bush on Air Force One were sworn to secrecy about the trip and instructed not to leak their whereabouts even to their editors or mommies (Bush himself held an imaginary cell phone and drew a finger across his throat to underline the no-call rule), otherwise we're going to turn this plane right around and head home. For security precautions, the presidential jet landed without lights at the Baghdad airport, the electricity in the city itself partially blacked out to deepen the cover of darkness. After making his surprise special guest star appearance at the Thanksgiving dinner emceed by Paul Bremer, a cameo reminiscent of Bob Hope's dropping in on the old *Tonight Show*, Bush held up a roasted gobbler for the cameras to make a nice picture for tomorrow's front pages and spent three hours boosting troop morale before hightailing it out of Iraq. (Which was two hours more than he was willing to grant the

9/11 commission to interview him over the deaths of three thousand people.) News bulletins of his visit were brilliantly timed for the Thanksgiving festivities in America, when millions of families express their gratitude to their Pilgrim heritage by loading up on mashed potatoes and resting up to hit the malls on "Black Friday," the first shopping day of the Christmas season.

Bush's hi-good-bye visit to the troops was greeted with derision by the foreign press, those cynics. "The turkey has landed," chortled the *Independent*. "I came, I saw nothing, but I will conquer," scoffed a Lebanese newspaper. But American reporters lucky to be invited were still rubbing the wonder from their eyes. Terence Hunt of the Associated Press: "At that moment President Bush strode forth from the wings in an Army track suit emblazoned with a First Armored Division patch. The bored crowd shot from their seats and whooped. As he surveyed the crowd, a tear dripped down the president's cheek." A tear as glistening as any that graced the cheek of the divine Norma Shearer. The next day a couple of the reporters who had accompanied the president were interviewed on cable news, beaming as if (to lift a phrase from James Boswell) they were still hugging themselves in their minds at their good fortune. And why not? Flying on Air Force One and keeping big secrets are fun. Even more fun is the thrill of being on the *deep inside*, embedded with the president and Condi while your colleagues snore unawares. Follow-up stories knocked some of the shellac off of Bush's Festivus miracle—articles about how the turkey was a prop that was never actually served to the soldiers, how some troops were turned away from the meal (attendees had been preselected), and so on. But Bush's approval ratings spurted over the weekend, and a satisfied Karl Rove could pat his tummy with pride over a con job well done.

To Rick MacArthur, the publisher of *Harper's* and a critic of the propaganda/censorship campaigns in both Gulf wars, Bush's Thanksgiving visit was an incriminating farce, a coffin nail the size of a railroad spike driven into any semblance of press independence. The press, he argued, should have declined to play along with the White House's strictures. "The proper thing to do in this case is to refuse the secrecy agreement and say we're not going to be participants in a photo opportunity, which is merely done to help your re-election campaign, and if that aborts the trip, well, it aborts the trip," he told Amy Goodman, the radio host of Pacifica's *Democracy Now!* Brave sentiments, but nobody likes a spoiler and, as MacArthur concedes, any reporter nervy enough to break the news embargo would have been committing an act of career hara-kiri; banished from the Washington press corps, his or her name scratched off the team trophy, such ingrates would have to hang up their bylines and start a blog. A press that avoids colliding with the government edges closer and closer to collusion. "More and more," MacArthur muses, "I'm thinking the proper response for Americans, for readers and viewers of the news, is to…assume that the press is now part of the government."

If so, it's a part of the government that wanders off on its own, becomes preoccupied with peccadilloes, sinks into self-reflection about its Role in a Changing World, and occasionally gets up to mischief. But a perceived threat to national security and American well-being nearly always tugs them back into formation. They get snowed, help snow the American people, and later suffer sucker's remorse when the mobile lab for bioweapons turns out to be a Good Humor truck. This is followed by a cycle of contrition and self-reflection on the op-ed pages and journalism panels. The difference between the Washington correspondents who imitate an oil painting during a Bush press conference and the attack poodles who masticate the press conference afterward is that the attack poodles aren't fooled (apart from the easily fooled Andrew Sullivan). They stifle no qualms, never look back, and aren't snowed or misled because most of them are on board with the program from the outset. They don't need much convincing. A simple nod will do. But what can undo the damage when attack poodles become dogs of war?

The Year
of Lying Dangerously

The president responded abruptly when a reporter suggested that war was inevitable.

"[Y]ou said we're headed to war in Iraq. I don't know why you say that," Bush said. "I'm the person who gets to decide and not you."
—CNN.com, reporting from Crawford, Texas
(December 31, 2002)

NEAR THE END OF HIS BILL OF INDICTMENT *Dreaming War: Blood for Oil and the Cheney-Bush Junta*, Gore Vidal foretells a sad end to the political fortunes of George W. Bush and his ministry of fear. "Mark my words. He will leave office the most unpopular president in history. The junta has done too much wreckage."

Gore, ever the cockeyed optimist. His faith in the slow-burn wrath of the American people is touching, considering how little we've done to deserve it. Never before have so many put up with so much for so long from so few. Despite corporate robbery on a Russian mafia scale, a rapist urge to ram a paved road or oil pipeline through every nature preserve...despite a trampling of civil liberties that makes the detainment camp at Guantanamo—Gitmo—"a physical and moral black hole" (according to the first civilian lawyer allowed to visit a prisoner there)...despite the corny spectacle of the president beseeching Americans to visit a shut-in and say, "I love you" (bringing a casserole would be nice too), and an unaccountable and unlocatable vice president who pops out of his groundhog hole only to raise money for the Republican Party, to play bad cop on *Meet the Press*, or—batten down the irony hatches—to bestow the ailing pope with a gift of a "crystal dove of peace"...despite all this and more, the huddled, befuddled masses have been as quiet as church mice. Those in power can't be accused of thwarting the will of the people, because the people seem to have lost their will, or traded it in for Powerball tickets. Most enigmatic was the quiet resignation, the iceberg drift of collective apathy, which marked the buildup to war against the Saddam Hussein regime in Iraq. But perhaps it wasn't mysterious at all. If George Bush is the one who gets to decide, nobody else has any real say, so why bother getting worked up?

The Year of Lying Dangerously

The Iraq war was the black triumph of the attack poodles and their political handlers. It was their greatest victory and, given how magnificently they misled the American people, misread the Iraqi people, and bungled the occupation, it may be their last. Failure and disgrace will trail the architects of this war into history, just as the chain-dragging ghosts of Vietnam have haunted the "best and brightest" who guided the nation into the big muddy. But history has a lag time, and the perpetrators are still at large. How did they and their poodles organize this propaganda coup?

They instilled an overpowering sense of fait accompli into the almost one-sided prewar debate, as if administering a futility drug. Even those of us who opposed the war knew that the bombers would be leaving the airfields, no matter what anyone said or did.

Fast-acting malaise is not a new brand of brainwash, of course. In past wars, citizens were browbeaten into bending their heads toward the inevitable. "Once the war is on," wrote the radical intellectual Randolph Bourne at the outbreak of World War I, "the conviction spreads that individual thought is helpless, that the only way one can count is as a cog in the great wheel.... We are told to dry our unnoticed and ineffective tears and plunge into the great work." Intellectuals and ordinary citizens alike are urged to jettison their Jiminy Cricket consciences and board the redball express. "Be with us, they call, or be negligible, irrelevant. Dissenters are... excommunicated." Excommunication through the traditional stigmatizations are employed by the nation-state. Advocates for peace, diplomacy, or a simple easing of the gas pedal to permit further debate are slandered as spineless, foolishly naive about the nature of evil and the planet-carving plans of America's enemies, and unpatriotic, perhaps treasonous. Under this onslaught, many of those harboring qualms let them drop with a shrug. Once war seems inevitable, the wise, pragmatic course is to accept harsh reality. Accepting reality always seems the grownup, responsible thing to do. "The realist thinks he can at least control events by linking himself to the forces that are moving," Bourne observed, anticipating the rationales of those liberal Democrats who rubber-stamped a resolution for Bush to pursue war with Iraq rather than risk being completely sidelined. Silly rabbits, they thought Bush would welcome their input later or at least, as John Kerry put it aphoristically in *Rolling Stone*, not "fuck it up as badly as he did." They learned the hard way the lesson of Bourne's warning that linking yourself to the forces in motion offers no guarantee of influence. War can turn into a runaway train that won't stop or change tracks no matter in what compartment you're seated. Especially if there's an incompetent crew at the throttle.

What was novel this time is that the prowar camp didn't wait for American convoys to caravan into the sandstorms before it began bashing and mashing dissent. As befitted a preemptive war, a preemptive strike was launched against the antiwar camp. The blitzkrieg bop came in three waves.

Wave One was the think tank pundits, policy analysts, and neoconservative proponents laying out the case for war against Iraq. What a familiar cast they became. *Ken Adelman*, the former U.S. ambassador to the United Nations, with his American flag ties and his confident prediction that the invasion of Iraq would be a "cakewalk." Said he, "Hussein constitutes the number one threat against American security and civilization." *Michael Ledeen*, the dyspeptic, monotonal author of *The War Against the Terror Masters*, who argued that Saddam Hussein's Iraq belonged to a jihadist consortium that included Syria, Saudi Arabia, and, "the mother of modern terrorism," Iran. *Frank Gaffney, Jr.*, the founder and president of the Center for Security Policy, who, citing the testimony of an Iraqi defector, wrote in his column that there may be WMDs "concealed in a tunnel complex built by Chinese engineers beneath Baghdad's sewer system." *Richard Perle* (a.k.a. "the Prince of Darkness"), of the Defense Policy Board, who told PBS, "[Hussein] is probably the most dangerous individual in the world today.... Capable of anything. Capable of using weapons of mass destruction against the United States...." *Paul Wolfowitz*, the deputy secretary of defense, who also warned of "weapons of mass terror." *Laurie Mylroie*, the author of *The War Against America: Saddam Hussein and the World Trade Center Attacks: A Study in Revenge*, and named "the Neocons' favorite conspiracy theorist" by the *Washington Monthly*. Mylroie believes Hussein was responsible for the first World Trade Center bombing, a view shared by herself and nobody else with any cred, and warned that Hussein might infect America with anthrax and smallpox if we let him run wild. *James Woolsey*, the former director of the CIA, who pronounced that America was now waging World War IV (World War III being the decades-long Cold War). Woolsey was also fond of repeating one of Thomas Friedman's favorite slogans, "Give war a chance." *Benjamin Netanyahu*, the former prime minister of Israel, who would helpfully fly across the Atlantic and scare the bejesus out of us with dark tidings about "suitcase nukes." And of course *Condoleezza Rice*, repeating that spooky refrain about how failure to act could mean that the next smoking gun would take the shape of a mushroom cloud.

None of the above wanted America to rest on its haunches after overthrowing the Taliban but to drain the swamp in the Mideast where terrorism festered and bred. They located the swampy epicenter in Iraq, even though there was the flimsiest of dental floss ties between Iraq and the terrorist hijackers of 9/11, most of whom were Saudi nationals. (No matter how many times the story was knocked down, prowar advocates such as *New York Times* op-ed columnist William Safire insisted that the disputed meeting between Mohammed Atta, suspected ringleader of the 9/11 attacks, and an Iraqi representative in Prague was proof positive of sinister commingling—proof the CIA spooks were inexplicably trying to smother). They reminded ad nauseam that Saddam Had Gassed His Own People. That he was a madman. They trotted out the Churchill quotations and the Hitler analogies and the auguries of apocalypse that could result should we pull a Neville Chamberlain and duck under an umbrella from the challenges ahead.

Wave Two was discrediting opponents or fence-sitters by committing character assassination by the buckshot-load. One by one, entire groups caught shotgun spray from the attack poodles. Their opinions, reputations, qualifications, and love of America were impugned, their right to speak up redefined as the duty to shut up. Too much back talk undermined the war against the Axis of Evil, and certain someones needed to get their mouths corked. A partial list:

A-list celebrities. In December 2002 Sean Penn visited Baghdad. Earlier, the actor and director paid for a full-page ad in the *Washington Post* to publish an open letter to the president, urging him to cool his jets and rethink the consequences of invasion. The letter had stilted and ingenuous passages, but was written in a respectful tone and reflected a serious moral concern; it wasn't a fiery salvo from a Hollywood hothead. (I interviewed Penn once and found him soft-spoken to the point of inaudibility.) Penn's trip to Baghdad demonstrated a similar brooding modesty. He toured hospitals, spoke to Iraqis, snapped photographs, and avoided posturing before the news cameras and microphones; in fact, he was so concerned about being used as a propaganda device by the Hussein regime that he immediately issued a disavowal when an Iraqi press report attributed quotes to him claiming the country was squeaky-clean of weapons of mass destruction.

None of the pains Penn took spared him the inevitable pelleting. He was branded a traitor and bracketed with Jane Fonda, "Baghdad Sean" to her "Hanoi Jane." In a column in the *Wall Street Journal*, Clifford D. May, a gratingly familiar attack poodle and president of the Foundation for the Defense of Democracies (one of those dorky think tanks with impressive stationery), reached deep into the fish barrel:

> Lenin, father of the Soviet Union, had a name for people like Mr. Penn: "Useful idiots." Lenin's successor, Stalin, was even able to dupe Walter Duranty, the *New York Times* correspondent in Moscow whose Pulitzer Prize–winning reporting helped convince the world that no government-orchestrated famine was occurring in the Ukraine.
>
> Similarly, during World War II, the Nazis took representatives of the Red Cross to the model concentration camp at Thereisenstadt, where they established to the Red Cross's satisfaction that those nasty rumors about Hitler's mistreatment of the Jews were unfounded and really quite outrageous.

In this amazing guilt-by-association hit-and-run, May managed to lump Penn, who had never uttered word one in admiration of the Iraqi dictator, with commie sympathizers and Nazi apologists. Words were not enough to convey the contempt felt by other powerpuff boys on the right. After mentioning Penn's shutterbug activities in Baghdad, the *Weekly Standard* editorialized with a sigh, "We must admit, we were kind of hoping some poor Iraqi citizen, mindful of his privacy, would make like stateside Sean Penn and punch him in the face."

B-list celebrities. Also in December, one hundred lesser Hollywood celebrities lent their names to another quixotic open letter to Bush, publicized at a press conference attended by signatories Martin Sheen, Mike Farrell, and Tony Shalhoub, among others. Unlike Penn, "the Hollywood 100"—a deliberate allusion to the blacklisted Hollywood Ten?—weren't roasted as useful idiots but were derided as attention-hungry has-beens hoping for guest spots on a gala *Love Boat* reunion. Grilled by cable news hosts doing their populist shtick, among them MSNBC's late editor in chief Jerry Nachman, whose anachronistic set was decorated like a dumpy newspaper office out of a Mickey Spillane novel, the hapless celebrity reps were barely able to defend their position, they were so busy being fitted for dunce caps. Nachman sneered to an unflappably cool Janeane Garofalo that most celebrities were dopes "whose knowledge of the subject seems to be informed by a bumper sticker and not much else." Garofalo later became the pet target of Nachman's colleague Joe Scarborough. She would be invited on shows in order to be told to go away. A-list or B-list didn't matter; the message to the celebrities was the same: Clam up and leave the political discussion to the seriously intentioned and well-informed. You know, jeweled minds like Jerry Falwell and Hungry Man entrée G. Gordon Liddy.

Un-Americans. The quickest way to dismiss a dissenter is the old-fashioned tradition of labeling him un-American, a worm-from-within who harps on what's wrong with the U. S. of A. instead of what's right, or plays a devious game of "moral equivalence" that he probably learned from some pointy-headed professor (see below). Typical of this tack was a George Will column in which he chided (and no one chides like Will—he's Mr. Belvedere and we're his young charges), "The left, its anti-capitalism transmogrified into anti-Americanism expressed in the argot of anti-globalization, will repeat that of course Iraq and North Korea are dangerous, but so are McDonald's and Microsoft." Those vegetarian, Linux-code-lovin' bastards! Combating such nattering null nodes of negativism is a cottage industry for prolific attack poodles such as William J. Bennett (*Why We Fight*) and Dinesh D'Souza (*What's So Great About*

America); also decking himself in the red, white, and blue was Fox News gabber Sean Hannity, whose inspirational book *Let Freedom Ring* had the grinning author posed on the cover with an American flag—apple pie pride beaming from every airbrushed pore. As long as such patriots are strutting the ramparts, the bestseller list would be safe for democracy.

Scrambled Eggheads. The most insidious cells of anti-American bad-mouthing are sheltered behind the ivy walls of our over-endowed universities. According to conservative dogma, former sixties radicals have thickened into affluent, middle-aged, saggy NPR listeners whose gray ponytails flop limp against their wattled necks (and those are the *men*—the women waddle around as Doris Lessing look-alikes in peasant skirts and ponchos). They remain nostalgic for the revolutionaries they might have been back when they were burning their draft cards and making free love on unsheeted mattresses to the smell of scented candles, indoctrinating a new generation of misguided idealists and trust-fund brats to despise corporate logos and make excuses for America's enemies. Happily, help was riding over the hills. Campus gurus who pollute the skullfuls of mush taking up space in their classrooms are being put under watch and on notice. Daniel Pipes (a.k.a. "Mr. Sardonicus"), the director of the Middle East Forum and frequent cable news attack poodle, presides over something called Campus Watch, which keeps tabs on college professors antagonistic to Israel and the United States, or, as he called them in a *New York Post* op-ed piece, "Profs Who Hate America." Pipes's ideological bunkmate, David Horowitz, another fiery, bearded prophet and demagogue who's never found a controversial issue he couldn't bugger senseless, fronts the Take Back Our Campuses campaign, which, like Pipes's operation, lists and excoriates left-wing hypnotists in college classrooms. (A donation at Horowitz's hothead Web site will "Help David Expose the Leftist Campaign to Shape America's Young Minds.") Along with taking down names, conservatives have sought to defund Mideast studies departments that are deemed seething hotbeds of anti-American/anti-Israeli hostility.

Non-Americans. After expressing sympathy and solidarity with America post-9/11, too many foreigners got uppity again. How dare they criticize the actions of this country? Especially those pampered, effete, coddled, ungrateful, deodorant-averse European wussies. Didn't they remember how we bailed them out of two world wars? God knows we remind them of it often enough. We drag it out of the attic every time they make a minor objection to one of Dick Cheney's or Donald Rumsfeld's Darth Vader schemes. "Europeans are the ultimate free-riders on American power," Charles Krauthammer snipped in the *Washington Post*, and hawks like him were fed up with their backseat driving. After German chancellor Gerhard Schroeder said, Include me out of a preemptive invasion of Iraq, Donald Rumsfeld snubbed Germany's defense minister at a NATO meeting and Condoleezza Rice was widely quoted as saying in policy meetings that France needed to be "punished" for its obstructions. What was different this time was that the hostility in conservative journals and Web sites wasn't limited to German and French officials but was lavished on the German and French peoples, who were scolded for being whiners and ingrates harboring a snake pit of renascent anti-Semitism (as if our own prisons weren't boot camps for white supremacist groups). Entire nations were now being written off as unworthy, no matter what sacrifices they had made in, say, Bosnia.

Even our geographically closest ally wasn't spared. Jonah Goldberg, swinging hard from the heels to be the next P. J. O'Rourke (and missing by a mile), ambled north to do a cover story for *National Review*, which branded the words "Wimps!"

across a photograph of Royal Canadian Mounties. The article itself, cheekily titled "Bomb Canada: The Case for War," argued that carpet bombing might be the best comeuppance for this socialistic North American neighbor and politically correct winter wonderland. It would shake them out of their smug, bland lethargy and learn 'em not to sass the United States and call our president a "moron." Even as a Swiftian modest proposal, "Bomb Canada" made for unhappy irony, given that four Canadian soldiers recently had been killed in Afghanistan in a "friendly fire" incident when American pilots, allegedly amped up on amphetamine, fired a laser-guided missile at their position. Many Canadians were understandably sore with the United States over the government's weak apology for the incident, and then Goldberg came a-gloating.

The subsequent backlash, played out in the Canadian media and on CNN's *Crossfire*, didn't deter Goldberg's foxhole buddy at the *National Review*—John Derbyshire—from daydreaming about what a few kabooms might teach another of our wayward allies, South Korea. Derbyshire, the journalistic charmer who once wished for the murder of Chelsea Clinton (otherwise, "the vile genetic inheritance of Bill and Hillary Clinton may live on to plague us in the future"), wrote that since our longtime ally on the Korean peninsula had tilted anti-U.S., perhaps it wouldn't be such a sad thing if a hard rain fell below the 48th parallel. "It would be a shame, of course, if a few dozen of those glittering malls, luxury apartment blocks, fast-food franchises, Hyundai showrooms, and Ikea outlets were to be smashed up by North Korean missiles.... In any case, given that the South Korean people keep electing leaders who sound like Walter Mondale, and register positively Parisian levels of anti-Americanism when polled, it's hard to see why we Americans [Derbyshire, an Englishman, received his citizenship in 2002] should mind if their nice prosperous little country gets knocked about a bit...." That thousands of human beings would perish amid this upscale property damage was a peripheral concern, perhaps because violent daydreamers like Derbyshire don't see nonwhites as human beings but as extras in a *Godzilla* movie.

Goldberg and Derbyshire weren't just funning. The retaliation and devastation they played with in print had filtered down from the deadly serious might-makes-right policies of the neoimperialists inside the administration—Richard Perle, Paul Wolfowitz, Doug Feith, Lewis "Scooter" Libby, Elliott Abrams, et al. The antics of the attack poodles and the deadly tricks of the neoconservative ideologues are light and heavy modes of the same crackdown approach to world affairs. In the sixties and seventies, militant lefties (parroting Mao) would spout, "Political power grows out of the barrel of a gun." What pikers they were. For righties, geopolitical power flows out of the bomb-bay doors: Seoul or Baghdad, friend or foe, wherever the payload hits the road.

Liberals. I know, I know: what liberals? Way back in 1973 Wilfrid Sheed wrote, "Although I myself have not met a self-confessed liberal since the late fifties... hardly a day passes that I don't read another attack on the 'typical liberal,' as it might be announcing a pest of dinosaurs or a plague of unicorns." Three decades later, the mythological liberal still remains at large in paranoid fever-dreams, Out There somewhere gnawing on the electrical wiring and subverting our defenses. Ann Coulter (*Treason*), Mona Charen (*Useful Idiots*), and Michael Savage (*The Savage Nation*) were among those heroically having their research assistants pore over news clips and scroll through hundreds of obscure Web sites to root out the scruffy saboteurs who had somehow escaped extinction. It was Coulter, mistress of understatement, who affirmed, "Even Islamic terrorists don't hate America like liberals do." (There's even an Ann Coulter Talking Action Figure, who'll recite similar koans words at the tug of a string.)

It wasn't just conservative kooks on the warpath who belittled and berated the Last of the Liberals. Even so-called liberal publications couldn't keep their snickers to themselves when antiwar liberals shuffled by holding hand-painted signs. That's when you know you've reached Wave Three—when the establishment media abandons the lifeguard stand and lets itself be swept along with the surge, servicing the administration's claims by running front-page articles with a flurry of quotes from anonymous sources within the administration and a few fubsy caveats (see Michael Massing's damning autopsy of the press performance, "Now They Tell Us," the *New York Review of Books* February 26, 2004), and warily distances itself from any bottoms-up dissidents. Restless natives make the major newspapers nervous, and they're relieved to report all quiet on the Western front, even if it isn't true. "So where are the antiwarriors?" a stumped George Packer asked in the pages of the *New York Times Magazine* in December 2002. The antiwar marches that moseyed down the streets of a few major cities underwhelmed Packer, as did the rhetoric. "Speakers at the demonstrations voice unnuanced slogans like 'No Sanctions, No Bombing' and 'No Blood for Oil.' As for what should be done to keep this mass murderer and his weapons in check, they have nothing to say at all." (By "mass murderer," Packer was presumably referring to Saddam Hussein and not the current occupant of the Oval

Office.) In the *Washington Post* reporter David Montgomery pre-
viewed an antiwar rally and found the protesters an amusing
menagerie of freaks and fogies. "Don't forget the suburban seniors fixing to march on the White House in spite of arthritis and
titanium kneecaps, women wearing pink keeping vigil in the
cold, Quakers in the basement debating slogans that are too
long and nuanced to fit on a bumper sticker...." Nor should we
forget, one might add, that a contingent of Quakers was arrested
during the 1967 antiwar march on the Pentagon and refused to
eat, drink, or wear prison uniforms, whereupon they were
thrown into the Hole of the D.C. jail. "There they lived in cells
so small that not all could lie down at once to sleep," Norman
Mailer wrote in *The Armies of the Night*, "these naked Quakers
on the cold floor of a dark isolation cell in the D.C. jail, wander-
ing down the hours in the fever of dehydration." In the pre-Iraq
war climate, however, Quakers and their peace activism were
considered quaint, antiquated.

So here we had two supposed liberal bastions, the *New York
Times* and the *Washington Post*, chiming that (a) there was no
peace movement; and (b) well, there is one, sorta, but it's a soft
parade of fringe lefties, college kids, and historical retreads
stretching their legs in a creaky exercise in uselessness. Policy
debate was best left to the manly, heavily stocked foreheads of

those East Coast "liberal hawks" Packer quoted with approbation, such as Paul Berman, author of *Terror and Liberalism*. Such anemic readings of the antiwar movement proved to be premature, as mass protests were mobilized in the United States, Great Britain, and Europe for February 15, 2003; hundreds of thousands marched, hoping against hope to head off a war erected on a tottering scaffold of fear and deceit. The marches were less scoffed at than the ones Packer and Montgomery covered, the protesters being too numerous, boisterous, and varied in makeup to be trivialized as a political hobo parade. In New York City the marchers, numbering from 150,000 to 300,000 (depending on estimates), were restricted by so many choke-points and no-go areas that the crowd's energy was segmented, mazed off. Since Bush and Blair had declared themselves unswayable no matter how many thousands took to the streets, and since lefties of all shades and follicle conditions had been categorized as running on little more than fumes, faint hopes, and impotent furies, even the most sympathetic coverage of the protest marches lacked the urgency of true contention, of history in the offing, there for the taking. Birnam Wood was not marching upon Macbeth's castle that wintry day.

The Year of Lying Dangerously

Weapons inspectors. This was perhaps the most peculiar and perverse wrinkle in the whole disgraceful shriekshow, the discrediting of career professionals by a jury of jeerers in the conservative media. The U.N. weapons inspectors led by Hans Blix were ridiculed and minimalized even before they reentered Iraq. It was assumed they would find nothing because it was assumed that they didn't want to find anything, the United Nations being a parliament of doves and Third World despots. It was also assumed that they'd find nothing because these idiots abroad were no match for the wily Hussein. Frank Gaffney, Jr., told the Australian Broadcasting Corporation in 2002, "The inspectors are at best going to be run around Iraq by the nose. Made fools of, as they were before, and left with, at best, the most fragmentary of evidence as to what Saddam is actually up to." Hans Blix was singled out for special slagging. His equanimity infuriated the hawks, who called him a "milquetoast" whose "most salient characteristic is politeness." Gaffney referred to Blix as the "hapless Swedish diplomat," and to Charles Krauthammer, Blix's nationality indicated that he was neutral to the point of neutered. ("He's Swedish, what can you expect?" I remember him saying, shrugging on Fox News.) But the rap that was hung on him the most was that he was an Inspector Clouseau figure, an unflappable bumbler. George

Will went even further, saying Blix was "a combination of Mr. Magoo and Inspector Clouseau." Again, the attack poodles set the tone, and the establishment press fleshed out the melody, with even *Saturday Night Live* getting into the act, doing a skit in which the Iraqis shifted weapons around under the clueless noses of U.N. inspectors. As Michael Massing documents in his *New York Review of Books* essay, "The press's submissiveness was most apparent in its coverage of the inspections process," where it largely ignored the findings of the International Atomic Energy Agency, headed by Mohamed El Baradei, which after visiting 150 sites announced on January 9, 2003, that "no evidence of ongoing prohibited nuclear or nuclear-related activities has been detected." The IAEA believed that Iraq's nuclear program had been "neutralized" since 1998, thus demolishing the claims of George Bush, Condoleezza Rice, and others who had warned about rogue nukes. By contrast, the press wigged out with Beatlemania at Colin Powell's shoddy show-and-tell demonstration at the United Nations on February 5, 2003, complete with diagrams, satellite photos, audio tapes of cryptic dialogue, and ominous warnings about aluminum tubes and a "sinister nexus" between Iraq and Al Qaeda. Massing: "The next day's *New York Times* carried three front-page articles on Powell's speech, all of them glowing. . . . the *Washington Post* was no less positive."

(Here's a helpful tip for future fun seekers. Play a tape of Dan Rather's exclusive interview with Saddam Hussein, conducted before the war began, and then play a tape of Colin Powell's U.N. speech, or any tape of Condoleezza Rice, Dick Cheney, and Donald Rumsfeld from *Meet the Press*, or any one of Tony Blair's full-wingspan flights of eloquence—then judge who was the most veracious.)

It would be remiss to leave the topic of weapons inspectors without noting that noisy squawker Scott Ritter, a member of the previous inspection team who insisted that Iraq didn't have weapons on the scale and capability that Bush-Blair maintained. Where Blix was droll, Ritter blasted away in BOLD CAPS, which made him a more powerful presence on TV, but also easier to designate a member of the screwball family—so deliriously out of orbit that CNN's Paula Zahn said that there were those who accused him of "drinking Saddam Hussein's Kool-Aid." The facts that Ritter had agreed to do a documentary in Iraq at the invitation of Saddam Hussein (shades of Leni Riefenstahl and Adolf Hitler) and had been arrested once in what was reported to be an Internet child-porn sting added immeasurably to his targetability. (The case was dismissed and the state records sealed until, in the words of Alexander Cockburn, "some kind soul in favor of bombing kids in Baghdad leaked the file to the press.") Even though Ritter was able to back up his assertions with facts, he was shouting into the whirl-wind. Facts are stupid things, as Ronald Reagan so memorably said, and the war hawks didn't believe in letting stupid facts get untidily in the way of what they intended to do. Destination: Baghdad.

IT WAS ONLY A YEAR OR SO AGO, this slice of scoundrel time, and yet it seems less like recent history and more like a bad dream, a shared hallucination. "What a difference a year—and the truth—makes, huh?" mused writer, gay activist, and radio host Michelangelo Signorile in a February 2004 column for *New York Press*. "A measly 365 days ago, if you believed there were no weapons of mass destruction in Iraq, you were a nut-job, a dangerous leftist ideologue and/or on Osama bin Laden's or Saddam Hussein's payroll. Perhaps you were one of Andrew Sullivan's 'fifth column' of pundits trying to under-mine the president. Or maybe you were one of those traitors who should have been bombed yourself, as Ann Coulter opined back in August of 2002 regarding the supposedly liberal editors and reporters at the *New York Times*." This was when

The Year of Lying Dangerously

Annie Get Your Bazooka tickled her own funny bone by asserting Timothy McVeigh had parked his bomb in front of the wrong building. Oui, so much had happened in that thrill-packed period. The weapons inspectors were forced to leave Iraq so that the United States could enforce its phony deadline. On March 21, 2003, "Shock and Awe" lit the Tigris River with fiery reflections. Embedded TV reporters photographed American tanks rolling through the desert and churning dust. Saddam Hussein's statue was toppled. The looting began, then the insurgency. Car bombs, rocket-propelled grenade attacks, oil pipeline explosions, entire towns ringed with barbed wire. Instead of being able to parade through Baghdad as liberators, Tony Blair and George Bush didn't dare attempt anything more than swoop-ins to visit the troops, and Paul Wolfowitz had to comb broken glass out of his gray hair after his hotel was shelled. The impending menace to America turned out to be paltry. As Signorile implied, David Kay's testimony to Congress about the nondiscovery of WMDs—"we were almost all wrong"—vindicated the good name of nut-jobs everywhere.

After the Kay bombshell, *Washington Post* columnist Richard Cohen, like Signorile, found himself trying to recover from the woozy hangover of this hysterical yellathon. "It would be instructive to examine the yahoo mood that came over much of the nation once Bush decided to go to war. The decision—its urgency—seemed to come out of nowhere. Yet most of America fell into line, and in certain segments of the media, the Murdoch press above all, dissent was ridiculed." Gee, ya don't say!

If in retrospect it all seems like a bad dream, it's one in which the dreamer awakens to find the sheets sopped with blood and fires breaking out down the hall. Hundreds of American troops dead. An alarming rate of suicides. The airport landings and funerals of the returning dead kept off-camera. Untold thousands returning home wounded, blinded, deafened, crippled, psychologically ravaged, financially strapped. The abominations of Abu Ghraib. The beheading of Nic Berg. The desecration of the dead bodies of four U.S. contractors. The car-bombing of the head of the Iraqi Governing Council. The massacre of a wedding party by U.S. strikes. Here at home, the repercussions of the war will ripple underground through our culture for years, decades, much as the repercussions of Vietnam did, erupting in small explosions of violence, tragedies that will seem inexplicable until the larger backstory is told.

Did the news media learn anything from the year of lying dangerously? Tonally, the treble knob has been temporarily turned down on cable news and the political chat shows. The attack poodles are subdued, somewhat chagrined, revising earlier statements and restating old points with less gusto. Going one-on-one with Tim Russert on *Meet the Press* in January 2004, President Bush looked for the first time since 9/11 like a shrunken executive, too small for the chair in which he was seated. White House reporters no longer have their noses completely stuck in the carpet. But in the faultfinding for the hysteria over Iraq and WMDs, the media positions the blame as a choice between the CIA and the Bush administration without reflecting on its own fat part in this tragic farce. It failed to scrutinize the claims of the war pushers or pay any notice to their affiliations with think tanks and corporate boards, letting them quack as if they were simply town criers in a time of trouble. Even the worst offenders are still welcome on cable news. But as Bob Somerby documented on his *Daily Howler* Web site, those who weren't wrong aren't extended the same courtesy. He noted that Scott Ritter, who had been all over the dial before the war, became MIA on the news programs, even after David Kay validated the truth of Ritter's previous rants. He was only invited on a smattering of programs. Somerby thundered, "Readers, Ritter's been dumped *because he was right*. Within this hopeless, Potemkin 'press corps,' you only get to stay on the air *if you're conventionally wrong!*"

Which is how the celebrity hosts of cable news hold down their jobs—by being proudly, defiantly, conventionally wrong. It's all a matter of maintaining consistency and, as we shall see, one channel has mastered the game while its competitors scour the countryside for a clue.

Fox Populi

W**HO IS THE IDEAL AUDIENCE FOR ATTACK POODLES?** Who gets the greatest high from listening to their beefy rhetoric and flag-draped pieties? It's the Angry White Male and—assuming he isn't foraging for dinner in the frozen-food aisle—his Vexed Wife. Aggravation is one of this couple's favorite forms of fun. They find nothing more relaxing than spending a quiet evening at home, getting aggravated. Like the talk-show hosts and pundits on whose barbed wired words they hang, Angry and Vexed get turned on by being turned off. They can get their gums in an uproar over each and any insult to decent folk, and something as fleeting as a flash of Janet Jackson's right pacifier can put them in a tiz. (One caller on Rush Limbaugh compared the unleashing of her shameless frontage to a terrorist act.) Of course, there are those who are sincerely offended by the slick garbage chucked at them by popular culture—by the TV ads that seem to have been created by frat boys during a kegger, the compulsive crotch-grabbing of the bulge-toting hip-hop artiste, or excited reports of Paris Hilton putting something in her mouth. The difference is that Angry and Vexed politicize their disapproval. Each affront to their taste buds becomes another reason to blame licentious liberals for the depravity streaking butt-naked through western culture, and another excuse for the professional liberal-blamers—the attack poodles—to politicize it even further, get some extra exploitation mileage out of it, along with valuable airtime to push their latest books on America's whirling descent down the drain. And if nothing big and awful is happening, attack poodles bring to their attention shockers that they wouldn't have known about otherwise—imported outrages, antireligious displays or spotty insults to the red-white-and-blue that can be magnified into a major rash. Angry Caucasians feel a certain sedentary oomph when they're having their hot buttons pushed, and no cable news channel has proven a better button-pusher than Fox News, which tailors itself to the red-hot libido of the easily riled.

"We went to war just to boost the white male ego."
—Norman Mailer, April 29, 2003

With the election of George Bush in 2000, the Angry White

Fox Populi

Male has reasserted and reestablished himself as a member of the privileged underprivileged class, waking up with a fart after a half decade in hibernation. In the early nineties, an irate mob of Angry White Males seemed to pile full-born out of the crackling static of talk radio, their fists, faces, and buttocks clenched. This newly formed posse was intent on righting the wayward path America had taken since the tribal sixties. Jutting their jaws like Charlton Heston defying his ape masters, getting their daily load of humorous indignation from radio host Rush Limbaugh, its members were fed up with the entire menu of liberal intrusion: high taxes, gay rights, gun control, feminist harping, yuppie snobbery, affirmative action, political correctness, multiculturalism, speed limits, Oprah's scented-candle affirmations, and illegal immigrants grabbing good jobs that nobody else wanted. Angry White Males felt like a persecuted minority themselves as the complexion of America began to shade from white to beige, tailing toward burnt sienna. The Angry White Male insurgence triumphed with the Republican takeover of Congress in 1994, as AWMs rose up like an army of marshmallows to mutiny against a political system that had too long discounted their complaints and stigmatized them as poster boys for patriarchy. This rebel yell was led by House Majority leader and Pillsbury Doughboy stand-in Newt Gingrich, who saw himself as a general on horseback (pity the poor horse) waging a second civil war. "This war has to be fought with the scale and duration and savagery that is only true of civil wars," he saber-rattled in a speech in 1988. This uncivil war would be fought without Southern gallantry. Gingrich's deadliest weapon was his incontinent mouth and a vocabulary of smear and loathing that would have brought a nostalgic grin to Joe McCarthy's unshaven mug. Democrats weren't simply wrong, or working from different premises, they were "sick," "insane," "grotesque," "decadent," a *Marat/Sade* group of polymorphous-perverse saboteurs. "I can't speak for others," David Brock wrote in *Blinded by the Right*, "but to me, Newt's appeal was based less on political philosophy or ideology than on raw emotion."

Raw emotion is hard to sustain, however, even for rabid believers, and this macho uprising suddenly went poof. Like Bigfoot, the Angry White Male exposed himself only to retreat into the berry bushes, replaced on the political stage by the Soccer Mom and, later, the NASCAR Dad. The most plausible explanation for this rapid fade is that the public turned against AWMs after Republican freshmen on the Hill overplayed their hand with the government shutdown of 1995, when a fool-hardy Newt was rope-a-doped by a wily Bill Clinton. What appeared at the time to be a temporary defeat dissolved into a total rout. Gingrich's switchblade gang of budget cutters and regulations slashers lost the "big mo" until they were left with no mo' mo, and came to a dead dumb stop. As John Dilulio, President George W. Bush's former adviser on faith-based initiatives, said later in a panel discussion, "[D]espite this earthquake election, within two years this supposedly new, cohesive, powerful bloc of angry white male voters had disappeared. They were gone."

No, not gone. Only gone into hiding. The White Angries had beaten a strategic retreat, taking their apoplexy and heartburn medicine with them. In October 1996, a month before Bill Clinton decisively beat Bob Dole in the presidential election, Rupert Murdoch launched Fox News Channel, a twenty-four-hour news service intended to provide a punchy alternative to the liberal mush of mainstream media. Named as Fox News czar was Roger Ailes, a former Republican strategist who had produced Rush Limbaugh's Howdy Doody talk show on TV. Ailes prides himself on being a cigar-smoking carnivore in a media stratosphere of mineral water, salad fork dainties. He told *Newsweek*, "The media elite think they're smarter than the rest of those stupid bastards, and they'll tell you what to think. To a working-class guy, that's bullshit." Fox News would do things differently. It would tell those stupid bastards what to think by pretending *not* to be smarter than them—by pretending to be *one* of them, only with more money, a better address, and a nicer wardrobe. Despite his longtime Republican track record, Ailes assured doubters, cynics, and other scoffers that Fox News wouldn't serve as a conservative propaganda spout, telling a reporter from E! Online News that it would be a fat-free, no-frills, no-bull, crew-cut operation. "We're going to provide straight, factual information with less 'spin' and less 'face time' for anchors." Fox's motto—"We Report. You Decide"—proclaimed that it would be the Joe Friday of cable news, just the facts, ma'am. One wondered even then whom Ailes thought he was conning, or why he was even bothering. Ailes is a loyal agent to his boss Rupert Murdoch, just as Murdoch is the loyal tool of Moloch ("Moloch whose mind is pure machinery! Moloch whose blood is running money! Moloch whose fingers are ten armies!"—Allen Ginsberg, *Howl*), and Fox News Channel is today what it was always intended to be: an organ grinder for the Republican Party and a vanity showcase catering to the Angry White Male in his autumn plumage. Matt Gross, a former editor at Foxnews.com, revealed in a letter to Romenesko's Media News site in 2003 that the first directive his unit received from a top suit at the channel was: "Seek out stories that cater to angry, middle-aged white men who listen to talk radio and yell at their televisions." A policy that unfairly discriminates against angry, middle-aged black men—what about their yelling needs? Or Asian women—they probably have a few gripes. But it's the white man who is used to thinking of himself as being at the front of the line (no matter how put-upon and powerless he may be as an individual), and who feels the most threatened by social reshuffling. For him it can seem like it's all downhill from here.

Since its inception, Fox News has cornered the market on this Angry White Male resentment and has been stealing everybody's lunch money on cable news. Bolting hard and fast out of the gate, Fox has raced to number one in the ratings, forcing the older 24/7 news outfits on the cable grid—CNN and MSNBC—to play anxious catch-up, a dramedy of errors that will be examined in the next chapter. As these two laggards take turns in the mirror wrestling with their identity crises, Fox lays down the heavy rhythm tracks for news coverage. At its conquistadorial core, it's an ideological aggressor, which endows it with a more purposeful drive, a sharper sword thrust than traditional news operations, and a longer horizon. When one submits to the channel for any spell, the ideological goals of the right click through the broadcast day like dominos: privatization of public services, unquestioning support of Israeli might, putting Jesus in the center of the public square, crediting the economic success of the Clinton presidency to anyone but Clinton, glorifying Ronald Reagan as our Great White Father with the rosy cheeks, and ungirdling corporate power, even if it means ravaging the environment and cramming the entire lard-ass country into one mother of an S.U.V. Conservatives detest small waste. They believe in big waste. Small waste fritters taxpayers' money. Big waste builds corporate wealth. How apt that after stepping down as Speaker of the House, Newt Gingrich was scooped up by Fox as an on-air political consultant (i.e., Republican mouthpiece). The first network with an agenda, Fox News Channel is the continuation of the Gingrich Revolution by other means.

In pushing the political center of gravity right, Fox News has succeeded perhaps beyond even Roger Ailes's and Rupert Murdoch's diabolical dreams, and earned its bragging rights. Which doesn't make its bragging any prettier. Fox's on-air hosts and contributors, an all-star squad of attack poodles, can't resist strutting around the sawdust like circus strongmen, snapping paper chains with their chests. It's a wonder Bill O'Reilly, Neil Cavuto, Brit Hume, Sean Hannity, and John Gibson haven't herniated themselves with all their anchor desk he-man heroics, cuffing their guests around and editorializing as if dictating a stern memo to the Almighty (on paper, God may outrank Rupert Murdoch, but He's been letting too many things slide lately). Years of being massaged with the tasty perks lavished on TV personalities—cocktail parties, rising speaking fees, proximity to power brokers, beckoning glances on the shuttle—have contoured their anger into a sleek contempt for those who don't share their mezzanine view. Just as Rush turned into the very sort of country-club Republican he professes to scorn (before entering rehab for addiction to Oxy-Contin, colloquially known as "hillbilly heroin"), he would enthrall listeners with anecdotes about the celebrity golf tournament he'd played the previous weekend, the anchors at Fox News are elitists who pretend to be firebrands fighting for you, the average angry white bozo.

It takes a bully to run a bully pulpit, and the biggest bully at Fox News is Bill O'Reilly, host of *The O'Reilly Factor*, bestselling author, and chronic crybaby. He's the Angry White Male's Angry White Male, master of a thousand tirades and a single throwaway look of disgust. A former newsman at CBS and ABC, O'Reilly came to semiprominence as host of the syndicated tabloid show *Inside Edition*. There he showed a knack for taking a hot story and shaking it like a maraca; this made him a natural for Fox News, which was looking for noisemakers. A tall, imposing man who uses his size and gruff, mercurial temper to destabilize the normally dormant air of the studio (much as Tom Snyder did on his old late-night show, his interviews often couched within a larger, darker psychodrama), O'Reilly is willing to scrap with anyone, which can make for good TV—"good TV" in this context meaning momentary flare-ups of genuine heat amid the staged pillow fights. He can't always keep up the appearance that he cares—he can only fake so much. In the middle of a question or response, his eyes will sometimes flip a switch of existential boredom that says, "Aw, what's the point? This is all a farce anyway," as his voice trails off into the commercial break. His unpredictability extends to his political opinions, but only so far. Although not a doctrinaire Republican like Cavuto, Hume, Hannity, and Fred Barnes, a barbershop quartet of Bushspeak, O'Reilly proclaims through his every word and defiant cock of the head that he made it where he is today without any handouts from bleeding hearts or bureaucrats, and if he could succeed without any coddling, so can you. Stand up and be a man! (You too, lady!) Following the Rush Limbaugh personality-cult playbook, O'Reilly has capitalized on his Fox News success by repackaging his on-air sound bites—he begins each show with a "Talking Points" memo—into number-one best-sellerdom with his straight-shooting, back-patting manifesto *The O'Reilly Factor.* This was followed by a book that was an even more self-congratulatory hodgepodge, *Who's Looking Out for You?* and a novel called *Those Who Trespass.* He postures as a Lone Ranger versus "the elites," distributing his own version of frontier justice.

O'Reilly's glowering portrayal of himself as a working-class hero has been derided as pure salami. His background, Michael Kinsley contended in *Slate,* is middle-class; he grew up in Levittown, New York; his father was an accountant. Kinsley took his most mischievous swipes at O'Reilly's poignant account of being a graduate student at Harvard's Kennedy School of Government, where he felt like a pair of brown shoes in a sea of tasseled loafers. "The notion that the Kennedy School of Government, populated by swells out of P. G. Wodehouse, reached out to O'Reilly, a poor orphan out of Dickens," beggars credulity, Kinsley wrote. He accused O'Reilly of reverse snobbery, quoting as evidence a passage in a *Newsweek* profile in which O'Reilly spurned Starbucks for a Long Island coffee shop, "where cops and firemen hang out." You know, real guys, not a bunch of frappuccino pussies. When opportune, he can play the class angle in reverse, as he did recently when he made fun of a couple of Lehigh University political science students who were on his show semidefending the display of a bawdy George Bush caricature in a college art gallery exhibition. In the offending picture, Bush is shown copping a breast feel in a crowded bar with a roguish gleam in his eye. In the post–Justin Timberlake moral environment, this was indeed incendiary, and yet, in O'Reilly's aesthetic judgment, crass. He snorted that such cheap provocation would be laughed out of a sophisticated college like Harvard. "I went to Harvard," O'Reilly emphasized with a finger jab, and reiterated that this sort of nonsense wouldn't fly there. If O'Reilly had been keeping closer tabs on his old alma mater, he might have known that the same week of the Lehigh flapdoodle, Harvard was embroiled in a similar so-what controversy about a campus publication called *H Bomb*, which intended to publish nudie pix in its premiere issue. In fairness to O'Reilly, it's hard to keep track of all the rampant breasts out there.

O'Reilly may be the number one prime-time host in cable news, but it has not brought him peace and serenity. This towering inferno is as sensitive to criticism as Patty Duke in *Valley of the Dolls*, and as prone to volcanic eruptions. This is what makes needling him such fun. He can't take it, has no humor about himself, a single well-placed zinger sending him into a blowhard's version of 'roid rage. On May 31, 2003, a day that will live in ecstasy, O'Reilly found himself on a Book Expo panel in Los Angeles with one of his chief hecklers, Al Franken, *Saturday Night Live* alumnus and the author of the lyrical studies *Rush Limbaugh Is a Big, Fat Idiot* and *Lies and the Lying Liars Who Tell Them: A Fair and Balanced Look at the Right*. Among the lies that Franken wanted to illuminate was O'Reilly's repeated claim that while he was host, *Inside Edition* had won the prestigious Peabody Award. Where a conservative ambusher might have blurted out a rude gotcha at O'Reilly's expense, Franken did something far more methodical and slow-torture. He *teased* out the accusation, detailing the phone calls he had made to the Peabody committee and the responses he had received, pacing this detective story as if he were doing a classic deadpan Jack Benny routine, complete with laugh-getting pauses, before delivering the coup de grace—that in fact O'Reilly and *Inside Edition* had never won the Prestigious Peabody Award. It was another one of O'Reilly's hollow boasts. On his own show, Franken's slow-peeling monologue would have been interrupted or his mike would have been cut off (as O'Reilly ordered the producer to do on *The Factor* with an antiwar protestor whose father died on September 11), but on neutral turf, playing by somebody else's rules, he had to sit and wait his turn before popping his radiator cap. Which he did, cutting off Franken during his rebuttal by snapping, "Hey, shut up! You had your thirty-five minutes! Shut up!" Had there not been cameras present, O'Reilly's hot flash would have remained pop lore, like jazz drummer Buddy Rich's legendary tongue-lashings of his band musicians (one of which survives on bootleg audio). Not only were there cameras present, they were recording live for C-SPAN, which helpfully rebroadcast the event again and yet again as excited word spread through the media of O'Reilly's temper tantrum. O'Reilly wasn't done overreacting. That summer Fox News tried to torpedo *Lying Liars* by launching a lawsuit charging "trademark infringement" over the use of the phrase "fair and balanced" in Franken's subtitle and the jacket design, which (argued Fox's attorneys) might mislead buyers into thinking the book carried the Fox News imprimatur. The case was quickly tossed by the court, another humiliation for O'Reilly and his sore ego, which were widely believed to be pushing the lawsuit (which the big O denies). Still sore, he huffed out of an interview on NPR's *Fresh Air*, complaining that host Terry Gross was being unfair and unbalanced in her pointed questioning, throwing him nasty fastballs after she had made only nice little underhanded tosses to Franken when she had *him* on the show. Reviewing the episode, NPR's ombudsman, Jeffrey Dvorkin, agreed with old grouchy, saying that he too was troubled by Gross's uncivil tone and inquisitorial approach. "[An] aspect of the interview that I found particularly disturbing: It happened when Terry Gross was about to read a criticism of Bill O'Reilly's book from *People* magazine. Before Gross could read it to him for his reaction, O'Reilly ended the interview and walked out of the studio. She read the quote anyway." That blade-twisting little sadist! Clearly, it doesn't take much to disturb the muffins over at NPR, and even if one accepts that what Dvorkin called the "empty chair" tactic—i.e., directing comments at a guest who is no longer present to respond—isn't quite kosher, it still reflected badly on O'Reilly that he was too thin-skinned to stand up to Gross. Or stand down to her, given his height advantage.

O'Reilly's self-sabotage continued apace. After he boasted that the sales of *Who's Looking Out for You?* were breathing neck and neck with Hillary Clinton's *Living History* in nonfiction sales, an unlikely debunker, Matt Drudge, reported that not only did O'Reilly's sales lag Hillary's but that he was trailing Al Franken by 30 percent. Ignominy upon ignominy, and yet O'Reilly still can't let the scabs heal, alluding as late as December 19, 2003, to Franken as an unnamed "smear merchant." Once rankled, O'Reilly never gets unrankled.

I got my own personal whiff of the eau d' O'Reilly charm

in the summer of 2001, when I was invited to be abused on *The Factor* after a column I'd written about Fox News was published in *Vanity Fair*. I found myself waiting in the green room with, among others, political maven Dick Morris. I forget whom Morris had been booked to slime-coat that evening, but in the green room he was a jovial chap, full of bonhomie, or at least a plausible facsimile. After he finished his segment, he returned to the green room and parked himself a second time in its motel-lobby splendor. "You know why I'm hanging around, don't you?" he said. "They're hoping to get you so mad you'll walk off the set, and they want me around to fill out the segment, just in case." Thanks for the tip, I thought, or maybe even said. After hearing that, I was determined to last out the segment whatever the provocation; they'd have to use a claw hammer to pry my fingers off the table to get me out of there. I had my manly pride, and I wasn't going to let that big meanie make me cry!

I was led into the studio, stepping over the usual anaconda coils of thick wires to reach the host's table, where I was miked. The set uptruded like a small island surrounded by a moat of darkness, so small that O'Reilly could easily reach over and slug one if he were so inclined, something that never crossed one's mind while sitting across from, say, Charlie Rose. Other

talk show hosts make regular-guy small talk or goof around
with the crew to put the guest at ease. But O'Reilly didn't want
me at ease, he wanted me simmering in the witness chair, and
he made no attempt to be chummy, grumbling while he did the
patented busy-anchorman paper shuffle at the table. His eyes,
when he finally looked generally in my direction, were blue,
cold, and mean. Isotonic. Then the interview began. During
the preinterview with a Fox staffer, we had gone over a wide
range of Fox-related topics, but on the broadcast O'Reilly
wanted to vent solely about a passage I'd written regarding his
middle-class upbringing, his father's job and salary. He complained, with exclamation marks at the end of every complaint,
that I had relied on published sources (like Kinsley's column)
instead of calling him personally to correct these lies! You call
yourself a reporter!? What kind of a reporter are you anyway?!
It was a typical steam-valve explosion from O'Reilly, who made
the (thoroughly fact-checked) article and the interview all
about *him*, and for a few moments I was flummoxed, since
O'Reilly's background hadn't received anything more than a
passing mention during the preinterview. Then I got into the
stride of it, accusing Fox of being antilabor and claiming that
ever since joining Fox News, John Gibson (a cranky independent on MSNBC) had "gone over to the dark side." "The dark

side!?" O'Reilly snapped. He and I traded verbal spitballs, and then *blink* it was over (everything happening twice as fast in TV time as it does in real life).

I didn't take O'Reilly's gruffness personally, and after the show had gone to commercial, I was ready to shake hands and let bygones, etc. I've made up with much worse ego-monsters than him. But he continued to sit there sulking, saying like a guy giving me a tip at a back table in Little Italy, "Tell your boss I don't like what he did" (that is, run my column). And I thought, Yeah, I'll get right on that, Graydon'll be crushed. I picked my way through the tenebrous dark, and when I reentered the green room, Dick Morris was still sitting and hoping. "Shit!," he cried with a laugh, "I was hoping to get more airtime." That's why I can never bring myself to dislike Dick Morris, though he does try a soul's patience.

BILL O'REILLY: Let me ask you about Jesus in the temple, driving the money changers out with a whip. Was he affording those people dignity, Father?

FATHER RYSCAVAGE, Jesuit priest: He was protecting the dignity of the temple, the people who prayed in it, and the merchants who worked in it.

Fox Populi

O'REILLY: That's exactly what President Bush and the U.S.A. was doing when they went in to remove Saddam. They were protecting the dignity of the Iraqi people and they were protecting the dignity of the world so we wouldn't have to deal with a guy who clearly was out to hurt people. So we were doing exactly what Jesus did in the temple, weren't we?

FATHER RYSCAVAGE: No, I don't think so.
—from *The Factor*, December 16, 2003

It's the measure of a true man to admit he was wrong, a gracious quality that has so far eluded Bush, Cheney, Rumsfeld, Gingrich, Limbaugh, and other plaster of paris idols in the Angry White Male pantheon. Which is why the ramparts trembled when O'Reilly conceded in blunt language that, on the issue of WMDs in Iraq, "I was wrong," adding that he would be "much more skeptical about the Bush administration now." O'Reilly managed to admit being hoodwinked without violating the infallibility of Fox News by confessing his error not on *The O'Reilly Factor* but on ABC's *Good Morning America*, where he got characteristically tetchy having to taste humble pie. Enough with the mea culpas already. "I just said it. What do you want me to do, go over and kiss the camera?"

Like O'Reilly, Neil Cavuto, the host of Fox's afternoon business news hour and of his own weekend show, *Cavuto on Business*, buttonholes the camera like a barroom philosopher who's had it up to here with these fancy cuff link types who think they can tell us regular slobs how to run our lives. His "Common Sense" commentaries, like O'Reilly's "Talking Points" memos, are sprinkled with colloquial icebreakers such as "Hey, maybe it's just me, but..." and "I don't care how the heck I sound saying this, but I gotta tell ya...." Unlike O'Reilly, however, Cavuto doesn't use his soapbox solely to stand up for the little guy; he also uses it to stick up for America's most mistreated and unloved minority, the oppressed rich. Irked over the trimming and second-guessing of President Bush's tax cuts by various Bolshevik groups, Cavuto harrumphed that those in the higher brackets were being slandered and vilified. "Why? Because they're rich, that's why. And because they can take it. That's why. And because no one will defend them. That's *really* why. I mean when is the last time anyone said anything good about rich people? Think hard. I dare you, because it isn't going to happen." Cavuto's weeping violin solo for unloved and unappreciated billionaires (Jack Welch staring out his penthouse window, as Suzy lays a consoling hand on his shoulder, or someplace further south) was almost touching in its romantic pathos. Hardly a day goes by that Rush Limbaugh doesn't laud the pioneer spirit of America's maligned plutocrats, every shelter book fawns over rich estates as if they were the halls of Versailles, and the political system is a millionaires' club, yet Cavuto is determined to do a Clarence Darrow on behalf of the rich. (His 2004 book *More than Money*, which he hawked shamelessly on Fox News, does this to an almost maudlin degree.)

Bossy as he is, O'Reilly will lean back now and then and let guests finish a stray sentence. Cavuto has an itchier trigger finger. He's a chronic, smart-aleck butt-in, breaking his guests' answers into bits of peanut brittle and trying to top them with quippy comebacks. He interrupts everyone but steps up his fragmentation campaign with liberals less besotted with Gulfstream owners than he. Former secretary of labor Robert Reich, vainly trying to have an adult conversation about Bush's tax policies, was peppered with darts from Cavuto that were capped with the parting question, "Admit it, you hate rich people, don't you?" "Oh, Neil," Reich sighed in disappointment. For comedy relief, Cavuto parries viewer e-mails about his hideous ties and the balloon size of his head with self-deprecating humor, something alien to O'Reilly's nature. On those rare occasions O'Reilly laughs at himself, he shakes his head and no sound comes out, as if he were rattling an empty box. What he and Cavuto share is the habit of trying to muzzle anybody who disagrees with them. According to a handy list compiled by Jack Shafer at *Slate*, O'Reilly, who was taught to shut up by his father at the dining table—"Shut up. Eat your food"—is carrying on Dad's noble legacy, telling everyone from Jimmy Carter and Alec Baldwin to Rosie O'Donnell and Tom Daschle ("with all due respect, Senator, shut up") to stifle, sentiments Cavuto echoes in his own editorials, telling war protestors to think of the soldiers and their families; "Then before you act up, may I suggest you consider them, and just shut up." Why did our parents bother telling us never to tell our siblings to shut up? That's all we hear now as adults.

Fox News would argue that its perceived political bias isn't an institutional mind-set, but rather is simply on-air personalities such as O'Reilly and Cavuto unbuttoning their tufted individualism and not stealth-communicating their opinions and emotions through a phony façade of objectivity. At least our bias is out in the bare open and not being coyly conveyed by subtle eyebrow semaphores and even subtler intonations—Peter Jennings's virtuoso specialty. But the individualism of the Fox News team is as synthesized as its populism. In the letters section of Romenesko's Media News site, a former writer-producer at Fox News named Charlie Reina divulged what many suspected when he revealed the existence of Fox's daily briefing to its staff, The Memo. Reina, who had spent the previous twenty-plus years at other news organizations, said none of them had ever asked him to toe the management line the way Ailes's ballet company did. Fox staffers were not only expected to toe the line but do barre exercises—unwobbly pliés. "The roots of FNC day-to-day on-air bias are actual and direct," he wrote. "They come in the form of an executive memo distributed electronically each morning, addressing what stories will be covered and, often, suggesting how they should be covered. To the newsroom personnel responsible for the channel's daytime programming, The Memo is the bible." The Memo establishes the dominant chord of that day's coverage; Cavuto and company supply the horn section. When the Bush administration launched a PR campaign to combat the bad news coming out of Iraq called "Operation Pushback," Fox mounted its own Operation Pushback: every host, headline, and news crawl at the bottom of the screen accentuated the positive—how many schools had opened, how many new Internet cafés were open for business, how the insurgent attacks were the work of "a relative few," etc. (MSNBC must have gotten a similar memo, because the network managed to outdo Fox, sending reporter Bob "Blonde on Blonde" Arnot to wander, microphone in hand, through coffee shops, bazaars, and busy streets to show us not everything in Baghdad was getting blown up.)

The Memo has proven to be an efficient tool of mind massage. A few valiant bloggers dedicated themselves to detailing Fox's Jackson Pollock drip canvas of distortion during the Iraq war, when the straightforward, flak-jacket reporting of Steve Harrigan was overshadowed by the putziness of Geraldo "of Arabia" Rivera, but it was too Herculean a task for a few isolated mammals. A more detached collaborative overview was prepared by the Program on International Policy Attitudes (PIPA) and Knowledge Networks, a polling research firm based in Menlo Park, California. Their report, titled "Misperceptions, the Media, and the Iraq War," explored the stratified depths of ignorance Americans had displayed about a conflict that was still streaming across their television screens. The PIPA/Knowledge Networks researchers discovered that a "substantial minority" of Americans polled believed that WMDs had been found in Iraq following the invasion—that a substantial minority even believed Iraqi forces had *used* WMDs against American soldiers. And of course there was the chestnut that, despite all evidence to the contrary, nearly half of

Fox Populi

Americans believed that Saddam Hussein had close ties with Al Qaeda. But there were degrees of ignorance, the researchers found. "The extent of Americans' misperceptions vary significantly depending on their source of news. Those who receive most of their news from Fox News are more likely than average to have misperceptions. Those who receive most of their news from NPR or PBS are less likely to have misperceptions." Misperceptions, such a nice euphemism. Fox News, building better morons the American way.

Sean Hannity, the cohost of *Hannity and Colmes* (or, as many people think of the show, Hannity and That Other Guy), is the Angry White Male putting on a sunny disposition. If O'Reilly is the channel's most erratic and ferocious attack poodle, Hannity is the most steadfast and pettable. Despite being the author of *Deliver Us from Evil: Defeating Terrorism, Despotism, and Liberalism*, yet another squirt of lighter fluid on the bonfire of liberal witch-burning, Hannity doesn't look and sound like a hater; he's able to smile without pulling a facial muscle (unlike O'Reilly, whose smiles appear to be held hostage), talks warmly of his family, and acts like a real happy-go-lucky guy—the perfect delivery man for all those calculated misperceptions. Never for a sec are you persuaded that the charged-up opinions or hostile questions Hannity hurls at guests are the result of independent thought, wheels turning in the windmill of his mind. Everything evacuating from his mouth sounds as if it were dictated by somebody else, somebody tapping the talking points right into his toy brain. Sean Hannity is an ideal mouthpiece for Fox News because he's the simulacrum of Fox News's ideal viewer: the middle-aged white man with the refillable, flip-top head who's told what to think and repeats what he's been told in a brash voice, convinced that he thunk it up himself.

> "This is a Republican network. You don't know that? Look around."
>
> —investor Jim Rogers to his fellow panelists
> on Fox's *Cavuto on Business* (February 14, 2004)

If one Fox News program could serve as a stand-in for the network, the entire schedule in miniature, it would be *Special Report with Brit Hume*, a nightly hour-long political news show that bleeds Republican blue. A former White House correspondent for ABC News, Hume was an occasional contributor to the *American Spectator*, outlet for the infamous "Arkansas Project" (a rat-fuck operation intended to bring down the Clintons), and a longtime critic of liberal bias in the news establishment. Lodged behind the anchor desk like an impasse, Hume scarcely masks his contempt and impatience toward those who disagree. He gets testy in interviews with Democrats, behaving like an angry dad whose word is law, or wishes it were. His grumpiness becomes most pronounced during the nightly "Fox All-Stars" panel discussion, where he can barely rein in his negative energy field. Among the rotating "Fox All-Stars" jawboning about the day's events are Fred Barnes, executive editor of the *Weekly Standard* (the perishingly thin opinion journal whose ads on *Special Report* tout its inside status with the Bush administration and which, like Fox News, is owned by Rupert Murdoch); Mort Kondracke, editor of *Roll Call* and Barnes's cohost on *The Beltway Boys*; Bill Kristol, Barnes's boss at the *Standard* and the prince regent of neoconservatism; the genially clueless Jeff Birnbaum of *Fortune* magazine; Bill Sammon, a correspondent for the *Washington Times* and author of those impartial, poetic studies *At Any Cost: How Al Gore Tried to Steal the Election* and *Misunderestimated: The President Battles Terrorism, John Kerry, and Bush Haters*; and NPR's Mara Liasson, who's interrupted the most because she's a woman, and who cares what women think?—not these guys.

One of the lab-rat fascinations of *Special Report* is how it alters the behavior and attitudes of those sharing its confined quarters. The show is so claustrophobically right-wing that anyone who appears regularly on the panel contracts a slow-progressing case of Stockholm Syndrome. The most notable experimental subject is the panel's only panelist of color, the hapless Juan Williams, former host of the NPR's *Talk of the Nation* program. To Yosemite Sam conservatives, always hoppin' mad about something, the soothing voices of NPR— where the women sound as if they're making a clay pot on the turntable and the men sound as if they've gotten in touch with their feminine side and can't leave it alone—are the pigeon coos of upscale liberalism, progressivism as a tone poem. The courteous tolerance of these gentle sisters and brothers of NPR of disparate points of view make Mara and Juan the most vulnerable to peer pressure. (Whereas the invulnerable Brit and Fred seem to have jamming devices in their brains to ward off liberal juju and the seductive beat of the samba.) When the camera is on Poor Juan, he begins to wobble, unsure of himself, trapped in enemy territory and suffering Hamlet indecision. *The war was a bad idea—but we can't pull out, can we?— drilling in Alaska—it's gotta be bad for the caribou or whatever's up there—but these conservatives make a lotta sense—I can't see me driving a solar car anytime soon—oh God now they're going to bring up partial-birth abortion—I guess I'm against that but I'm also for a woman's right to choose—I wish the other guys would stop glaring—Brit looks like he's about to snap at me again, and Fred—Fred's snickering again—Fred's always snickering at me!—someday I'm going to stuff those snickers back down his throat!* Then, his eardrums beating from the pressure of the voices inside his head *that won't leave him alone,* Juan often concedes the argument but shakes his head to show he's not fully convinced, his way of salvaging some scrap of dignity. We will know this pressurized process of osmosis is complete the day Williams walks into the Washington studio as a black man and walks out as a disgruntled honky—then he'll really blend.

Fox News has so successfully consolidated its conservative base that it can make overtures to the center, something George Bush might emulate, if he gets desperate enough. In October 2003, Fox hired Chris Wallace of ABC's *Primetime Thursday* to fill the host chair of *Fox News Sunday* formerly warmed by Tony Snow, who now has his own radio talk show time-waster. This was a master stroke by Ailes. The son of CBS iron man octogenarian Mike Wallace, Chris Wallace would bring a hard crust of mainstream journalistic cred to Fox News, an aura of adult supervision and a bass note of Edward R. Murrow gravitas. Even in the yappy attack-poodle era, a few well-sounded vowels can resonate with an audience. Installing Wallace in the host's seat also would enable the show to book high-level Democrats who had hitherto resisted being double-teamed by the conservative duo of Snow and Hume, who had a bad cop–bad cop interrogation routine going. When the surprise acquisition was announced, media skeptics (myself included) speculated that Wallace might succumb to the mindwarp culture of Fox News, inching right by immeasurable degrees until he conformed to the channel's prevailing tilt, and started snapping at Juan. But so far his self-containment core has not been breached, and his terse, uninflected questioning of political guests achieves the *Dragnet* tone of dry factuality that Ailes claimed was the original aim of Fox News. Wallace even resembles Jack Webb, minus the jug ears. For one hour a week, Fox News Channel provides a flinty reminder of what real broadcast journalism looked like before Fox News Channel helped ruin it.

Bungle in the Jungle

NEWS COVERAGE HAS CLAMOROUSLY ENTERED the void of what George W. S. Trow famously described as "the context of no context," a rootless realm where history is made up on the spot and new narratives are woven every day. How can legit cable news operations compete when the news itself becomes politicized, polarized, and postmodernized? What do the watchdogs do when rival attack poodles overrun their positions, ransack their dressing rooms, and carry off their most prized on-air personalities into the barbarous night? Do they dig in and tough it out, rededicating themselves to their original mission, or try to regroup by copying their conqueror and peeling off of some of its market share? Or hope to buy time by tinkering around until they hit on the right combination of the two? This is the wavering plight of MSNBC and CNN as they seek to devise a counterstroke strategy against Fox News before it bulks into an invincible franchise, like the New York Yankees in full Ruthian swagger.

Of the two, MSNBC is the more precariously dazed and confused. CNN at least has its early footloose glory days as the "Chicken Noodle News" to nourish it through this barren cold snap. To sustain an institutional culture, a proud legacy, it can draw on the memories of Peter Arnett in Baghdad with bombs bursting in air during the first Gulf War and the august Bernard Shaw at the anchor desk. MSNBC has no wondrous scrapbook to page through. It tripped coming out of the gate, and has been trying to sustain rhythm and direction ever since. Founded in 1996, when the words "convergence" and "synergy" were bandied about without ironic quotation marks, the channel joined Microsoft and NBC in corporate matrimony, a wedding of new media and old. The moment was propitious for futuristic endeavors and bold wayfarers. Soon we would all be singing the body electric and feeling foreglimpses of immortality. The third millennium was approaching, and a "new era" had dawned in computer technology, the financial markets, and the economy. Dot-com millionaires barely out of their underwear-strewn dorm rooms were puffing on fat stogies and splurging like *Miami Vice* drug kingpins; floppy T-shirted entrepreneurs were hailed as garage-band geniuses of capitalism-in-the-untamed-raw; and ad-thick, text-packed bibles of desktop messianism such as *Wired, Red Herring,* and *Fast Com-*

pany clogged up mailboxes and newsstands. MSNBC wanted to feed the flippy heads of the plugged-in MTV generation and help make informed citizens of those party dudes and dudettes.

The original MSNBC set, with its sweeping lines and blinking, flashing computer terminals and TV monitors, resembled the captain's deck of the Starship *Enterprise*, prepared to warp-drive into the data stream. New media were represented on board by freshly baked hosts such as Soledad O'Brien (currently cohost of CNN's *American Morning*) and a multiculti mod squad of regular rotating guests who were hip, casually photogenic, and fluent in geek. These cadets did their part. They hung out on the set and said their cool piece. Their elders, however, chose to remain in their cabins. The established stars of NBC News largely failed to lend their dry-cleaned presence to the flight crew, depriving MSNBC of their silvery highlights and crisp gravitas. "Right off the bat, they [MSNBC] made a mistake," media strategist and former CNN executive David Bernknopf told *CBS MarketWatch*. "They promised all their big stars from NBC News would appear. Of course that was impossible." With the experienced warhorses reluctant to converge and synergize, the burden of success fell on the cybernauts, and as went the Nasdaq and the dot-com boom (ker-plop), so went MSNBC. Having lost both the old guard and the new vanguard, MSNBC had to scramble for a fresh reason to exist, rebrand itself as a non-nerdy news operation, and periodically restock the talent pool in the hope that a star would foamily rise like Venus on the halfshell. Under the itchy triggerfinger of former NBC president Andy Lack, MSNBC became infatuated with info honeys only to burn them out with overexposure. "It was all Ashleigh Banfield all the time," Bernknopf said. "I mean, think about how much time and effort they spent on trying to turn her into a hot celebrity." One moment she was banging around in a jeep through Afghanistan and anchoring her own show *Ashleigh Banfield: On Location*, and before you knew it she was serving appetizers stateside, covering such nonstories as a class offered at Yale devoted to deconstructing Michael Jackson.

Over the years MSNBC's schizoid nature, under severe pressure from the ascent of Fox News and its kennel of attack poodles, intensified into a seismic crack. MSNBC evolved into the cable news channel with two brains, one operational and rational, the other glitchy and prone to spazzes. The two brains are News Brain and Chatter Brain. News Brain gathers information, Chatter Brain dispenses opinion. News Brain works the day shift, Chatter Brain punches the time clock at night. News Brain has no reason ever to be ashamed of itself.

Bungle in the Jungle

Its team breaks hard-news stories and keeps the inane patter to a tolerable minimum. Professional newscasters such as Sam Shane, Lester Holt, Bob Kur, Dawna Friesen, Chris Jansing, Natalie Morales, Tom Aspell, Forrest Sawyer, Alex Witt, and Kerry Sanders still practice the disciplines of broadcast journalism, and there is no glossier newsreader than glamourpuss Christy Musumeci (content isn't everything). Unlike their counterparts at Fox, the MSNBC first-stringers don't chorus administration talking points as if they were riding in Karl Rove's Captain Kangaroo pouch, and unlike their counterparts at CNN, they don't josh around at the anchor desk in the afternoon like local news airheads. During the Iraq war, MSNBC's news unit outperformed any cable outlet—faint praise, perhaps, given the babysitting service most of the American media provided for Operation Neocon Boondoggle—and the leap in viewership reflected this relative strength, the ratings skyrocketing 124 percent. Having been so long forsaken in the ratings basement listening to the lonely drip of the water pipes, MSNBC could be forgiven for feeling that deliverance was finally at hand. "If credibility needed to be restored, it has been," MSNBC President Erik Sorenson told the *Wall Street Journal* with chesty pride. "I want MSNBC to be known as the 'straight shooter' news channel." If only he had listened to himself. But some perverse imp played with his mind, and MSNBC proceeded to squander the momentum and credibility it had accrued by not shooting straight but veering right—politically right. It was as if News Brain had handed the car keys to Chatter Brain after putting in a tough week, only to watch Chatter Brain go joyriding through red lights, careen into a ditch, and puke away its hard-earned efforts. Chatter Brain is a constant trial and a constant disappointment. Chatter Brain never listens, Chatter Brain pays no attention, Chatter Brain got no sense.

> "You see, meatballs can tell us a lot about a society."
> —Michael Savage, *The Savage Nation*

Ideally, News and Chatter Brain might have found harmony together, complementing each other like *Seinfeld*'s Jerry and George, Mayberry's Andy and Barney. Instead, MSNBC became a Frankenstein's monster of dug-up spare parts. Under the direction of Erik Sorenson (whose Viking warrior name could be Erik the Unsteady), MSNBC embarked upon one star search after another to fill spots in the chatter department. It looked high, re-signing the mercurial Keith Olbermann, who returned to MSNBC after several testy tours of action elsewhere. It was a welcome homecoming. Olbermann is the thinking person's

thinking person—quick, imperturbable, commanding, tele-
graphic in his delivery, enveloped in electrical tension, a Clark
Kent with attitude. Pure fuel cell efficiency, he looks as if he
doesn't sleep at night but recharges in a Borg alcove. Where
some anchors wax folksy in their humorous takes on the news
or act pose-strikingly pensive (Aaron Brown and his thoughtful finger), Olbermann is a throwback to the old school of
newsroom cynics, his irony urban, caustic, platinum-edged.
He originally left MSNBC nauseated by the nightly Monica-
thrash he had to referee, writing scathing columns for *Salon* on
the slimy wallow that cable news had become. The format of
his current show, *Countdown*—five segments on timely topics—prevents one fit of manufactured hysteria from flooding
the full hour.

The network looked sideways, hiring Deborah Norville,
formerly of the *Today* show and *Inside Edition*; often trivialized as
a beauty pageant fluff bunny, she has an underlying rigor and
poise and mainstream appeal that makes her show a plausible
counterprogramming move against CNN's aging Larry King.

Mostly, however, MSNBC looked low. Real low. And when
that wasn't low enough, it looked lower, draining swamps,
scouting the bus depots, recruiting from the mole people.
Nonpolitical picks such as Olbermann and Norville were the

quality exceptions. Intent on finding a conservative super-patriot to out-flag-wave Fox News, MSNBC kept reaching deeper into the sack and digging out Mr. Wrong. Each trumpeted discovery blew up in its face like an exploding cigar, making an Elmer Fudd spectacle of the network. And no matter how many times it backfired on MSNBC, it couldn't give up the quest for an attack poodle the public would accept and welcome into its humble chateau.

Exhibit A: the bizarre prime-time experiment with political preacherman Alan Keyes, whose gloomsday harangues on the amusingly misnamed show *Alan Keyes Is Making Sense* drove spiders out of their holes, bats out of their belfries. Keyes is one of those spellbinding orators so hyperarticulate and ruminative that he's completely incoherent, possessing the ability to split a simple thought into a billion non sequiturs. Connoisseurs of bad TV, the sort of media pathologists who have tapes of Jerry Lewis telethons lovingly filed in their video collection, tuned into *Alan Keyes Is Raving Like a Man Possessed* with their VCRs running, hoping for that magic meltdown moment Keyes's overwrought performance seemed to promise, but there weren't enough fans of the macabre to make up a quorum, and Keyes was canceled before he could set himself ablaze. Not so for our next model coming down the runway.

Bungle in the Jungle

Exhibit B: A mangy charmer named Michael Savage, whom Sorenson praised as "brash, passionate, and smart" in the press release announcing the latest acquisition to the MSNBC team. Each week Savage attempted to foment a native uprising on *Savage Nation*, its title taken from Savage's syndicated radio talk show and best-selling collection of polysyllabic belches. Based in San Francisco, the beauteous, progressive city conservatives love to loathe, Savage—real name, Michael Weiner—was a former herbal products pitchman who discovered his true métier was peddling homemade remedies to rid us of "Turd World" immigrants, naive do-gooders catering to social parasites (such as student volunteers slumming for sick kicks by feeding the homeless—"There's always the thrill and possibility they'll be raped in a Dumpster while giving out a turkey sandwich"), and, the most nefarious group fouling our minds and sapping our vital essences, no-good liberals ("You liberals should drop dead for what you've done to my country"—*his* country?). Like Charles Bronson in *Death Wish*, but more talkative, Savage saw himself in the scum removal business. But it was difficult to figure out what civilization this uncivilized clown thought he was protecting, what culture this uncultured boob thought he was preserving. Here is a man ignorant of literature and basic grammar ("Back in college, I remember Sartre and Camus were big in those days... I had no idea that Sartre was a commie"), and illiterate in his chosen field of communications, managing to misspell the name of radio great Jean Shepherd in his book. He brought nothing to the broadcast table except garlic breath.

But that was okey-dokey with MSNBC. All it asked of Savage was that he be himself. Unfortunately, he obliged. He let it all hang out until viewers begged him to tuck it back in. It was as if MSNBC had hired Boxcar Willie to host a political hour: *Savage Nation* was as low-rent in taste, imagination, and production values as anything filling a time slot on cable access. Gay activist groups and liberal blogs organized boycott campaigns of the show over the Internet, persuading Procter & Gamble, Dell, and Sharper Image, among others, to withdraw sponsorship. This left *Savage Nation* with the dregs of daytime advertising—hair-restorer commercials, mortgage refinancers, etc. It was also noted that Microsoft had enlightened policies regarding gay rights and benefits, as did the foundation headed by Microsoft founder Bill Gates and his wife, Melinda—did the "MS" in "MSNBC" mean nothing to them?

Unable to entice "name" guests into this flea pit (although Peggy Noonan, a poodle who hath not shame, made an early appearance), Savage ate up the clock with mock irate monologues and call-in segments. On July 5, 2003, during a special Fourth of July weekend broadcast, the "Savage Weiner"—as he was unfondly known in blogland—committed suicide by sound bite. The Supreme Court had just handed down its decision striking down Texas's sodomy law, which *Savage Nation* saw as another triumph for decadence, deviancy, and the friends of Dorothy. It referenced the ruling with slug lines on the screen that screeched COURT SODOMIZES AMERICA and SODOMY DEMEANS OUR CULTURE. During the call-in segment, a prankster identified himself as a "sodomite" and blurted an insult at Savage that was swallowed by the five-second delay. It must have been a nasty insult, one unworthy of a gentleman, because Savage pulled a Joe Pyne on the caller. (For you youngsters, Joe Pyne was a once popular jingoistic West Coast talk show host, the prototype for Morton Downey, Jr., and Wally George, who would order hippies to go home and get a haircut, or tell a heckler, "I could make a monkey out of you, but why take the credit?") In a comeback that will forever haunt Savage's conscience, once he retrieves it from the lost and found, Savage told the caller, "Oh, you're one of the sodomites. You should only get AIDS and die, you pig." He sputtered a bit more, muttering that another snarky caller "didn't have a nice night in the bathhouse," and ordered the producer to cut to commercial, he didn't need these bums, the hell with them. *Savage Nation's* special "sodomy and sausage" edition (his words) ended with the host sampling barbecue on camera, the "Savage Weiner" chewing on a savage wiener. It would prove to be Michael Savage's last meal as host of his own cable show. He was fired the following Monday, his photo and biography scrubbed from the MSNBC Web site like an unsightly stain. A spokesman announced Savage's hasty departure by issuing one of those we-deeply-regret corporate apologies for Savage's "extremely inappropriate" comments.

It was too late for sorry. Media critics and Savage head-hunters, aroused with that special warm-all-over feeling of schadenfreude, chorused that MSNBC had nobody to blame for this debacle but itself, and to spare us the manicured hand-wringing. What did Sorenson and the other brass expect when they hired this bigoted pop-off artist? Savage had a long rap sheet of minority group smears ("ghetto slime") on talk radio. Rewarding him with his own cable show only encouraged him to keep spraying pesticide. Having achieved notoriety and best-sellerdom as an abrasive divider, Savage wasn't about to start wearing a Clifton Webb carnation and making pleas for brotherhood. He was hired to raise a considerable but contain-able stink, and from MSNBC's perspective, Savage's toxicity was a risk worth taking. There was even speculation that MSNBC had given him a weekly show to test-pilot him for a possible weeknight slot, angling for its own O'Reilly factor. After all, apart from his AIDS outburst, Savage is an attack poodle loyal to nearly all of the standard Republican dogma, faithful to every article in the (neo)conservative hawkish agenda: pro-gun, antienvironment, pro-Israel, anti-French, pro–family values, antifeminist, etc. Like Rush Limbaugh, he thinks global warming is a lot of hooey, and his anti-Arab sneers are indistinguishable from those of Ann Coulter, who appears frequently enough on MSNBC to warrant her own dressing room and bikini waxer. (A chapter in *Savage Nation* called "Crimes of the Democrats" reads like a trial run for Coulter's *Treason,* which in turn reads like a prequel to Savage's *The Enemy Within* and Sean Hannity's *Deliver Us from Evil.* They are all riding carousel ponies, pretending to be Paul Revere.) Once he had been canned, Savage was dismissed as a fringe kook, an urban mountain man. But that The Weiner was ever employed at all on cable TV showed how the kooky fringe had wormed closer and closer to the political center, and how much the political center had lurched to the right.

CONSIDER HOW MSNBC MISTREATED ITS ONE PASTY, unabashed liberal, Phil Donahue. Hiring the daytime veteran Phil Donahue was a play-it-safe retread move that might have paid off, given patience. Lots of patience. Donahue's hokey attempts to bump up every argument with body jazz (Jewish-mother shrugs, rainmaker arm-waving) were grating, and his Mario Cuomo brand of liberalism was smothered with schmaltz. He also played into the stereotype of liberal masochism, of being so open-minded that he let any loony fanatic inside to flap around the studio, allowing white separatist publisher Jared Taylor to have an entire hour to expound on how an influx of "cannibals" and "lesbians" can ruin the neighborhood. Although underperforming initial projections, Donahue's ratings were respectable, and the show was finding its niche on the channel, a secure grip. Whenever something began to take hold at MSNBC, that was the moment to step in and stamp it out. The channel canceled Donahue after eight months, citing weak numbers, an explanation that industry watchers found fishy. "While Donahue does badly trail both O'Reilly and CNN's Connie Chung," Rick Ellis wrote on AllYourTV.com in February 2003, "those numbers have improved in recent weeks. So much so that the program is the top-rated show on MSNBC, beating even the highly promoted *Hardball* with Chris Matthews."

Bungle in the Jungle

Donahue's real sin was that he was perceived as a dove in hawk-infested airwaves. In times of peace, this wouldn't be a problem, but America was about to rumble with Iraq, one of the axes of evil, and there was no space for pink-pantied appeasers in the steel cage death match between George "Texas Executioner" Bush and Saddam "Butcher of Baghdad" Hussein. "Although Donahue didn't know it at the time," Ellis reported:

> his fate was sealed a number of weeks ago after NBC News executives received the results of a study commissioned to provide guidance on the future of the news channel.
>
> That report—shared with me by an NBC news insider—gives an excruciatingly painful assessment of the channel and its programming.... But the harshest criticism was leveled at Donahue, whom the authors of the study described as "a tired, left-wing liberal out of touch with the current marketplace."
>
> The study went on to claim that Donahue presented a "difficult public face for NBC in a time of war.... He seems to delight in presenting guests who are antiwar, anti-Bush, and skeptical of the administration's motives." The report went on to outline a possible nightmare

scenario where the show becomes "a home for the liberal antiwar agenda at the same time that our competitors are waving the flag at every opportunity."

Couldn't have that. Once battle lines are drawn, it's the patriotic duty of every talk show host to suck in his puffy gut, stifle his doubts, and learn to cakewalk. It didn't go unnoticed that the same week MSNBC dropped tired, out-of-touch, liberal Donahue, it signed conservative former Republican congressman and House Majority Leader Dick Armey, Exhibit C, as a commentator. He had quite a résumé. It was the debonair Armey who was once overheard calling gay congressman Barney Frank "Barney Fag," who told Hillary Clinton, "Reports of your charm are overstated," and who—according to Sidney Blumenthal in *The Clinton Wars*—"employed the wife of Supreme Court Justice Clarence Thomas on his staff, [who] helped him target Democrats who they thought should be investigated." He was the perfect anti-Donahue.

MSNBC'S CHATTERBRAIN IN CHIEF IS CHRIS MATTHEWS, who says whatever's on his mind whether there's anything there or not, vamping until a fully formed thought finally shows. He refuses to govern his galloping mouth, riffing and free-associating like Elvis on his last tour, letting all the gremlins out of the attic. But Elvis Unedited was slouching toward the end of the line in drug-addled bondage, trying to squirm out of the imprisoning corset of his bejeweled jumpsuits. If Matthews has demons, they're poking him with Q-tips. Plump and sassy inside his own hotdog skin (a self-described "happy troll"), Matthews splashes and spills his noisy presence around the studio like a man supremely assured that he's at the top of his game, the life of the party, the zeitgeist zapping from his pores. His lucid flashes and slashes of insight on *Hardball* are spaced farther and farther apart as he rides his ego up and away on the beating wings of Pegasus. It isn't that he lacks political knowledge or historical perspective, but that he prefers to be infected by the latest cocktail chatter inside the Beltway, enjoying the feverish high it gives him, the babbling rush. His weekly half-hour syndicated talk show, much more evenly paced and less filibustering than *Hardball*, proves that he can keep his tongue tucked when he tries. He just so seldom tries. Although his politics can't be neatly categorized as conservative, he goes after his liberal aversions as viciously as any rightwing attack poodle, and with as little concern for fairness and factuality. He was at his most manic-euphoric during the Monica mess, because it offered the perfect train wreck of gossip, wild conjecture, character sideswiping, political infighting, Constitutional drama, and national soap opera: a Watergate for wankers. It also allowed Matthews to bombard Bill and Hillary Clinton with flying spittle, obsessing over their every gloved political move as if they were the last of the Borgias, plotting a coup in the pantry. In his memoir *The Clinton Wars*, Sidney Blumethal ascribes personal pique to Matthews's political vendetta. "Matthews had been a speechwriter for President Carter and a press secretary for the Democratic Speaker of the House Thomas P. "Tip" O'Neill before becoming a talk-show host. He had lobbied the White House to replace DeeDee Meyers as press secretary, but the job had gone to Michael McCurry. Even before the impeachment Matthews had turned into a detractor of Clinton. He freely told perplexed friends that as a consequence, his ratings had improved."

Although like Tim Russert and Mike Barnicle, Matthews spouts a lot of beer-sudsy rhetoric about average hard-working blue-collar guys, he's developed an impacted sneer against liberal Democrats, the traditional champion of blue collars, despising them as (to borrow a word from the Nixon era) effete. In the world according to Chris, Republicans are manly (upright, proactive, astride the globe), the Democrats womanly (fearful, carping, tied to domestic apron strings). Republicans strap on the holster and get the dirty job done, while Democrats stand in the doorway, attaching caveats and wringing their dishpan hands. Sexual chauvinism infuses Matthews's political impressions and responses. He's rude, interruptive, and peremptory toward female guests, particularly feminists, with whom he gets thin-nostrilled, as if they were trying to take all the fun out of roughhousing and spoil things for the guys at the lodge. That Bill would be married to a harpy like Hillary, that Al Gore would need a Naomi Wolf to advise him on alpha malehood, only confirmed his worst suspicions about how emasculated the Dems had become.

Give him a real fake sun-bronzed stout-hearted man every time, such as Arnold Schwarzenegger, the crowd-pleasing, self-parodying cyborg (who in his bodybuilding prime resembled, as Clive James immortally observed, a fistful of walnuts stuffed in a condom) whose run for governor of California had Matthews effusing all over his lobster bib. For Matthews, elections equal erections, and the recall election would be an affair to remember. Night after night on *Hardball* he dropped any pretense of being a disinterested journalist (none of that finicky David Brinkley dryness for him), and turned flak-catcher and fire extinguisher for the Schwarzenegger cam-

paign, having a fierce fit of pique when the multiple accusations of sexual harassment by Schwarzenegger over a stretch of
decades broke in the *Los Angeles Times*. No sooner had feminist
lawyer Gloria Allred recited the accusations on *Hardball*—the
breast-grabbing, the butt-groping—than Matthews dashed
into damage control, dragging in Clinton's affair with Monica
Lewinsky as a diversion tactic. Undiverted, Allred observed
that what happened between the chief executive and the
thong-twanging intern, though inappropriate and, yes, icky,
was consensual; Schwarzenegger's advances weren't. Each time
Matthews tried to overtalk Allred, she stubbornly repeated her
point about consensuality until any dope could understand her,
except one determined to miss the point. To cut her off,
Matthews said, "My producer is telling me to shut you up.
Okay? I'm trying to be polite." So caught up in the heat of the
Schwarzenegger campaign was Matthews that he even showed
up at the victory rally, receiving a hug from the earthmover he
had helped elect.

Even when Matthews deplores a politician's policies, a
well-struck pin-up pose will lay him out in the grass like one of
the girlish swooners in *Bye Bye Birdie*. Although he took an
admirable, forthright stand against the Iraq war, and was one
of the first to sniff out the malignant influence of the neocons

in bamboozling the country into this desert mirage, he still can get as gaga as Andrew Sullivan and Peggy Noonan over that hickory-smoked hunk of masculinity, George W. Bush. That wide-stanced walk of Bush's, wowee wow wow wow. One of the more goose-pimply TV moments in recent memory was Matthews and G. Gordon Liddy plotzing over the spectacle of Bush on the carrier deck in his flight suit as he proclaimed the end of major combat operations in Iraq, his parachute harness showcasing the presidential bulge—or, to use Liddy's inimitable phrase, "his manly characteristic." One guy to another, Liddy put Matthews wise. "You know, all those women who say size doesn't count—they're all liars. Check that out."

MATTHEWS: And I've got to say why do the Democrats, as you say, want to keep advertising this guy's greatest moment?

LIDDY: Look, he's coming across as a—well, as women would call in on my show saying, what a stud...

To borrow a line from the late Marvin Mudrick, the two of them should take a cold shower, preferably not together.

In fairness to Matthews, Liddy, and their keen appreciation of the male anatomy, conservative women also oohed at the box lunch Bush was packing as if he were a Chippendale's dancer defending our precious freedoms. The *American Enterprise* magazine rounded up a number of conservative fun gals and ardent antifeminists for a symposium on politics and modern manhood, including Mona Charen, Kate O'Beirne, Jessica Gavora (author of *Tilting the Playing Field* and the wife of attack poodle Jonah Goldberg), and Erica Walter, who was identified as an at-home mom and Catholic writer. An Emma Bovary clearly waiting to happen, Walter purred, "In George W. Bush, people see a contained, channeled virility." O'Beirne also marveled over the container. "Bill Clinton couldn't credibly wear jogging shorts, and look at George Bush in that flight suit."

Exhibit D is Joe Scarborough, an MSNBC host and attack poodle who launched his show in 2003, hoping that Bush's virility mojo would rub off on his own manly characteristic, metaphorically speaking. The montage for his weeknight broadcast, *Scarborough Country*, stitches together shots of Bush in *Top Gun* gear with shots of Scarborough in flyboy drag, sending the message that these two belong to the brotherhood of the sky. "I am the hawk's hawk," Scarborough declared. He didn't see actual bullets-flying military service any more than Bush did, but, like the president, there's nothing he won't do to protect the country, as long as there are cameras present—

that's the Republican way. A former Republican congressman from Florida, Scarborough was a bright-eyed Boy Scout in the insurgent freshman class that, led by Newt Gingrich, seized control of Congress in 1994. Gingrich had instructed the troops to denounce liberal Democrats as sick, contagious, permissive, and morally relativistic heathens who'd leave their *Playboy* magazines out in the open for children to see, and Scarborough hopped to, whooping it up and playing the happy warrior on *Hardball* and other chat venues, casting stones at the sinning Bill Clinton. But—like Gingrich and a number of his fellow crusaders—Joltin' Joe had secrets hidden in his own sock drawer. His moral relativism had some bend to it. An "epidemic of ruined marriages swept through the freshman class of 1994," Joe Conason wrote in his book *Big Lies*, the casualty toll including Gingrich himself, Oregon's Jim Bunn, and Iowa's Jim Nussle. Keeping a valuable scorecard, Conason writes, "Other freshmen soon joined the list of broken vows, including Jim Longley of Maine, Enid Waldholtz Green of Utah, and, a year or so later, Joe Scarborough of Florida."

On the evolutionary scale, Scarborough is a step up from Michael Savage. Unlike Savage, Scarborough knows how to dress himself and smile without scaring toddlers. You can imagine him mingling in society, as long as society doesn't expect too much. He's more moderate than many of his conservative cronies on gay rights, the environment, and corporate responsibility, and doesn't treat pop culture as products forged in Satan's workshop. He's been quite amiable and almost witty on his subsequent Imus visits. But—his major liability—he still practices the divisive politics that Gingrich taught his marching band several chins ago. Scarborough's *Scarborough Country* is a Republican red state of mind where Americans are hard-working, God-fearing, flag-waving, gun-loving, straight-talking, and looking forward to the next county fair. Where all of the children of Garrison Keillor's Lake Wobegon are a little above average, the goobers in Scarborough Country are all a little below par, rudimentary figments of cartoon populism. The show is a drastic effort by MSNBC to cure what (Roger) Ailes it, with Joe's "Real Deal" editorials mimicking Neil Cavuto's daily diaper rash complaints and the fighting words of Bill O'Reilly's "Talking Points" editorials. Scarborough acknowledges the copycat comparisons, informing the *New York Observer* that MSNBC staffers call him "Little O'Reilly." Perhaps they do, one blogger joked, in the sense that Elvis spoke of his penis as "Little Elvis."

Where Scarborough strives to out-Fox Fox is in the lopsidedness of his partisanship. "Obviously, Fox is conservative,"

Scarborough told the *Observer*. "If I can help tip the scales at MSNBC, which is currently more down the middle, I think that's a victory." He certainly tips the scales on his own show. Even Fox's prime-time lineup presents a more balanced mix of opinion than does the slanted booking on *Scarborough Country*, a forum for Republican spin and unpaid political advertising where Democrats aren't the loyal opposition but the hapless obstructionists, or, worse, useful idiots. Scarborough is never chummier than when greeting Saxby Chambliss, freshman Republican senator from Georgia, as a guest. A man without scruples, Chambliss defeated Max Cleland in the 2002 midterm elections by running ads soiling his opponent, a paraplegic and Medal of Honor winner who lost three limbs in Vietnam, as soft on terrorism. Chambliss has since graduated to impugning John Kerry as deficient on national defense in a conference call set up by the Bush reelection campaign, while Ann Coulter, Mark Steyn, and *National Review* editor Rich Lowry have wheeled round to disparage Cleland yet again, taking turns rhetorically kicking a cripple. There is no low blow of which these cowards are not capable.

As if hiring two former Republican congressmen, Armey and Scarborough, weren't already too much, MSNBC's chief analyst of public opinion is Republican pollster Frank Luntz,

Exhibit E, who should be wearing a letter sweater, carrying a Rudy Vallee megaphone, and leading the pep squad. He is the most domesticated-looking and deceptive of attack poodles. Luntz, the head of Luntz Research Companies and the architect of Newt Gingrich's "Contract with America," coaches Republicans in how to package their hostile indifference or aggression in soothing words and warm fuzzies. Perturbed that Republicans were losing the PR battle over the environment, he issued a memo counseling them to mellow their language (i.e., substituting "climate change" for the more highly charged "global warming") and put on a good show of caring without actually exerting themselves. Stress the "scientific uncertainty" of most environmental issues, and call yourselves conservationists, since "environmentalists" has such a negative radical connotation (thanks to the demagoguery of Rush Limbaugh). Then sit back, count the votes, and let the earth sizzle while species perish. During the California recall, Luntz unveiled a strategy to unseat Gray Davis that relied upon similar Uriah Heep humbuggery: "While it is important to trash the governor," the memo advised, "it should be done in the context of regret, sadness, and balance." Or as they say in the British satirical magazine *Private Eye*, Take out onion, wipe away tear. Considering Luntz's flagrant partisanship and conflict of interests, MSNBC did the only thing it could do under the circumstances: it gave him his own crappy show. *America's Voices*, hosted by Luntz, was a weekly focus group on the issues facing this country in which the audience members—citizens like yourself, but duller—sat and waited their turn to speak, as if participating in the most medicated P.T.A. meeting ever held, before being shipped out of the studio and converted into soylent green. The late *New Yorker* journalist Joseph Mitchell (*Joe Gould's Secret, Up in the Old Hotel*) once explained that the reason he gave up doing human-interest stories was because over time his interviewees stopped talking like individuals with their own unique vernacular and started imitating the characters they heard on TV. Likewise, people who participate in focus groups have become gifted in speaking focus-groupese, supplying the placebo comments expected of them. "Education's definitely a big priority in our household." "Trust is high on my agenda when I'm considering a candidate." "I want to consider all the issues before I make a decision." Kill me now. The only traces of comedy were Luntz's frustrated attempts to coax Republican responses from these Concerned Citizens, only to hit one bland wall of moderation after another. Few things are sadder than a pep rally with no pep. *America's Voices* made for a deadly hour and underlined the difference between MSNBC and Fox News, which never would have allowed a show this amateurish and energy-depleted to bounce off the satellite. Fox powers up its programming, makes a complete fist when it stamps its logo on a show, and has the conviction of its cynicism. MSNBC wanders the ward like an amnesia victim, hoping someone will solve the mystery between its ears.

In the futile hunt for an incredible hulk, MSNBC signed former pro wrestler and governor of Minnesota, Jesse "The Body" Ventura, to host a talk show. He, they prayed, might be the long-sought rabble-rouser to turn things around before the network lost any more audience share and ran out of rabble. After so many false starts, dashed hopes, and rainy Mondays, MSNBC didn't want to rush this hunka junk on the air and delayed the show's debut so that it could tinker with the format, get Ventura comfortable in his new role, and make sure the backdrops didn't wobble every time the beefy host shifted buttocks. (The sets for *Savage Nation* looked as if they couldn't survive a sneeze.) From his *Meet the Press* appearances, Ventura came across as a man (and what a man) who was all talk and no listen, full of himself, and impatient with other points of view. So in that sense the incredible bulk should have fit right in at MSNBC, even if he did sound as if he gargled with gravel. But MSNBC soon learned to its migraine misery that it had another flounder on its hands. His weekly show found him galumphing around the studio in Saint Paul, Minnesota, dressed as if he were grand marshal at a Harley-Davidson rally. On one broadcast, he swapped hunting stories with long-tressed rocker and Rush Limbaugh fan Ted Nugent, who rhapsodized about the Hemingwayesque thrill of luring and killing bears ("Jesse, I put a worm on my hook when I'm fishing and I like to sit over a pile of doughnuts when I'm bear hunting"), at which point I found myself wishing Nugent's head could be mounted on a wall as a hat rack. This dismal experiment lasted only two months before it was put on hiatus, and in television, everyone knows what "hiatus" means. It's Hamlet's undiscovered country, from which no traveler returns. Jesse Ventura, Exhibit F.

F as in flunk. The failure of Ventura's show may not have been the final straw, but it certainly weighed heavily in the loss column. Unable to stomach any more erosion with a presidential election looming, in February 2004, MSNBC hired Rick Kaplan to replace Erik Sorenson and stride around the executive offices and apply charismatic leadership. A producer at ABC News, where he spirited *Nightline*, *Primetime Live*, and *World News Tonight* to success, Kaplan became news chief of CNN in 1997. It was under his command that conservatives began jibing that CNN's initials stood for the Clinton News Network, Kaplan guilty of being a golf buddy of Bill's and a frequent guest in the Lincoln Bedroom during the Clinton presidency. One conservative firebrand, L. Brent Bozell III (he of the orange beard), labeled him the "personification of liberal media bias." Selecting Kaplan to rescue MSNBC from itself thus made for a distinctive and perhaps portentous break with the rightward swerve of the network in the Bush era. As Eric Alterman, the author of *What Liberal Media?* wrote on his blog, welcoming Kaplan, "With MSNBC he's got a near clean slate and plenty of resources to work with. Not everything he tries will work, but I'm guessing the days of Faux-Fox are over." Kaplan's most immediate task is to heal and seal the breach between News Brain and Chatter Brain. In the eloquent words of *Seinfeld*, "A George divided against itself cannot stand," and neither can a network undecided about what it should be.

IF MSNBC HAS BATTLED AN IDENTITY CRISIS SINCE infancy, CNN has been bogged down in the longest midlife crisis since film critic and soul searcher David Denby joined the *New Yorker*. When CNN originally hopped on the air in 1980, its maverick founder Ted Turner, a dashing loudmouth with a Rhett Butler mustache and a cutlass manner (his oft-quoted motto: "Lead, follow, or get out of the way"), made the network sound like a window seat on the saga of mankind. "We're gonna go on the air June 1," he proclaimed, "and we're gonna stay on until the end of the world. When that time comes, we'll cover it, play 'Nearer My God to Thee,' and sign off." The dark, sardonic tint of Stanley Kubrick had infiltrated the news business, which would never be the same. In its early days under Turner and cofounder Reese Schonfeld (the network's first president, who would recount their story in *Me and Ted Against the World*), CNN resembled a start-up, cut-rate airline where the ride was bumpy but the exhilarations intense and the curvature of the earth always in view. CNN's global vision reflected Turner's cockeyed optimism and ambition. He wanted to wrap the planet in his arms and squeeze some sense into it, before war, famine, and environmental ravage shredded it apart. The buccaneer spirit that made CNN nimble and daring in the beginning dissipated as the network expanded and stratified into a bureaucratic behemoth. It lost altitude and amplitude. "I suppose there comes a time for the mavericks to pick up their marbles and go home," Schonfeld later philosophized. Once the mavericks move out, the managerial class moves in and prepares its PowerPoint displays. Commemorating the twentieth anniversary of CNN, media critic and executive editor of MediaChannel.org, Danny Schechter, lamented how establishmentarian the network became. "What may have been innovative and adventurous long ago soon lost any upstart edge and sense of mission. CNN today is slickly and professionally produced, by network veterans groomed in corporate news culture. It is designed to be homogenous, a seamless flow of predictable formats and personalities like Larry King." Schechter also noted CNN's loss of authority as it emphasized lighter, viewer-friendly featurettes, symbolized by the switch from James Earl Jones as the basso profundo voice of CNN (*"This ... is CNN"*—such Godlike intonation!) to promos featuring cute celebrities chirping, "I'm watching you, CNN."

The gargantuan merger of AOL and Time Warner, the parent company of CNN, compounded the corporatization. It was the mating of dinosaurs, the awkward, unworkable coupling of two mammoth organizational charts. As in so many corporate mergers intended to benefit shareholders and management, the first ones sacrificed on the altar of greater efficiencies were hundreds of lower-level employees no longer required in their cubicles. Reducing redundancies is standard operating procedure in any corporate merger, but as the media business faltered through the nuclear winter following the popping of the dot-com bubble, the layoffs kept coming at AOL Time Warner in successive waves. Veteran anchors and correspondents such as Brooks Jackson, Garrick Utley, Bruce Morton, Charles Feldman, and Mike Boettcher were let go, and behind the scenes and overseas, cutbacks of stringers and freelancers spattered the walls. Crowning Walter Isaacson as president of CNN in 2001 was a significant bungle, one that seemed to sum up the media-merger era. Isaacson is the epitome of an Eastern media establishmentarian, a Harvard grad and Rhodes Scholar, the former managing editor of *Time* magazine, the biographer of Henry Kissinger, and the author of *The Wise Men: Six Friends and the World They Made*. Isaacson had no broadcast experience, and no boyish Charles Foster Kane zest to see what he could do with a new set of toys. He was an impeccable, cautious, poll-watching caretaker, warning his staff (as reported in Alterman's *What Liberal Media?*), "If you get on the wrong side of public opinion, you are going to get into trouble." He remained sure CNN stayed on the right side of public opinion, issuing a memo instructing reporters to balance citings of Afghanistan casualties with reminders of how many Americans lost their lives on 9/11. Use our dead civilians to keep their dead civilians in perspective. After a couple of years at CNN, Isaacson left to run a think tank in Aspen,

Colorado, where it's much easier to stay out of trouble, unless your skis lock on the slopes.

The attrition at CNN over the years has yielded a legion of the disillusioned. You don't have to walk too long a stretch of sidewalk in New York to hear bitter stories from current and former CNNers about the network's spit-'em-out treatment of talent. Or its clumsy juggling of big names—how it tossed hastily conceived and overhyped star vehicles for Connie Chung (whose embarrassing magazine show, packed with human-interest stories featuring unfortunate people weeping in close-ups, CNN soon canceled) and Paula Zahn on the air in a state of dishabille, making them easy pickings for reviewers and a gloating Roger Ailes (Zahn being a Fox News defector). This lack of bench strength and initiative at CNN has left it shifting the same ivory chess pieces defensively around the board, overrelying on the old reliables. It's as if Wolf Blitzer is always available and never on vacation, ageless, tireless, affect-less, a key cranked in his back during commercial breaks to keep him fully wound, a sheaf of papers glued to his palms. Judy Woodruff, who seems to have a filmy layer between her and whatever burning political topic she's lightly addressing, is Washington's Avon Lady of conventional wisdom. She's too genteel to pose a tough point-blank question to a politician or pundit; she alludes instead to vague unnamed shadows in the capital that are raising questions, qualms, and objections. "Critics say you haven't done enough to..." "Some of those on the other side of the aisle dispute your assertion that..." "There are those who suggest..." It's like being pelted with powderpuffs. Bill Schneider, Jeff Greenfield: they've seen it all, they've said it all; they're bored, we're bored, let's order another round of yawns.

And then there's political analyst Bob Novak, a staple on CNN for decades. He should be unstapled. His Danny DeVito butt should have been put on suspension as soon as the investigation into the leak of Valerie Plame's status as a CIA agent in his syndicated column was announced. It is widely and plausibly suspected that Plame's name was divulged as retaliation against her husband and former ambassador Joseph Wilson, who had embarrassed the administration by shooting down Bush's claim in the State of the Union address that Iraq had tried to purchase uranium from Niger—those infamous sixteen words he was forced to retract. Getting even against Plame and Wilson qualifies as dirty tricksterism worthy of Nixon's henchmen, and Novak has long been a favorite Republican garbage chute. "A reporter doesn't reveal his sources," Novak smugly repeats, maintaining that he was informed that

Plame was a CIA analyst, not an operative, but according to Terence Smith's report on PBS's *News Hour with Jim Lehrer,* "The CIA [said] it tried strenuously to dissuade Novak from identifying Wilson's wife so as not to endanger her or any agents she might have worked with." Until it's clarified as to whether Novak was played for a dupe by his source or was a willing partner in this payback operation, he shouldn't be allowed to appear on CNN's *Inside Politics,* to share the contents of his "Reporter's Notebook" segment with a credulous Woodruff, or to pound the desk with phony indignation on *Crossfire.*

The one old pro who exemplifies what CNN was and still can be is Lou Dobbs, the rotund host of CNN's *Lou Dobbs Tonight* and a forceful battering ram. So full of self-assurance himself that it seems to be spilling out of his shirt collar, so confident in his opinions that he acts as if he bowled a ten-strike every time he delivers a smart comeback to some pencil-neck economist, Dobbs nevertheless is not your average cable news know-it-all demagogue. He has become what Bill O'Reilly, Neil Cavuto, and Chris Matthews only pretend to be, a broadcaster outraged on behalf of the screwed American worker, fleeced investor, and betrayed pension-holder. A champion of capitalism whom no one could accuse of being a liberal weenie, Dobbs has been pounding the beat on the outsourcing of American jobs and the hollowing-out of the industrial base with an unswervable fervor that sets him above and apart from everyone else on financial news. While they're orgasming over every jump in the stock market, he's outpaced them in comprehending the slow-motion convulsions and dislocations under way. Each night he holds apologists and guilty parties responsible for their answers without making it all about him and his amazing interrogation techniques. There's nothing wrong with CNN keeping a few attack poodles such as Tucker Carlson and Jonah Goldberg around as pets, but if it is to depose Fox News from the throne CNN once held, it must let more lions like Lou Dobbs out of the den. Because the wrath over what George Bush has done to this country and its economic future is going to feed a hungrier roar in the years ahead, and his defenders and fellow deceivers will become prey for the big cats. In fact, I can think of a couple of fine dining prospects who might want to start lacing up their running shoes....

Peggy Noonan: Best in Show

"George W. Bush didn't grow up at Greenwich Country Day
with a car and a driver dropping him off, as his father had.
Until he went off to boarding school, he thought he was like
everyone else. That's a gift, to think you're just like everyone else
in America. It can be the making of you."

—Peggy Noonan,
WSJ Opinion Journal, February 19, 2004

N O MATTER WHAT IT SAYS on the marriage certificate,
Peggy Noonan is a bride of George W. Bush. He is the
butch side of her, she the femme side of him, and together they
are ideological lovebirds, united in holy sanctimony. They
share the mission vision of world transformation through
American might, subscribing to the same polarities of good
and evil, innocence and guilt, love and hate. Both draw a line in
the sand between those with us and those against us, seeing the
world in black and white (even if Noonan's prose style tends to

misty watercolors). Although they talk the same language, their line readings have caricaturized in opposite directions. The longer Bush is in office, the more his sentences lose the connective tissue of consecutive thought. They've become as clipped as a Marine crew cut. As anyone who watched his interviews with Diane Sawyer on *Primetime Live* and Tim Russert on *Meet the Press* knows, the president uses judo jabs to link nouns to absent verbs, verbs to missing nouns. As Bush has mimimalized, Noonan has luxuriantly budded, weaving ever more extravagant garlands of blushing-maiden mannerisms. She has entered the Tallulah Bankhead phase of punditry, fussing over herself like crazy, tinka-tinking her nose like Samantha on *Bewitched*, tossing her hair at every turn of thought, wincing with disapproval whenever someone criticizes her heartthrob, and deepening her sighs until they could cup a gentle rain. No one seems to mind how ridiculous are the vain airs she puts on, perhaps because her words and responses are so reliably soothing, it's like listening to a lullaby. She can make the lethal use of force sound so lilting.

Noonan is sunshine, cotton candy, barefoot walks on the beach. She thinks good thoughts, and she thinks them for all of us, whether we want her to or not. She thinks troubled thoughts, too, thoughts that cloud the sky and bring raindrops falling on her brain. She doesn't so much know what she knows as she believes what she believes, and she believes with every trembling cell of her being, her soul oozing an unequivocal *yes*. The sole proponent of the Impressionist school of political journalism, Noonan is the only attack poodle of any prestige and credibility whose writing aspires to bad transcendental poetry—the schlocky sublime. She seldom allows annoying obstacles (such as facts; reality) to inconvenience her creativity. They would only impede the creamy flow of her thought-feelings. She is compassionate conservatism's answer to Anna Quindlen and Ellen Goodman, womanly-wise, her observations bearing none of the sharp corners, serrated edges, and joy-buzzer shock effects of shrieking cockatoos such as Ann Coulter or Laura Ingraham. Speaking on TV in a crushed-velvet voice, she tips her head to the side, turning political chat into pillow talk. Yet she is innocent of coquetry. Her sighs are not come-ons, boudoir purrs, but expressions of wistful regret that not everyone has received the light. She shakes her head more in sorrow than anger at liberals and other imperiled souls who know not what they do. Her persona is that of the good Catholic girl all grown up and still good, still firm in the belief that most people are good too. Like her hero Ronald Reagan, she believes in accentuating the positive. Upon closer inspection, however, Noonan bears less resemblance to Ingrid Bergman's radiant nun in *The Bells of St. Mary's* than to Betty White's "Happy Homemaker" on *The Mary Tyler Moore Show*, all sugar and spite. No poodle is more faithfully protective of George W. Bush, more avid to fill in the dull blanks in his sentences with deep understanding. And no poodle is smarmier in going after anyone who would get in his, her, and God's way.

Peggy Noonan carries a unique strike capability as an attack poodle. Unlike other poodles, many of whom seem to have popped out of a torpedo tube, ready to be fired, she embodies and narrates a personal and political journey, a journey that's a metaphor for America's postwar odyssey. She didn't stake out a set of positions and stick to them; she grew as a person and evolved into her conservative convictions, bittersweetly wised up. And in doing so has persuaded herself and her followers that she is a representative figure of postwar America, someone who speaks not just for herself but for a huge branch of her generation. Noonan is the quintessential Reagan Democrat, a Kennedy Catholic baby boomer who migrated right and set up camp. Born in Brooklyn, New York, in 1950, she was the third mouth to feed in a lower-middle-class family of seven children, and shared her family's love of the Kennedy clan. "They were Irish Catholic just like us, and they were smart and glamorous with their tuxedos and silk dresses," she writes in *What I Saw at the Revolution* (1990), "and they always said the right thing and had a wonderful humor—and with a little time and money and education we could be just like them." Young Peggy bought two goldfish and named them Jack and Jackie, and papered her walls with pictures of brother Bobby and Secretary of State Dean Rusk, a precocious sign of her propensity to moon over powerful men behind powerful desks.

"We were in love with the Kennedys but they died," Noonan writes. The sixties turned into the time of the assassins, claiming Martin Luther King as well, and each slaying disrobed Noonan's mystical gifts. As she slept, death murmured into her unconscious. One evening in 1968, a teenage Peggy dreamt of Lincoln's assassination, only the face of the man in the theater box was black. The next day she told her friends at school, and that night—*that night*—King was assassinated. Spooky. Later that climactic year she had another dream, a liquid swirl of images from which she thought she heard the words, "Forty-four days." The next morning she informed her friends of her latest premonition, and forty-three days later Robert Kennedy was killed. Noonan hasn't received dark tidings of deaths foretold since, but she's still sensitive to tremors in the ectoplasm and gets frequent mailgrams from the great beyond. She's become the media elite's foremost storefront gypsy fortune-teller, but no one on television ever scoffs at her hunches and predictions, or goggles in disbelief. Her colleagues humor her and it is we, the public, who suffer.

The political convulsions of the sixties that disillusioned and radicalized many in Noonan's generation had the reverse effect on her. They drove her to the straight and narrow. During a bus ride to an antiwar demonstration, she realized that the blue-collar Democratic liberalism of her childhood had been hijacked by a mutant strain of hippie snobs. To this ragtag army of unshaven armpits, America wasn't the land of the free and home of the brave but "a racist, genocidal nation with an imperialistic lust." The haughty contempt of her fellow protestors sounded as if it had been scripted in a French café under Sartrean supervision. "What can you expect of a culture that raises John Wayne to the status of hero?" sneered some snotnose on the bus. Noonan's ears burned. She felt protective of the Duke, safe in the idea of being sheltered in his huge, meaty arms. Trying to bring down this mountain of a man was a symbolic act of patricide. Years later, in *Life, Liberty and the Pursuit of Happiness* (1994), a still saddened Noonan conducted an autopsy and reindicted the left for Wayne's cultural eclipse, each faction having plunged a dagger into his carcass like the passengers in *The Murder on the Orient Express.* "And I was there in America [as opposed to exploring the Amazon] when they killed John Wayne by a thousand cuts. A lot of people killed him—not only feminists but peaceniks, leftists, intellectuals, others. You could even say it was Woody Allen who did it, through laughter and an endearing admission of his own nervousness and fear. He made nervousness and fearfulness the admired style."

Just as America seemed to have lost faith in itself, another aging cowboy trotted to the rescue atop a sagging horse. Ronald Reagan and wife Nancy Reagan became the Roy Rogers and Dale Evans of the new American morn. A mighty oak hewed into a man, Reagan restored Noonan's belief that there were still tall quiet-spoken men among us who seemed to have sprung from the earth under a cloudless sky of limitless possibilities. Smitten, Noonan quit her job at CBS News, where she wrote and produced radio commentaries for Dan Rather, to volunteer her talents in 1984 to the Reagan White House, where she served as speechwriter and special assistant. Her first glimpse of her hero aroused tender, maternal yearnings. "I first saw [President Reagan] as a foot, a highly polished brown cordovan wagging merrily on a hassock. I spied it through the door. It was a beautiful foot, sleek. Such casual elegance and clean lines. But not a big foot, not formidable, maybe a little...frail. I imagined cradling it in my arms, protecting it from unsmooth roads...." His other foot would just have to fend for itself.

Despite such Harlequin Romance moments, *What I Saw at the Revolution*—Noonan's memoir of serving as a speechwriter in the Reagan White House—remains her best book, indeed her only good book, the first and last of her titles in which she occupies physical space in the here and now. When she describes being a girl in the boys' club of blue suits and crisp authority or running afoul of the ferocious butterball that was Maureen Reagan ("Her face was like the face of Bette Davis in *The Private Lives of Elizabeth and Essex*"), she zooms in on other people at eye level, sizing them up in vivid snapshots as individuals with individual strengths, weaknesses, and velocities. She's an equal among equals, a status that her subsequent media stardom and rise to queen of the attack poodles would remedy.

Political speechwriters usually peck at the keyboard in semiobscurity, seldom upstaging their bosses, but big events can tilt the spotlight. As a presidential speechwriter Noonan not only could strum harpsichord phrases on the page but proved she could come through in the tense clutch. On the morning of January 28, 1986, the space shuttle *Challenger* exploded after liftoff at Florida's Cape Canaveral, killing all aboard, a catastrophe all the more traumatic because among the passengers was the first civilian to fly a mission, Christa McAuliffe, a third-grade teacher; millions of schoolchildren had been watching the launch from their classrooms. A speech had to be written—fast—to console the stunned nation and to salvage hope from the shower of debris. Noonan came through with a eulogy that had the tremolo of sad trumpets, a peroration that would be her finest moment as a speechwriter, fusing past, present, and future into a single valedictory note: "The crew of the space shuttle *Challenger* honored us by the manner in which they lived their lives. We will never forget them, nor the last time we saw them, this morning, as they prepared for their journey, and waved good-bye, and 'slipped the surly bonds of earth' to 'touch the face of God.'"

The "surly bonds of earth" and "the face of God" were courtesy of a poem called "High Flight" by a pilot named John Gillespie Magee, Jr. A few quibblers questioned what made the bonds of earth "surly," but such poetry critics numbered few in the press, which hailed Noonan's text and Reagan's delivery as dramatic achievements of grace under pressure. From then on in the White House it was look homeward, angel, whenever grim circumstances called; spiritual manna as mother's meat-loaf became Noonan's specialty d'house. After 248 soldiers in the 101st Airborne died coming home for the holidays when their transport plane crashed, Reagan publicly addressed the deity he referred to privately as "the fellow upstairs": "Receive, O Lord, into your heavenly kingdom the men and women of the 101st Airborne, the men and women of the great and fabled Screaming Eagles. They must be singing now, in their joy, flying higher than mere man can fly, and as flights of angels take them to their rest." The American way of death: a painless transition into a Hollywood afterlife, with a touch of Shake-speare for class.

When Noonan wrote for George Bush senior, her prose became prosier, her words clamped into his mouth like a set of wooden choppers. It was she who supplied him with the defi-ant line-in-the-sand declaration "Read my lips: no new taxes" for his acceptance speech at the 1988 Republican convention, a pledge that would haunt his presidency and reelection bid after he acceded to a deficit-cutting tax hike in 1991 and was tarred with the dreaded epithet of flip-flopper. This was also the speech that conjured "a thousand points of light," a metaphor for the spirit of volunteerism dotting the country (and not, as one late-night comic claimed, the number of candles on

Ronald Reagan's birthday cake), and the occasion when Bush pleaded for "a kinder, gentler nation," which had a nice laxative sound to it.

After Bush was denied a second term by a nation of ingrates, a shadow fell across the capital, a shadow as big and wide as Bill Clinton after a hefty meal. Although Noonan once thought Clinton had promise, glimmers of greatness, she became so distressed by his prevarications and hee-haw antics that she assumed everyone shared her revulsion for this political Elvis imitator. She predicted Clinton would be denied a second term, and was dismayed when he wasn't. To millions of Americans, the Clinton-Gore nineties was a decade of relative peace and runaway prosperity, lifting the leftover deficits from the Reagan era into surplus. To Noonan, those millions of Americans who gave Bill Clinton high approval ratings even after his impeachment were deluding themselves, deceived by this "gifted phony." He debauched himself and the office he held, and accomplished little of substance. (She alludes to the long economic expansion during Clinton's presidency as if it were just something that happened while he was standing around combing his hair for eight years.)

In 2001 Noonan published a personalized biography of Reagan and his prelapsarian presidency called *When Character Was*

King, its Camelot title a rebuke to Clinton and his amoral slob-dom. Noonan averted her gaze from Reagan's cold, aloof side, painting his portrait entirely in autumn-leaf fleshtones. As Jonathan Chait noted in the *New Republic*, "She glides over Reagan's divorce and indifferent parenting; instead, she lavishes attention upon his poor, character-building childhood, his kindness to underlings, and other personal virtues...[For] Noonan and her ilk, conservative ideology and personal virtue are so deeply intertwined that it is virtually impossible for a good person to pursue liberal policies or for a conservative politician to be morally flawed." A bad liberal bears bitter fruit, and Clinton produced a bumper crop. Chait, again: "Just as Reagan's policies were seen as an extension of his inner goodness, Clinton's policies were deemed an extension of his inner evil."

Hillary Clinton, hard to believe, was even more evil than her husband in Noonan's outraged eyes. Bill had a loose handle on himself. He was a rambunctious man of wide-arced mood swings, delivering warm fuzzies when he was pleased and blowing his top until the wallpaper wilted when he wasn't. He was volatile and yet reachable; a big softie who just wanted to be loved. Not Hillary. Her protective shell was uncrackable. She was mistress of her domain, a frozen fish stick that never thawed, the imperious superego to Bill's junkfood-junkie id.

Her warmth, passion, and approachability were simulated, as self-conscious and calibrated as Nixon's creaky biomechanics. Unlike Republican spouses, who maintained a wedding-cake pose on the political stage, Hillary Rodham Clinton insisted on butting into the act. She had ambition, which she had the poor taste not to hide.

Shortly after Hillary Clinton announced her intention to run for the Senate seat in New York being vacated by Daniel Patrick Moynihan, Noonan dive-bombed into action. Her nation needed her. Published in 2000, Noonan's *The Case Against Hillary Clinton* was marketed as nonfiction, a Nabokovian conceit. It is in fact Noonan's first novel, written with the haste and white heat of pulp fiction, but with a chastity of purpose, a selfless desire to save us from our starstruck selves. The good people of New York should not reward the former First Lady for helping drag the country into the pig slop of Whitewater, the travel-office scandal, the health care task force fiasco, Vince Foster's suicide, and her husband's midnight orgy of presidential pardons—all the while insisting that her own hands were Ivory pure. The good people of New York should not indulge Hillary's insatiable appetite for attention by throwing her a cookie, for she only looks humanoid from the exterior. Behind those unfeeling, searchlight eyes lurks a political cyborg of ruthless calculation. Should Hillary Clinton be elected to the Senate, warned Noonan, she will feel vindicated, and prepare for the greatest vindication of all, a return to the White House, with Bill as First Man. She must be halted. Nothing personal, understand. "I wish her a long life with good health, much friendship, and many grandchildren. But I do not wish to see her succeed in continuing Clintonism in our national life." Clintonism being a tough stain to remove from the carpet.

The Case Against Hillary Clinton doesn't contain footnotes or an index. It doesn't need such trimmings, not when it has this much woman's intuition and missionary zeal working overtime. Noonan was peddling a morality tale, playing with adult-sized dolls—in this instance, a voodoo doll. Pin after pin is poked into Hillary's pretensions, failures, and performance as wife, political adviser, public figure, fancy dresser, and master of disguise ("like Lon Chaney in front of a mirror, building herself a new nose that will reflect a new pose"). Although Noonan calls the book a polemic "based on the public record," it is more of a séance where she invites herself into other people's minds for a cozy chat. "I think of the people I will sit on the beach with, my friends and their friends, and already I'm talking to them in my head." And they're talking back as Noonan practices her own unique brand of ventriloquism, putting her words into other people's mouths and piping it out as the voice of the electorate. She tunes up her psychic powers with a preface imagining Hillary's victory-night speech; trains her telepathy on Bill ("I actually suspect he has long believed, as the novelist Charles McCarry has his Clinton-like character believe in the novel *Lucky Bastard,* that he is JFK's unknown illegitimate son"); picks up steam with a confidential seventeen-page report of a secret meeting in which Hillary tears into entertainment executives for sleazing up the culture—"I am asking you to stop making the entertainment that is hurting us, and start making challenging, tough-minded, truly fearless entertainment that doesn't rely on sex and violence to keep the attention of the audience, and that doesn't drum bad messages into the minds of children"—before cutely revealing that Hillary's stand-up moment of integrity was all a fleeting dream (no dream has ever packed that much stagy dialogue); crests with a character sketch of a childhood friend named Christine, now married with kids, who contemplates voting for Hillary, contrasting her friend's hard slog in life with Hillary's smooth glide ("She was flying high while you and Bobby were getting clobbered by inflation and taxes and child care"); and climaxes with a finger-wagging warning to Christine: "She doesn't know your concerns, and she doesn't share them either. She is not like you. She was never like you." Never, I tell you, never!

From old friends to experienced pols, no consciousness is safe from Noonan's cat-burglar intrusions. She won't grant Hillary's admiration of Eleanor Roosevelt without trying to one-up her, dedicating *The Case Against Hillary Clinton* to Eleanor Roosevelt as if she, not Hillary, is the earth-daughter who truly comprehends her. "What would Eleanor think of Hillary?" Noonan asks in the book. The gaslights dim as Peggy closes her eyes and presses her fingers against her temples. *Earth to Eleanor*..."You can imagine her looking down and saying, 'She seems a strong woman certainly, which is always a good thing to see, but senses there is something... strange there, and I'm afraid one senses it with both of them. Tell me, what does she actually...stand for?" *Nothing* is Noonan's mute reply. In a bizarre fantasy scene, Noonan even implies that Hillary, unlike Eleanor, will not be truly mourned by friends and allies when she's lowered into the ground some fine day. The stature gap between the two First Ladies extends into the chilly grave. Or as she said in an interview, "Hillary only wishes she had Eleanor Roosevelt's seriousness and Jackie Onassis's class."

This is Peggy Noonan's favorite poodle tactic, pitting living Democrats against dead Democrats and always finding the living ones defective. A Democrat doesn't have to be dead for long to make the living look small. When Paul Wellstone, the liberal senator from Minnesota, died in a plane crash shortly before the 2002 midterm elections, his ashes were barely cold before Noonan began sprinkling them on his mourners from a great height. In her greatest feat of Rich Little mimicry to date, Noonan channeled Wellstone's voice from the great Senate cloakroom in the sky. Wellstone, a mensch in life, a greater mensch in death, was disappointed that his grieving followers had turned his funeral service into a political rally: "You hurt a lot of people," Noonan mouths for him. Wellstone wasn't alone in feeling let down. Widespread disgruntlement could be heard across the cotton patches of heaven. "Jack Kennedy was here, and you're not going to like this, but he said what he said the day Nixon had his meltdown in '62. He looked at you and said, 'No class.' John Adams is here too. He turned away from you in disgust. 'Faction!' is what he said. It was no compliment." I should think not. In Noonan's fertile fantasy life, the only good Democrat is a dead Democrat.

In *The Case Against Hillary Clinton* this sentiment sharpens into a death wish. All of Noonan's fantasies about Hillary lead to an open grave. "God, remember the Hillarys?" she writes, doing some high-school reminiscing. "The Hillarys would only be nice to us, would only look at us in the hall and say hello when they were running for senior council president. And then only because every vote counts. So she'd actually talk to people like us, and I wish I could say we told her to drop dead, because we didn't, did we?"

Cri de coeur, call to arms, and one-sided catfight, *The Case Against Hillary Clinton* failed to sway the jury or stir the villagers against the bride of Frankenstein. Hillary Clinton trounced her Republican opponent, Rick Lazio, a thumping repudiation of Noonan's counteroffensive. A lesser attack poodle might have retreated to her scratching post to pout over how the people of New York had ignored her counsel, gone their own fool way. But Noonan drew solace from knowing she had fought the good fight and satisfaction from thinking she had slithered under Hillary's polysynthetic skin. "It would be fair to say that Hillary and I hate each other," she later told a reporter from the *Spectator* of London with "genuine relish" in her voice. "I met Hillary recently at the funeral [another funeral!] of a mutual friend. It was bizarre; when she looked at me her face separated into entirely different halves. Her mouth smiled but her eyes told me quite clearly, 'I detest you and will do my best to destroy you.'" File this under Freudian projection.

From the foot of Reagan to the face of God, Peggy Noonan has searched with outstretched arms and wings to find the magic spot where rugged masculinity and religious faith meet. She has found it, at long last, in the gleam of George W. Bush's oversized cowboy belt buckle. As husband, father, president, and humble servant of God, George Bush is Ronald Reagan with a double scoop of hunkitude. "Mr. Bush also followed a charismatic leader, and I do not mean Mr. Clinton.... The charismatic figure Mr. Bush follows is the last big American president, the last who had the massive presence of a battleship, Ronald Reagan." It's been a tall order, filling those long johns, but Bush has done it. Like Reagan, he put the world on notice that the America of Frederic Remington's paintings rides again and is willing to trample anyone who dares get underhoof.

September 11 was his fiery crucible. To some literal heathen minds, the toppling of the Twin Towers and the gouging of the Pentagon represented an appalling breakdown of intelligence and airport security, a failure to gauge the full reach and vicious capabilities of Al Qaeda, a horror of a humility lesson. To Noonan, the black clouds billowing from the ruins of Ground Zero were smoke signals summoning the righteous. It was more than a wake-up call, it was an Awakening. Angels were flying V-shaped formations overhead, and God's hand was signaling to the bullpen for Bush to take the mound. "He found himself amid the rubble," she wrote. In *A Heart, a Cross, and a Flag,* a collection of Noonan columns for the *Wall Street Journal* written after the terrorist attacks, she announced, "God is back," and Bush's got Him. She describes President Bush's speech on September 20, 2001, to a joint session of Congress to calm and rally the nation after the terrorist attacks as "a God-touched moment": "He talked of prayer like a man who'd been praying, and who understood that tens of millions of Americans and others throughout the world were his powerful prayer warriors."

Noonan is a prayer warrior too, when her schedule permits. Like those conservative chickenhawks who want others to do the fighting while they stay home reading the *Weekly Standard*, Noonan asks others to pray with a diligence she herself can't muster. In an article for the now defunct *Forbes ASAP*, Noonan passed on a message from Jesus' mother. "When the Virgin Mary makes her visitations...she says: Pray! Pray unceasingly!" In the very next paragraph, Noonan hastens to add, "I myself don't, but I think about it a lot and sometimes I pray when I think. You don't have to be Catholic to take this advice."

I think about it a lot and sometimes I pray when I think. If only Noonan would think when she thinks—what an improvement that would be! Instead she has become captive to omens, superstitions, and Catholic kitsch. The bout of temporary insanity she suffered in 2000—when she mused that the dolphins that surrounded six-year-old Elián González after the boat taking him from Cuba was lost in a storm at sea were guardian angels, "commanded to protect one of God's children"—has become a permanent haze. In *A Heart, a Cross, and a Flag* she describes meeting a neighbor two days after September 11. "Years ago she told me that she saw a rat in her neighborhood, and he had risen on his haunches and then scrambled away. For no reason she could remember, she said a prayer at that moment: 'Dear Lord, if the big terrible thing is ever coming, will you warn me by having a rat rise like that?'" Another pal of Peggy's shares a different precognition of the big terrible thing. "The first e-mail I opened this morning was from a friend who said this: Peggy, the government fears a nuke has been smuggled into the United States, the Mideast is boiling, the weather is roiling, the church is reeling from sexual corruption in the clergy, and last night came a report that a statue of Padre Pio in Sicily is weeping blood."

On vacation in Mexico over the Christmas holidays to get away from it all post-9/11, Noonan receives her own special report from the ethereal. Her column begins, "I have not read a newspaper in seven days, nor heard a news report, gone online, or called the States in four. Apparently you're all well, or I would have heard about it on the beach." From a passing gull, perhaps.

A few newsless days later, however, the talk of the village is the spectacle of a perfect white ring encircling the moon like a wedding band. A doctor who has lived in the town for ten years tells Noonan he's never seen anything like it. The more scientific-minded beachcombers discuss it as a meteorological event, but she knows different. "I of course immediately apprehended what it was: a celestial gift. A nod from God. For three days earlier, in Rome, Pope John Paul II had approved the canonization of Juan Diego." Although some historians doubt he ever existed, Juan Diego is venerated as the humble Indian peasant who had seen and spoken to the Virgin Mary in the sixteenth century, helping inspire the conversion of Mexico to Catholicism. The moon ring was more than a thank-you for welcoming Juan Diego to sainthood. It was also God's A-OK sign, telling Peggy to tell us that all would be well, his blessing was with us.

Wonders abounded in the aftershock of September 11. The destruction of the World Trade Center not only allowed God to stage a comeback tour but exhumed the grizzled spirit of John Wayne, who wasn't about to let a bunch of pansy liberals keep him six feet under, not when he heard the bugle call. "I think he returned on September 11," Noonan wrote. "I think he ran up the stairs, threw the kid over his back like a sack of potatoes, came back down and shoveled rubble. I think he's in Afghanistan now, saying with his slow swagger and simmering silence, 'Yer in a whole lotta trouble now, Osama-boy.'" I think Peggy needs help.

Rescue dolphins, cautionary rats, weeping statues, moon rings, John Wayne's drawl rippling through the outlaw caves of Afghanistan—Noonan believes in celestial signs, spiritual rebirths, and Hollywood horseshit, which she tends to interpret sunny-side-up. She often quotes Carl Jung but barely sticks a baby toe into the Jungian shadows where the flapping demons and dark tempests dwell, her interpretations of weird events fitting snugly into an optimistic belief system. For her, heart, cross, and flag are as neatly packed as a box lunch. God loves America, America loves God, America loves itself, Bush loves God and America, and Noonan loves God, America, and Bush—a holy trinity of positive energy that no national trauma can sunder. She never entertains the unhappy notion that America has accrued a huge overdraft of bad karma with its bombing, monstrous appetites, and hubris; it never occurs to her that the gods may not be pleased—indeed, may be ready to teach us an expensive lesson.

As U.S. forces invaded Baghdad and the Stalinesque statue of Saddam Hussein was razed like a goalpost after a championship game, Noonan plucked daisies from the daily news. "Unanticipated good can come from misfortune," she wrote after a bunker blaster failed to disperse Hussein's atoms. This near miss meant that the war wouldn't be easy, but a hard war would be an opportunity for America to demonstrate it could hang tough for the long haul. She cited a news report about a soldier shot in the leg outside Baghdad, which picked up her spirits because his wound was treated with laconic humor on the gurney. "It has had me thinking a happy thought, about the success with which our country, for all its troubles the past few decades, has continued to communicate to new generations the simple idea of the goodness of loving America." She credits George Bush for the turnaround, of course. While "intellectuals, academics, local clever people who talk loudly in restaurants, and leftist mandarins" (easily spottable by their Fu Manchu fingernails) have been practicing their surrender poses, he has been "President Backbone," as she titled the column. Anyone can have brains, but it takes a special man to face adversity with firm abs. "Backbone is not an average gift. Guts are not an average gift. The willingness to take pain and give pain to make progress in human life is not an average gift." It's the gift that keeps on giving. "More and more this presidency is feeling like a gift."

No one, not even a loud-talking leftist mandarin sending back the consommé, would quarrel with the proposition that

George W. Bush has a gift for dishing out pain. He's been a world-champion pain giver since first being elected to public office, signing the execution papers of Texas death row inmates without losing a lick of sleep, laying waste to environmental protections as if the earth were his private Ponderosa (not caring if whales die from navy sonar), and beautifying the countryside of Iraq with cluster bombs and depleted-uranium shells. Allah only knows where Noonan got the goofy idea that Bush is willing to *take* pain, however. His entire presidency has been based upon the sacrifices of the many for the prosperity of the executive few. Doing Republican fund-raisers and playing golf as the casualty figures mount, attending as few funerals and visiting as few veterans' hospitals as possible, fighting the war on the cheap, letting Republican business cronies profit from the reconstruction, refusing to show any flexibility or contrition before the United Nations (thus ensuring that U.S. troops will be left holding the fort with the slimmest of international backup), these are not the deeds of a man willing to confront the human consequences of his decisions or consider the awesome possibility that he might be foolishly, tragically wrong. "Bring 'em on," he taunted, regarding the guerrilla attacks in Iraq; easy for him to say, thousands of miles from the theater of operations. It wouldn't be his cocky head in the crosshairs. This is the detachment of a CEO who delegates everything while adhering to his strict routine. George Bush delegates pain, and he delegates death.

But it's what's in his heart that counts, and Noonan had no doubt that Bush's heart is as tender as Reagan's shod foot. "This, truly, is a good man," she wrote after his 2003 State of the Union speech, his peanutty shell housing "a profound authenticity." In the foreword to *We Will Prevail* (2003), a selection of Bush's speeches on war and terrorism, Noonan again authenticates Bush's authenticity. "Bush is unafraid of sounding like what he is, a Christian reborn in faith who sees the world through a prism of belief. Life is not accident; it has meaning and governance. Bush is a pray-er. He has told me he is grateful to be the focus of the prayers of others, and that he feels those prayers. A prayer is among the most direct and succinct of communications. Bush speaks to the nation in a style that suggests he doesn't really think a public proclamation has to be fancier than a prayer." Among the prayers excerpted in *We Will Prevail* are Bush's addresses to the Missouri Farmers Association and the Iowa Republican Party Victory Luncheon.

In the summer of 2003 Noonan was granted an audience with his goodness. On assignment for *Ladies' Home Journal*, she was sent to the White House to interview the president and Mrs. Bush about their faith, their marriage, and whether the events of September 11 had enabled them to "grow." According to Noonan, it was his blossoming as a war leader that inspired the turnaround in America's self-esteem. "His palpable faith in our country, and his insistence that it could do any good thing it set its mind to, helped ignite a new wave of patriotism. It has become chic to love America again." The weather in Washington cooperated with the upbeat tenor of the story, Noonan's arriving on "a sparkling June day," one of those bright mornings after a dreary spell of rain that offers itself like, yes, "a kind of gift." Bush in the trim flesh did not disappoint. "[M]ost presidents fairly quickly develop a kind of screen in front of them, through which you can see them and they can see you. From behind the screen they talk to you, but they also, in some way, detach." Not this president. He was all there and then some. "[T]here is nothing detached about George W. Bush. He doesn't have the screen. There is a profound *presentness* to him." Of course, in her presence Bush had no reason to hide behind an invisible pane. He knew from the torch songs Noonan has performed praising his name that she would conduct herself with proper deference, each question making a little curtsey. She was no Helen Thomas angling to spring a rabbit trap. Instead, he was lobbed a volley of Wiffle

Balls such as "Do you talk to your mom every day?" (Bush: "No") and "Mr. President, you are drawn, I think, to strong women" (Bush: "Yes, I am"). The only dramatic moment in this demure interview is the solemn pause that falls after Noonan asks Bush about having tears in his eyes when he took the oath of office. He acknowledges that he may have misted in the weight of the moment, his voice trailing off into silent reverie. Noonan captions the expression on his face. "He stares off into the middle distance, eyes narrowed slightly, obviously lost in a private emotion or memory; his features soften, and he looks proud and awed and humbled."

Noonan's misty-eyed mythologizing of Bush and his gift of bringing good things to life (and bad things to death) finally got on someone's nerves other than mine and those of untold millions muttering at home. In December 2003 the unthinkable, the scarcely-to-be-wished-for occurred...Noonan was knocked off her plinth. Brought roughly to earth not by a political adversary but by someone with whom she had always been in such sweet harmony, Chris Matthews, host of MSNBC's *Hardball*. To her astonishment (and the audience's), the attack poodle found herself attack poodled. During a general political discussion, Matthews asked Noonan point-blank if Saddam Hussein had a guilty hand in September 11. Matthews: "Do you believe he was personally involved?" Noonan: "Chris, I don't think it can be asked as a crystal question." In the past, Matthews might have let it slide, but this time he kept pressing and pressing, and she kept fudging and fudging, and such was their former affinity and melting rapport that the quarrel became almost uncomfortably primal—like hearing Mommy and Daddy fighting upstairs (with Daddy in a real bad mood). He shunted aside her impressions and intuitions to shake real hard evidence out of her, something, anything, dammit! "I'm sure there is evidence that he has been helpful to bad guys who have tried to hurt us and who in fact have hurt us in the past," was the tepid best Noonan could do. "Peggy, you can't handle the question, because it gets to the heart of why we went to war. You can't handle the truth." After delivering his kiss-off line, Chris Matthews broke for commercial, the brute.

Of course, she can't handle the truth! Can't, won't, and probably never will. Like Blanche Dubois in *Streetcar* hanging paper lanterns over lightbulbs to spare her eyes the harsh glare of reality, Peggy Noonan spent her adult life adorning herself with illusions. The difference is that she's been wearing the lantern on her head. It's time she took it off. It's unbecoming.

The Miller's Tale

"Americans are always asking why the rest of the world hates them. Well, the reason is Dennis Miller."

—Elton John,
on stage in Las Vegas, October 4, 2003

DENNIS MILLER IS AN ATTACK POODLE masquerading as a laughing hyena. As a comedian he's always been his own best audience. He cracks himself up when he gets to the punch line, chortling a half-beat before everyone else joins in, assuming they do. Sometimes, sadly, he who laughs first laughs alone. Since assuming his new role as hipster-daddy superpatriot, however, Miller needn't worry any longer about the chance of his lonesome laughter hanging out to die. He found the perfect forum for his political rap on *The Tonight Show*, and the perfect setup man in its host, Jay Leno. A hardworking comedy professional who appreciates Miller's origami-like joke constructions, Leno delights in the comedian's wicked way with words almost as much as Miller does. He convulses into a laughing hyena when Miller's in the guest chair, and two hyenas equal one set of hysterics. But theirs is not the smarmy, backslapping camaraderie satirized by SCTV's "Sammy Maudlin Show," their over-the-top spoof of Sammy Davis, Jr.'s variety program, where each bad-toupee performer was toasted as a legend, a great humanitarian, and a helluva guy. Their shameless complimenting of each other was the naked neediness of applause junkies—Vegas velour kitsch. This is a less innocent spectacle. Since September 11, Dennis Miller has undergone conversion and embraced his inner avenger. Once considered a thinking person's comic (a kind of curse in show business, like being labeled "cerebral"), he has meaned down into a polysyllabic yahoo who caters to a mob mentality. His esoteric references are marbled into chunks of red meat flung out to incite the worst prejudices and dumbest instincts of the studio audience, which whoops and hollers as if it were at a hootenanny. Hack your way through Miller's hip convolutions and the sentiment that escapes is Kurtz's dying plea in *Heart of Darkness*, "Exterminate all the brutes!"

When Miller first started sounding like General Jack D. Ripper on speedballs, some dismissed his veer to the right as a crass career move, a midlife crisis turned malignant. He is in

his early fifties, no longer the tousled wisenheimer who delivered the fake news on *Saturday Night Live*'s "Weekend Update"
with switchblade phrasing and a pallor of sullen overcast. His
eyes look tired now, a little sour; the mousse in his hair has lost
some of its springy hold. His movie career never hit the highs
of fellow *SNL* grads Chevy Chase, Eddie Murphy, and Bill
Murray (while avoiding the mortifying lows of Norm Macdonald, Molly Shannon, and Rob *Deuce Bigelow* Schneider), but he
had not been a woeful vagabond. His topical talk show for
HBO, where he could curse unbleeped and turn up the jets in
his monologues (rants), thrived for nine years. He lasted only
two seasons making tossed-salad metaphors on ABC's *Monday
Night Football*, wedged inside the broadcast booth between veteran announcers Al Michaels and Dan Fouts. Hired to add a
little cultural zip to all the steroid freakazoid grunting on the
field, Miller drizzled his gridiron insights with literary/histori-
cal/media allusions so flossy and arcane that they were anno-
tated on Internet sites like passages from Spenser's *The Faerie
Queene*. Considering his inexperience as a color commentator,
he acquitted himself respectably on the air, but what he added
in IQ points to *Monday Night Football* was offset by the loss in
Nielsen shares. Beer-bloated viewers wagering on point
spreads in sports bars across America failed to ascertain what

the Council of Trent had to do with an incomplete pass. When ABC decided to restore jock cred to the broadcast by replacing him with some other pile of mashed potatoes, Miller was forced to pack up his thesaurus and peddle his unique take someplace else. But where?

The exciting growth opportunities in conservative grand-standing beckoned. It was an easy-entry occupational arena. All you need, apart from a microphone, is a soaring love of the sound of your own voice and the ability to hold forth on a variety of issues, regardless of how little you actually know or care. Scores of other AM-dial desperadoes and attack poodles have proven that millions of Americans had a bottomless belly for declarations of what's right about America and denunciations of those who disagree. Conservatives are true-blue brand-loyal, a solid base that knows what it wants and wants it all the time, not like those trendy liberals who like to dabble and try nouveau things. Entering a crowded field, Miller nevertheless would fill a need. Apart from country music "hat acts" vowing to introduce a boot up the enemy's ass, conservatives have few showbiz performers to voice their un-pent-up feelings. Professional comics with conservative convictions being as rare as village smithies, there was a daylight opening for a sass master like Dennis Miller to move in and set up a concession stand. Yet it was a risky gambit. Slanting right violated so many comedy norms. Comics tend to throw rude uppercuts. They're little bullies picking on big bullies, to lift a line from Groucho Marx, directing the firepower of their anger and ridicule at the adults in charge, whether it's Lenny Bruce taking on "Religion, Inc," Sam Kinison wailing against the Almighty, or Rodney Danger-field bellyaching like a modern Job. Comics are licensed to deflate egos and false prides, topple the plaster saints from their pedestals, say the unsayable. To side with authority, uphold the status quo, click their sandals together, and cry, "Hail, Caesar!" goes against the grain of most comics' contrarian nature. But Dennis Miller isn't most comics, and after September 11 he was willing to humble himself before a higher power.

The Caesar to whom Miller swore allegiance was George Bush, Jr. Here was a load he could look up to, a stalwart leader who didn't allow too much headwork to interfere with his deci-sion making. Bush goes with his gut, and Miller gladly goes with him, believing personal virtue and a moral compass take precedence over pulsating brainpower: "Bill Clinton has single-handedly reminded me that even if you are the smartest man out there, what matters more to me is if, as president, you are a good man." Like so many attack poodles, he fashions Bush as America's father figure post-9/11, but it isn't the father figure as protector and comforter that speaks to Miller. He's turned on by Dad the Strict Disciplinarian. He compared the war in Iraq to a long, squabbling family car ride with Bush in the driver's seat and about to lose it. "Bush is the father and he's been screaming, 'Don't make me come back there!' for around 200 miles now, and it just reached the point where we had to pull the car over and the bad kid is going to get the spanking of his life." On *The Tonight Show* broadcast of February 25, 2003, Miller, like a hopeful suitor proposing marriage to his fiancée on the Jumbotron, made a public overture to Bush. "[If] you're watching, I want to just say, I think you're doing a hell of a job and I'm proud that you're my president. I want to thank you and wish you Godspeed because you got a tough deal of the cards."

His gesture was appreciated and reciprocated. Miller was invited to ride in the president's limousine during the president's fund-raising swing through California and was given the honor of flying in Air Force One. "I spent an amazing couple of hours with Dennis Miller," Bush said at the Los Angeles fund-raiser. "He keeps you on your toes." While Bush was on his toes, Miller was dancing on air. Surrendering every ounce of dignity, happy to play the hallowed flunky, Miller took to describing himself as "a Rat Pack of one for the president in

Hollywood." Of course, it's hard to swing when you're the only rat in the pack. Frank could snap his fingers and order up a fresh shipment of showgirls to help him and his pals polish off a late round of martini-toonies. I picture Miller swigging bottled water in the blue of the night, wondering if he'll ever be able scrape up his own entourage or if all his former so-called friends in showbiz will shun him at the Golden Globes for buffing Bush's halo. This is the price one pays for the lonely decision to defend a popular president.

Original Rat Packer Sammy Davis, Jr. never lived down hugging Richard Nixon (our least huggable chief executive) on stage. Miller hasn't laid a full-body hello on the president, but he's shown himself willing to roll over and fetch with an enthusiasm even Sammy might have found uncool. Miller finds it a total gas the way Bush vows to go after terrorists. Our dude in chief has the tenacity of a bounty hunter, man. "Bush will just not go off message. He's like a Doberman on a hambone. The president is a real grinder, as far as the terrorists go, and that Mossad-like mind-set is simultaneously our best protection and their worst nightmare. I also like it when President Bush gets PO'd and starts dropping the 'g's at the end of his verbs. We're not 'hunting' anybody. We're huntin' 'em." On the "submicroscopic chance" that Bush loses reelection, Miller takes solace in knowing that the president's Steve McQueen steely blues will be scanning the horizon for human prey until the last nanosecond before his successor is sworn in. "I guarantee you, up until that precise instant he'll be intensely focused on killing all the bad guys. As a matter of fact, by then he might have dropped the whole 'ing.'"

A man of action when it comes to flexing his jaw muscles, Bush personally isn't doin' the killin' any more than he's doin' the dyin', but Miller, collecting dropped *g*'s as if they were spent cartridges, has convinced himself that talking a good war is some kind of wonderful. That's what befalls an educated mind once it starts jock-sniffing around the war room. He even ascribes Corleone *cojones* to Dick Cheney (if Bush is the country's testy dad, Cheney's the grumpy grandpa), as the veep hides in undisclosed locations and plays deathmaster via remote control. "You don't ever see Cheney any more since this hit the fan. Because he's in a bunker pushing buttons ending enemies' lives, you know? That's a tough guy. Cheney's thinking, Listen, I got a bum ticker, I'd like nothing more than to take a couple of you punks with me." This may account for Cheney's killing spree in late 2003, when he slaughtered seventy ring-necked pheasants in a canned hunt at the exclusive Rolling Rock Club, an orgy of blood and feathers. An estimated four hundred out of five hundred birds were blown out of the sky by Cheney and his fellow sportsmen, including Supreme Court Justice Antonin Scalia.

Dennis Miller functions as more than the toastmaster general for the fund-raiser in chief. He may still call himself a loose-floating "libertarian conservative," but he's fastened on the spiked collar of an attack poodle, taking on Bush's enemies as his own. Apart from a few lifestyle differences on gay marriage and such, he subscribes to the neoconservative agenda. Their target list is his target list.

Insult the French? Check. "I would call the French scumbags, but that, of course, would be a disservice to bags filled with scum." He also contributed to international comity by accusing the French of forgetting whose army liberated them from Nazi oppression. "You've got all those boys buried in Normandy. And after we had the good taste to chisel the armpit hair off the Statue of Liberty you gave us...."

The Germans? Another nation of no-goods. "You going to rely on the Germans?... They know they've got the skankiest track record on the planet earth, so now they'll be obstinate about being pacifists."

The loyal opposition? Pin the tail on the donkeys. "The Democrats continue to snipe at Bush. They'll never give it up to him. You know Teddy Kennedy and Tom Daschle pick more nits than a father and son spider-monkey team who know they're being followed by a *National Geographic* film crew." He called Congressman Jim McDermott a "punk" for criticizing Bush from Baghdad; diagnosed the "pop-eyed" look on House Minority Leader Nancy Pelosi's face ("I thought she might be hyperthyroid, but then I heard her speak.... She's stupid! The reason her eyes are so wide is that she's as shocked as we are that she made it that high!"); and mocked Senator Robert Byrd of West Virginia, whose denunciations of Bush's sloppy Iraqi-war planning proved prophetic, for having senior moments on the Senate floor. "I think he must be burning the cross at both ends," Miller quipped at a Bush fund-raiser, a low blow that provoked scattered boos from the Republican faithful. (Byrd was a member of the Klan a half century ago and has not only apologized but avoided race-baiting since, which is more than can be said of some of his Southern colleagues.) Temporarily losing his hepcat cool, Miller tried to scramble out of trouble. "Well, he was in the Klan. Boo me, but he was in the Klan." Once a comedian's reduced to explaining and defending his jokes, he might as well straighten his Easter bonnet and head home.

Oil in Alaska? Start drilling. "Screw the caribou! I don't give a shit about the caribou. I say you run a pipe in there and suck it dry."

Civil liberties? We don't need no stinkin' liberties. "[P]eople say it's not the American way to infringe on civil liberties. Well, it's not the American way to roll over for punks either. We've got to start kicking ass on these people because they don't care about us. They live for one reason and one reason alone, and that is to kill you and I." When Miller gets ungrammatical, you know he's riled. It's like the Bush Man droppin' his *g*'s.

Nowhere has Miller gone more neocon than in his hearty advocacy of hegemony through intimidation. In neoconservative circles this principle is known as the "Ledeen Doctrine," named after author and policy analyst Michael Ledeen, who reportedly told an audience at the American Enterprise Institute, "Every ten years or so, the United States needs to pick up some small crappy little country and throw it against the wall, just to show the world we mean business." The Ledeen Doctrine has become an article of faith for attack poodles such as Jonah Goldberg and Mark Steyn. Grenada, which President Reagan invaded in 1983 to rescue American medical students, qualified as a small mangy mutt of a country, complete with tin-pot dictator. (It was speculated that Reagan needed an easy win after the debacle in Beirut, where 241 servicemen died in a bombing of their barracks. America's swift withdrawal from

Lebanon was seen as a sign of weakness, which Reagan wanted to reverse.) Another example of the Ledeen Doctrine in action came in 1989 when, under orders from President Bush the elder, the American military swooped down on Panama to nab its military ruler, Manuel Noriega, on drug-running charges. Called "Operation Just Cause," the campaign, which may have cost the lives of more than three hundred Panamanian civilians, according to a report from Physicians for Human Rights, was cynically referred to by some U.S. officers as "Operation Just Because," as in, "Why are we attacking Panama? Just because we can." Even if such a smackdown fails to elevate respect abroad for the United States, it provides a temporary morale boost at home, making Americans proud to have watched their television sets during those crucial days. Iraq's long history of swallowing and eventually spitting out foreign occupiers should have cautioned those tempted to assign it to the crappy-little-country category of a Panama or Grenada, but Miller, like Ledeen, Steyn, and Goldberg, was undaunted.

"You've got to get in there and slap these guys around," Miller told Leno. The threat to the world from Hussein's suspected weapons of mass destruction, the torture and enslavement of the Iraqi people, the deliverance of democracy to that troubled region—this was just parsley on the plate as far as he was concerned. "Am I the only one who could care less about weapons of mass destruction? I mean, that wasn't the whole point of the war for me. It was just to, you know...kick somebody's ass to get the domino effect going around the world." America doesn't owe anybody an explanation. Let our gun barrels do the talking. "[T]he next time we go to war, don't give a specific reason for the war that the left can seize upon and later flog us with it ad nauseam, just do it. Remember, the first rule of the Fight Club is that you don't talk about Fight Club."

As Fight Club promoter, Miller wants the media to obey a code of silence as well. Forget all that civics class bunk about a free press and an informed populace. The Founding Fathers may have believed in those Enlightenment ideals, but in the age of terrorism they're as quaint as sewing bees. Americans reserve the right to wage war on foreign soil without getting overwhelmed or upset by too much information. "If the working press is listening out there," Miller said during one of his *Tonight Show* visits, "you always say that during this war it's the public's need to know about our ground forces being in there and stuff like that.... [A]nd I want to say to you tonight, 'We don't want to know!' Okay? They're young boys [Miller apparently having forgotten the military is sexually integrated], it's scary enough, leave 'em alone! Everybody say it, 'We don't want to know!'" And as Jay Leno chimed in with an amen, Miller and the studio audience chanted, "We don't want to know!" *We Don't Want to Know* could be the hear-no-evil, see-no-evil slogan of the American people during the Bush II years, a willed ignorance and apathy encouraged by a timid press and happy-dust sprinklers such as Miller and Leno.

Supporting the troops didn't always mean signing up for a lobotomy and forfeiting your humanity. Bob Hope was a Republican and unabashed patriot, entertaining the troops from World War II though the first Gulf War and cracking jokes about the enemy. But as America's chief morale officer and comic ambassador, he risked his life flying in and out of the theaters of battle and visiting hospital wards, trying to buck up young men lying in beds with severe burns, bandaged eyes, missing limbs. "Probably the most difficult, the most tearing thing of all, is to be funny in a hospital," John Steinbeck wrote in 1943. "The long, low buildings are dispersed in case they should be attacked. Working in the gardens, or reading in the lounge rooms are the ambulatory cases in maroon bathrobes. But in the wards, in the long aisles of pain the men lie, with eyes turned inward on themselves, and on their people. Some are convalescing with all the pain and itch of convalescence. Some work their fingers slowly, and some cling to the little trapezes which help them to move in bed.

"And Bob Hope and his company must come into this quiet, inward, lonesome place, and gently pull the minds outward and catch the interest, and finally bring laughter up out of the black water. There is a job."

A job Hope did again and again, for decades, his hospital rounds teaching him never to regard war as a lark, or human life as something to be sacrificed lightly. Even raffish comedians were more morally serious in Hope's generation; they had grown up in times of hardship and didn't treat war as a relief from boredom, a spectator sport. It takes a lot of jaded emptiness inside to be as nihilistic as Miller has become, so nihilistic that he can suggest setting off a nuke as if it were a no bigger deal than popping open a can of Bud. "I don't even understand why we've taken nuclear weapons off the table. I mean, we treat them like our mother's good china. We never use them. I think you've got to pick a day where there's no wind, in a desolate part of the Earth, just blow off a bomb just to let them know we're sitting on a nice hold card, okay?" We dropped a couple in Japan in the forties, as I recall. I think everyone's aware of the cards we're holding.

Sir Elton John was offended when he had to follow Miller on stage at a Las Vegas fund-raiser after the comic had spent twenty minutes being a naughty scamp about "not caring about blowing the Baghdad Museum to bits, and...advocating killing caribou and raping Alaska for oil" (Timothy McDarrah, *Las Vegas Sun*). Cable news executives apparently were less fastidious. In the summer of 2003, Fox News, the hard right's home of the whoppers, hired Miller as a weekly commentator on *Hannity & Colmes*. As if telecommuting from an isolation booth, Miller dished out his commentaries directly to the camera from a nondescript studio, hunched forward like a salesman trying to close the deal, repeating (or rehearsing) much of the same material trotted out on *The Tonight Show*. But here there was no laughter, applause, and banter with Leno to jewel-case the jokes. In this zero-atmosphere setting, the words and the sentiments behind them jabbed out in stark relief. It was like getting a raw feed from Miller's fume pipe, which made you realize that his militancy was no showbiz masquerade—he sounds, glares, and sneers like a man who has shriveled inside. The rancor of his opinions roils up his features, inflames his bleary eyes. Once I was watching him on Fox know-nothingly mocking concerns about global warming and, unable to endure any more of such Rush Limbaugh Limburger, I turned down the sound on the set. Miller was even harder to endure with the sound off. His mute, naked face looked as if he had entered the get-acquainted stage of damnation. It was the portrait of a man who'd found his creed only to lose his soul.

But there are a lot of lost souls floating around show business, and some of them enjoy very successful careers and win the respect of their equally soul-dead peers. Showbiz can be very accepting of the unliving, and with his arrival in the poodle parlor, Miller did seem to be back in the game. The bounce he received from his *Tonight Show* and Fox News soapbox routines landed him his own weeknight talk show on CNBC, a network in need. Ratings for the financial news channel had been in a rut ever since Wall Street entered a bear market in the spring of 2000, disillusioning and dejecting the legion of stock ticker addicts who once doted upon Maria Bartiromo's every sultry trading-floor report. To brighten its staid, stagnating brand, CNBC went on a hiring spree, adding personalities to its talk lineup with some colorful pop to their personas, live wires such as former editor Tina Brown, advertising whiz Donny Deutsch (touted as "last of the Madison Avenue wild men"), and, their big catch, Miller. Of the three, Miller seemed the safest selection, considering his seasoned record as a comedy performer and host.

Dennis Miller's talk show, *Millertime*, came rattling out of the assembly plant in January 2004, in immediate need of retooling. A few reviewers questioned his choice of a chimpanzee as an occasional sidekick. Miller explained that his diapered cohost was intended to be an homage to J. Fred Muggs, the banana peeler who shared the desk at the original *Today* show with television pioneer Dave Garroway. It was unclear as to why Miller was saluting the pioneer days of television, or what affinity he believed he shared with the gentlemanly Garroway. The simian sidekick seemed to be one of those whims that went too far. Still others retched at the transformation of Miller from smart-aleck iconoclast to suck-up extraordinaire. Even publications predisposed to embrace Miller's political conversion shied away from the damp spot he left in the studio after the orgy of hero worship he conducted opening week. "Just look at the guest list for his first three nights—Governor Schwarzenegger on Monday, John McCain on Tuesday, and Mayor Giuliani on Wednesday—and you realize how freely Mr. Miller has traded in his newfound right-wing capital for access," TV reviewer David Blum wrote in the conservative *New York Sun*. "The trouble with trading beliefs for interviews is that when you get them, you go limp." Miller fawned over Schwarzenegger, for whom he had campaigned in the recall effort, saving some obsequiousness for the following nights with McCain and Rudy. Gushing over three Republicans in a row—well, at least no one could say Miller wasn't consistent. He was little better with the guests, revealing himself as blasé and disdainful of soiling his hands with newsprint as the president he so admires. In the *Daily News*, TV reviewer David Bianculli, who rated the show one and a half stars out of a possible four, wrote, "When author Naomi Wolf sensed Miller wasn't fully informed about the news event she was discussing, she asked, 'Did you read the paper today?' Her question was rhetorical; his answer, a quick 'No,' stunned her so much, her head snapped back." Maybe he was busy cleaning out the chimp cage that day and needed the paper to line the bottom.

He's more at ease with pundits of his own persuasion, such as "my friend" David Horowitz, a right-wing provocateur who Miller introduced as "David Hero-witz." Horowitz feigned maidenly modesty at receiving so handsome a tribute, reverting to character later in the broadcast by telling left-wing journalist Greg Palast, "Just shut up, okay?" As with his Fox commentaries, Miller's CNBC show had no studio audience, which meant that he was playing to the stagehands, guys in thick-soled shoes. When a joke bombed, as it often did, or when an esoteric reference flew over everyone's head, an even more frequent occurrence, Miller's desperate cackle of nervous laughter to cover the dead spots was painful. Gallows humor, without the humor. After the curiosity factor wore off and the ratings from the first week sunk slowly in the west, veteran producer Steve Friedman (formerly the executive producer of NBC's *Today*) was brought in as a consultant to tinker and twirl the show up a notch. His first remodeling decision was to troop in a small studio audience for a more nightclubby atmosphere, and spare us further ordeals of a comedian drowning in dry air.

What a new producer can't do is prevent Miller's new kinda love from expiring beyond its sell-by date. Not even a miracle worker can reverse the zeitgeist, and Miller's plight is that he hitched himself to the popularity and political fortunes of George Bush when he was riding high, and, having bought into Bushism at the market top, is now stuck with him on the ride down. In the brief lag between Miller's leaving his Fox News gig and launching on CNBC, opinion rolled over on the president. Bush had finally exhausted his post-9/11 fund of good faith. The slow accumulation of all his lies, meretriciousness, mind-stunting banalities, and complacent simplicities reached a tipping point when his slippage became unignorable even to the most obtuse, i.e., the media elite. His flat State of the Union address and faltering *Meet the Press* appearance were too glaring to be gauzed over. George Will clucked with disapproval at Bush's "rhetorical carelessness and overreaching." It wasn't just the poodle class that began to see that the emperor had no drawers. Don Imus, a former Bush supporter, became so fed up over the WMD deceptions and the loss of life in Iraq that he switched allegiance, and shock jock Howard Stern pivoted against Bush with a vengeance after the FCC started cracking down on radio vulgarity. It's a bad omen when two vital indicators of the vox populi turn negative, early warning signs of deeper brewings of discontent. And sure enough, Bush's poll ratings soon confirmed a downturn in sentiment, his approval numbers dipping to their lowest levels since 9/11, and he began losing hypothetical presidential matchups against John Kerry, John Edwards, and an unnamed lump of dough. Bush's babysitters may mop up the mess, bury Kerry in guano, and divert attention by staging the overthrow of another weak Third World government, but Bush has lost the leadership aura of a president who rises to the challenge to meet History head-on. Behind his leather hide is just another political hack. Bush has lied to us for so long that (fatal error) he *bores* us, and our boredom has allowed us to see how bald the lies are, and how mechanical is the man behind them.

What's a poor attack poodle to do when his master goes astray? There seemed nothing but blue sky above when Miller began defying his fellow Hollywood phonies and defending George Bush to the roaring approval of the Leno audience. He could exploit that whole phony elitist/populist, blue state/red state, nanny-hiring/home-schooling divide that has yielded such valuable ore for Limbaugh, O'Reilly, Savage, Bennett, and other inflatable balloons. But Miller came late to the gold rush, and his ideological sex change was predicated upon the hero worship of one simple, godly, warmongering man. The others bought the entire conservative package. Most of them won't hesitate to abandon Bush as they did his father should the mark of the loser be upon him, then shop around for another chump. Miller can't express buyer's remorse after so howling a conversion. He repulsed his old liberal fans by swerving right, and if he starts bitching about Bush, he'll alienate his new conservative fans, leaving him with nobody, nothing. He's aware of the trap he's in. When Miller expresses his respect for the prez, his volume level drops and the words seem to wash out from under him. You could almost feel some cheap sympathy for him, had he not been so giddy at the prospect of playing court jester for a throne of blood.

Hour of the Wolfhound

T HE ATTACK POODLES no longer swish their tails as high and jauntily as they once did. They've lost some of the snap in their judgments, some of the gutturals in their growls. Their group coordination has been temporarily severed. Accustomed to being on the scented hunt, chomping after rumors and accusations that they usually planted themselves, attack poodles are milling around backstage, waiting for new pages from rewrite. The original script had to be chucked, and such a beautiful script it was, too, one with action, pathos, stirring dialogue, moments of suspense, and a satisfying payoff. Victory in Iraq would sweep all before it, confounding the dubious. "Once we have victory in Baghdad, all the critics will look like fools," Dick Cheney predicted to a British official in 2002, according to *Financial Times* editor Philip Stephens in his book *Tony Blair: The Making of a World Leader*. Liberated Iraq would become a model of stability, nascent democracy, and market capitalism in the Mideast, putting Syria, Iran, and others on notice that they might be the next beneficiary of regime change. At home, the twin injections of tax cuts and Fed easing would jazz the markets and give Larry Kudlow and Jim Cramer something to high-five about every night on CNBC. The Democrats, ricocheting around the rubber room with frustration over Bush's uncanny ability to win every immunity challenge—as telegraphed in the taunting subtitle of John Podhoretz's book *Bush Country: How Dubya Became a Great President While Driving Liberals Insane*, published in early 2004—would nominate a hothead with an autodestruct button in the middle of his forehead, like Howard Dean. Or, just as sweet a prospect, some designated patsy to take one for the team until Manchurian candidate Hillary Clinton could make her move in 2008, allowing Bush an easy trot to the winner's circle in 2004. At the Republican Convention in New York City, against the backdrop of Ground Zero a week before the third anniversary of September 11, George Bush and Dick Cheney would salute cheering throngs of white people like Roman coemperors, as a grateful nation paid tribute (and a gridlocked Manhattan grumbled). A Republican landslide in November would give coemperors the votes they needed in the Congress to make the tax cuts permanent, appoint whichever backwoods judges they wanted, aggrandize the military even more, and pave enough forests, wetlands, and wildlife preserves to protect future generations of fat kids from the pushy demands of songbirds and other endangered species. Yes, from the windows of the Bush White House, the future looked awful pretty.

But karma paid an early call on the Bush administration, which had pitched its mansion upon a mound of bleached bones and tattered truths. Victory in Iraq, far from making the critics look like fools, vindicated them. "Simply stated, there is no doubt that Saddam Hussein now has weapons of mass destruction. There is no doubt he is amassing them to use against our friends, against our allies, and against us," Cheney told a Veterans of Foreign Wars convention in August 2002, and what Cheney had no doubt of proved to be dead wrong. Our grand entry into Baghdad, meant to unreel like the liberation of Nazi-occupied Paris (with Geraldo Rivera substituting for Hemingway in dashing beret), montaged into *The Battle of Algiers*. On the one-year anniversary of the invasion of Iraq in March 2004, Colin Powell, Condoleezza Rice, and Donald Rumsfeld, making the rounds of the Sunday morning talk shows to trumpet the success of post-Hussein Iraqization, instead found themselves accounting for the amazing, invisible WMDs. A few days later, in a speech at the Ronald Reagan Presidential Library that was advertised in advance as a methodical amputating of John Kerry's record, Dick Cheney shared a split screen with live footage of the Lebanon Hotel burning in Baghdad after a car bomb explosion. The images of desperate shadows scurrying against smoke and flames clashed with the upbeat assessment of progress in Iraq from the shiny head being applauded at the podium.

The economy and the opposition party also declined to cooperate. Despite enough stimulus to revive the big-band era, the job market limped sideways, "outsourcing" became a dirty word, and the American consumer kept piling on debt like unwanted pounds, embedded in his own bloat, the deficit growing deep enough to produce an echo. And the Democrats, defying expectations, dropped out of kamikaze class. The subtitle of Podhoretz's *Bush Country* was mistaken: Dubya didn't drive liberals insane, he drove them sane. He made them realize the full awful, fanatical extent of what they were up against, the brutality behind his joshing banality. After a whirlwind infatuation with the hellzapoppin' Howard Dean, who articulated the anger they felt toward Bush and activated the mouse-clickers, trailblazing the use of cyberspace as a meeting place and fundraising tool, Democrats grouped behind a chiseled, reliable John Kerry, a Vietnam war veteran none dared call wimp. A decorated hero, as opposed to an action-figure doll.

After 9/11 Bush looked as if he could walk on water, as long as he had Karen Hughes and Karl Rove waiting on shore, clapping like seals. He then lumbered into 2004 barely able to take a step without falling into a well. His uninspired State of the Union address belonged on the rubber-chicken circuit. His "Mission to Mars" initiative was dead on the launchpad, prohibitively costly and transparently cynical, a grandiose-sounding stunt. The use of 9/11 imagery in his first positive reelection commercial provoked a backlash: a majority of Americans polled found the shot of the flag-draped coffin "inappropriate." The use of a swarthy male actor to signify the furtive face of terrorism in Bush's first negative commercial—jokily dubbed his "Muhammad Horton" ad, in honor of Willie Horton, the paroled killer whose scary black face glowered in attack ads against Michael Dukakis in 1988—was criticized for racially exploiting voters' fears. The Washington press corps nudged each other awake from their naps and began pecking press secretary Scott McClellan apart in the daily gaggle, refusing any longer to put up with Robby the Robot programmed reponses, the indomitable Helen Thomas once again flustering a presidential flak-catcher just like in the good old days. Best-selling exposés of the Bush administration by Richard Clarke, Bob Woodward, Joe Wilson, and John Dean set off successive bomb blasts in the media. Clarke's appearance on *60 Minutes* and his testimony before the September 11 commission—which was prefaced with an apology to the victims' families, and an admission of failure—was so compelling and authoritative that the attack poodles went after him *en masse*. Then they charged after commission members Jamie Gorelick and Richard Ben-Veniste, Democrats both.

For the first time in years, the attack poodles themselves met with more than token resistance. Chris Matthews once said that the purpose in booking liberals was so that they could have sand kicked in their faces by muscle-bound conservatives. (Never mind that the conservatives doing the kicking resembled beach balls more than Charles Atlas.) Tired of taking their daily whuppings, liberals began eating their spinach and building up their girly biceps. On Fox's *Hannity & Colmes*, Alan Colmes stopped playing chump and began standing up for himself and his opinions, to the amazement of those who had written him off as a lost cause. (One blogger attributed this to a long-distance spine transplant Colmes had received courtesy of Al Franken, whose example had emboldened him.) The best-seller list, which had been dominated by books with somber warnings such as *Evil Boll Weevil: Bill Clinton's Secret Plan to Make America Safe for Abortion, Satanism, and More*

Abortion, Hollywood Cesspool: How Liberalism Perverts the Movies You Watch with Your Children, and *Jesus Wept: Why Liberals Hate God and All That Is Good* made room for swashbuckling counterattacks by Michael Moore, Joe Conason, Eric Alterman, and Molly Ivins. Attack poodles met the counterattack with their own counterattack, bringing out even more titles brandishing the words "evil," "Clinton," and "liberal(ism)," such as Sean Hannity's *Deliver Us from Evil,* R. Emmett Tyrrell, Jr.'s *Madame Hillary: The Dark Road to the White House,* Rich Lowry's *Legacy: Paying the Price for the Clinton Years,* and Andrew Breitbart and Mark Ebner's *Hollywood Interrupted: Insanity Chic in Babylon—The Case Against Celebrity.*

That the attack poodles were reduced to recycling their bile should not be construed as a momentary lapse of imagination on their part. They never had any imagination to lapse on them, apart from the capacity to imagine the worst about their enemies and the best about themselves (how they would have defied Hitler had they been alive in those decisive years). No, the poodles were paddling in place because they had no new demons to demonize and the old demons wouldn't do. A decade or two ago, gay marriage would have been a gift-wrapped godsend for them. Lesbians in lumberjack plaids exchanging vows, leather boys in chaps clutching bridal bouquets, drag queens voguing down the aisle in glittery Cher gowns—so many stereotypes just dying to be dangled in front of decent folk for a good scare. But the popularity of *Will & Grace*, *Queer Eye for the Straight Guy*, *The L Word*, and Ellen DeGeneres's daytime chat show alerted attack poodles that gay-baiting no longer flew, that familiarity had bred affection. Gone were the days when Rush Limbaugh could get away with joking, as he did during the early nineties, "When a gay person turns his back on you, it's anything but an insult—it's an invitation." As Frank Rich and others observed, the outré spectacle of Gay Pride Day in San Francisco, with its parade floats of transvestite nuns and muscular men in dog collars, was supplanted with footage of just-married gay couples kissing happily on the courthouse steps, most of them middle-aged, middle-class, and as boring-looking as everybody else: a bunch of normos, to borrow a word from the late Tony Randall. When the Reverend Jerry Falwell wagged his jowls on TV and resuscitated the hoary wisecrack about how marriage was intended to be between Adam and Eve, "not Adam and Steve," you winced with embarrassment for him, that he was that old and out-of-it.

Attack poodles could count no longer on the culture war to furnish them a decisive wedge advantage. The same bottom-heavy, entertainment-drunk country that makes a megahit out of Mel Gibson's piously sado-mazzy *The Passion* watches *The Sopranos*, listens to Howard Stern, and makes pop tarts out of porn stars (Jenna Jameson) and supercool icons out of marijuana-wafting mack daddies (Snoop Dogg). Culture isn't an either/or proposition, despite what virtucrats such as William Bennett may claim. America doesn't want Family Values or Godless Decadence—it wants both, or neither; it pays its money and it makes its tacky choice. As Oliver Willis wrote on *Daily News Online*, "One of the reasons why right-wing media mogul Rupert Murdoch is shelling out billions of dollars for the DirecTV satellite network is that they generate cash like crazy from pay-per-view porn." The culture war isn't winnable, but it is losable, as witness the defections of Don Imus and Stern, proof that the president was alienating the key morning-drive-time white-guy vote. And when Mel Gibson, who had risen to the eminence of savage messiah among religious conservatives, mumbled his own doubts about Bush's mishandling of WMDs, it further smeared the chalk lines that the cultural warriors had so carefully drawn.

However, attack poodles are nothing if not tenacious. Retreat equals defeat in their lexicon. Confronted with adversity, they don't give in to doubt and discouragement. They take a long weekend by the pool to reflect, dig a millimeter deep into themselves and resolve to become even meaner and more uncompromising in their devotion to sowing fear and half truths. That's what they were put on this granite planet to do. In March 2004, Fox News queried guests about a new poll published in the conservative *Washington Times* claiming that a majority of Americans surveyed thought that terrorists would prefer Kerry for president over Bush. Terrorists, of course, are notoriously tricky to poll; they cherish the privacy of their clandestine cells, and don't tend to take phone calls from strangers with a slate of nosy questions. So the pollsters asked a sampling of idiot Americans to surmise whom terrorists would prefer as president if terrorists could be polled—polls don't get any more "meta" and tendentious than that. Intended message: Elect Kerry, and the terrorists win. Making this even more of a sham sandwich was that the sampling was conducted by a research firm with Republican connections: a partisan poll published in a partisan paper and disseminated by a partisan cable channel. The entire sordid charade made blogger Billmon bitterly question humanity. "Every time—*every time*—I think it can't get any worse, some tub of rancid pork guts masquerading as a human being crawls up out of the political sewer and proves me wrong again."

Can the attack poodles be spayed? It's difficult—but doable. Granted, they're hard to house-train. Most of them know not shame, never regret the deliberate or sideswipe damage they do. They leak no more sympathy for their ideological targets than Ann Coulter does for the victims of the McCarthy era. They adopt the attitude of William *Naked Lunch* Burroughs, who argued there are no such things as "innocent bystanders"—hell, what were they doing standing there in the first place? Dedicated attack poodles cling fast to their insincere convictions even in the cascade of evidence to the contrary, smoothing their eyebrows in the charming reflection of their own "moral clarity." And why should they reform their wicked ways? They didn't get where they are and make the money they do by nuancing their way up the best-seller list or sprinkling grace notes into their syndicated columns. Attack poodles such as Ann Coulter, Mark Steyn, Jonah Goldberg, and even John Derbyshire (hard to believe, but there are those who dig his Old World uncharm) have fan followings that would defect in droves should they detect any signs of softening or straddling. Poodle readers want poodle authors to remain at the same stage of immaturity so that they can all grow older but no wiser together. But there are steps that can be taken to limit the destruction that attack poodles do, confine them to the porch as much as possible, and diminish them to the insignificance they deserve.

Quarantine falsifiers and plagiarists. We're not talking about isolated mistakes or ugly splats of hyperbole. We're talking about patterns of misbehavior, a track record of muddy footprints tramped all over the facts. Journalists can hardly hold politicians and other public officials to even loose standards of veracity if they tolerate truth-molesters such as Ann Coulter, Matt Drudge, and other attack poodles. The cuddling of serial fabricator Jayson Blair is instructive. When Blair's memoir *Burning Down My Masters' House* was published in 2004, most of the print reviewers treated his self-serving account of his brief, inglorious career at the *New York Times* as if it were a patch of dried vomit. "Shoddily written," "A great big non-apology apology that would make Pete Rose proud," were among the kinder discernments. But on cable news, Blair was hugged with a hero's welcome. On *Hardball*, Matthews effused over this little punk as if he were ready to step into Thomas Wolfe's gargantuan shoes. "Why—you are such a damn good writer, a creative force," Matthews told Blair. "You have fluency and life.... [Your book] moves. It's got air. It's got oxygen, the thing you always look for in writing. What's it like to be that creative? You are obviously a guy who can knock out 120,000 words in a month.... You're one of these guys who can do it magically. Do you know that?" Blair modestly confessed that he didn't truly know what a fluent, oxygen-filled, magical life force he was until he left the *Times*. But now that he does believe in himself again, he's ready to make a grab for the bitch goddess of success and write a novel, earning the Maxwell Perkins nod from Matthews, who assured Blair of a promising future in fiction because he possessed the two most shining prerequisites: "You're a great writer and you know how to lie." It was intended as an unalloyed compliment. On Fox News, Bill O'Reilly also bounced Blair on his avuncular knee, happy to encourage this moocher, who has admitted swapping sexual favors for drugs, bemoan the "amoral" atmosphere at the *Times*. Unbaggaged with self-knowledge, Blair seemed to blame the *Times* for sustaining a sleazy environment in which a sleazy hustler like him could thrive; plus, they sometimes forgot to refill the snack machines. An item in New York's *Daily News* reported that Blair's numerous appearances and mentions on Fox News and Fox affiliates helped goose his book sales a tad, which had been lagging despite the ballyhoo. If the penalty for lying is repeated bookings on cable news and increased notoriety, what incentive is there to stay straight? A lax attitude is what lets attack poodles feel they can blurt anything without consequences. It's up to viewers, bloggers, and fellow journalists to restore the sting of stigma to journalism's betrayers, and to chastise their enablers. It'll take a lot of chastising but that's what e-mail is for.

Feed attack poodles their own questions. Political journalists traditionally portray themselves as fulfilling the role of the people's representatives, honest referees between the public and their elected officials, custodians of the commonweal. But increasingly many political journalists, even those who can't strictly be classified as attack poodles, see and conduct themselves as players, poking their own egos between the tent flaps and trying to midwife Defining Moments in the permanent campaign. They're less interested in eliciting information than in laying traps, and in so doing they've made themselves fair game. Any anchorman or reporter who dart-tosses "gotcha" questions at candidates about their marital histories, sexual pasts, drug use, and financial assets ought to be prepared to answer the same questions. If it's in the public's interest to know which lobbyists are funding a presidential contender's campaign to determine how they may be influencing policy decisions, it's also in the public's interest to know from whom the anchors, pundits, and other "influentials" have taken money from over the years through speaking and consulting fees, and what their stock holdings are—do a background check to determine *their* possible conflicts of interest. If it's considered the public's right to know about a candidate's messy divorce, let's lay everyone's messy divorces out there on the table; ditto, the history of drug and alcohol use. If talk show hosts are going to impugn someone's war record, get them to answer what they were doing stateside during Vietnam, make them discuss their deferments. Religion has become another refuge for reportorial scoundrels. When Elisabeth Bumiller of the *New York Times* snaps at Democratic candidates during the New York primary debate, "Really quick, is God on America's side?" I want to know what Miss Snippy thinks the correct answer is to the question, what relevance she thinks the question has to anything resembling reality, and if that's how they taught the art of interviewing in journalism school back in the little house on the prairie.

An effective display of batting a question back at the pitcher was demonstrated by Richard C. Holbrooke, former United Nations ambassador and author of *To End a War*, who was interviewed by CNN's Wolf Blitzer about Kerry's claim that unnamed foreign leaders told him *sotto voce* that they wanted him to beat Bush. At the end of the usual back and forth, Holbrooke was fed up with this dopey cha-cha lesson. "John Kerry said something everybody knows is true. And,

Wolf, you know it's true.... Why don't you, instead of staging a silly he said/he said between the White House, which is throwing all this mud at John Kerry after he said something true. Why don't you poll your foreign correspondents on CNN? And ask them who the population and leaderships in the world would prefer to see elected? Very simple." Too simple, which is probably why the Wolf Man didn't think of it. Like most TV interviewers, he works automatically in a binary mode of accusation and response ("How do you respond, Senator, to the accusation that you're cold and unfeeling?"), and clings to his sheaf of prepared questions like a play prompter. That's what attack poodles rely on—getting their bullet points into the news media's automatic repeaters. Jam the process, and the process will be revealed for the mindless ritual it is.

Beware of small concessions. Contest each inch of political ground. Nothing is too trivial for attack poodles to leverage into something larger. Every conflict fits somewhere on their spectrum of overarching dominance. Attack poodles excel at seizing upon emotionally fraught issues such as late-term abortion, child pornography, or wildfires and exploiting them to extend their reach into women's reproductive rights, curbs on artistic expression, and the logging of western forests. A victory in banning late-term abortion won't placate "pro-life" advocates; they will train sights on the next set of restrictions until the full realization of their goals, the revocation of *Roe v. Wade*, and the criminalization of abortion. Or take a nonsexy subject like partial privatization of Social Security. Free-market advocates speak as if they wish to shave off a minute slice of Social Security and allow people "to invest their own money in the market," but the larger goal, as anyone who has heard Grover Norquist and similar privateers proclaim, is to privatize the entire system and eventually raze this monument to FDR's New Deal. According to an article by Robert Dreyfuss in *The Nation*, Norquist conceives of the privatization of Social Security as a twenty-year project; his other dream projects include privatizing state and local pension plans, wresting control away from government. "We want to take that power and destroy it," Norquist said. Whenever attack poodles disparage the public sector, there's some industry's future profit opportunity they're pimping for, some safeguard they are looking to pillage. Assume every attack poodle is Attila the Hun until proven otherwise. It'll save time.

Adopt an attack poodle. The credit for this idea goes to blogger Steve Gilliard, who proposed what has come to be known as the Adopt a Journalist program, whose purpose is to hold political reporters accountable for their output. It's an exacting job, but it's become necessary to start following attack poodles around with pooper scoopers. The bungling performance of the press during the 2000 election must not be rerun, and one way to prevent a pathetic reenactment is to compile online dossiers of the couriers of slanted reporting and outright misinformation. "I think it would be a really, really good idea to track reporters word for word, broadcast for broadcast, and print the results online," Gilliard blogged. "Keeping score of who's right and wrong, how many times they repeat cannards [*sic*] like Al Gore invented the Internet and make obvious errors. Not accusations of ideology, but actual data and facts." An ongoing file on David Broder, the Alka-Seltzer dispenser of conventional wisdom from his pillar at the *Washington Post*, would provide a useful stream of box scores. Since fact–checking at newspapers is so hit and miss (mostly miss), this adoption program would have a secondary function of weeding out the undesirables. "If someone had actually checked Jayson Blair's work," Gilliard wrote, "the *Times* might have fired his ass years earlier." True, that might have cost future readers the lyric novel little Jayson has within him, but literature's loss would have been journalism's gain, and literature can take care of its own problems.

Some attack poodles have already been adopted by kind strangers. The blog SullyWatch, for example, has undertaken the Herculean task of cleaning out Andrew Sullivan's stall on a regular basis and keeping tabs on his political backflips. But there is ample room on the bandwidth for others. Some enterprising hobbyists should adopt Fox News attack poodles Fred Barnes and Mort Kondracke, the doddering "Beltway Boys." A running tally of their valentines to Republicans, neoconservative natterings, and foul-ball prognostications would be useful to political pathologists. Another attack poodle worth putting under flea watch is John Fund, who never goes anywhere without his ear-to-ear grin. He was a busy lad in the nineties. A former ghostwriter for Rush Limbaugh and an editorial writer at the *Wall Street Journal*, Fund, according to Eric Alterman in *What Liberal Media?* "spent a great deal of time" as a major mover in the get-Clinton conspiracy "meeting with members of the Arkansas Project and some of the more notorious figures in the Paula Jones lawsuit.... Fund acted as kind of a father figure to many of them, helping to guide their strategy in secret while simultaneously writing editorials in the *Journal* accusing

Clinton of all manner of unproven malfeasance." Proof, schmoof, it's all in the presentation. Fund has also been fingered, if you'll pardon the innuendo, as one of the sources for the *Drudge Report*'s spousal-abuse smear against former Clinton senior adviser Sidney Blumenthal. In *The Clinton Wars*, Blumenthal recounts a conversation with journalist Jennet Conant, who profiled Drudge for *Vanity Fair*. "'Fund spread the story,' she told me. 'He told the world. He told everyone in conservative circles. As soon as your appointment was announced, he started. I couldn't find anyone who didn't hear it from Fund.'" After some messy romantic contretemps involving a mistress, her daughter, and an abortion, Fund, who denied the charges, seemed to disappear for awhile. But he has popped up again for the 2004 election year, this time setting his salivary glands after John Kerry, joining those frog-bashers who allude to Kerry as "the junior senator from France." Considering how much vicious mischief Fund did during the Clinton presidency, his marauding mouth deserves monitoring.

Another in need of tracking is Katherine "Kit" Seelye, political correspondent of the *New York Times* and a chronic pain. She was one of the nastier scourges covering Al Gore's presidential campaign, a considerable achievement, and seems to apply a coat of clown makeup whenever she covers any

Democrat. Of Richard Gephardt's presidential bid, she shared this insightful pearl: "He has been on the inside for a quarter-century and has yet to solve the problems that he says he understands so well." Imagine, an incredulous Bob Somerby wrote on his *Daily Howler* site, "As a House member, Gephardt *failed to solve the nation's problems!* Where on earth—except in our press corps—can you find such consummate nonsense?" Where, indeed. After Gephardt withdrew from the race, Seelye directed her decoder ring on John Kerry, whose string of primary victories may have been impressive to some, but under closer divination were rather thin. "As a percentage of all 200 million potential voters nationwide, his support looks much smaller," Seelye informed *Times* readers. "Only 5 percent voted in the 20 Democratic primaries that produced the presumptive nominee; an even smaller percentage... voted for Mr. Kerry." This time it was the blogger Atrios's turn to be incredulous and a mite sarcastic. "Wow. Kit's so right. Not all people who voted actually voted in the Dem primaries so far. And, unbelievably, not all of those people voted for John Kerry! Wow! Gold star to Kit Seelye for Stupidity in Journalism." But is Katherine Seelye truly dunce material or is she *playing* dumb—a cunning attack poodle hiding behind a press badge and a bewildered expression? Her esteemed colleague at the

Times, La Bumiller, betrayed her attack poodle identity by barking at Kerry during the New York primary debate, "Are you a liberal?—Are you a liberal?" but Seelye should be presumed innocent pending investigation. That's the American way.

Unleash the wolfhounds! As mentioned in the opening chapter, liberals have their own attack poodles. But I prefer to think of them as wolfhounds, in honor of the Irish wolfhound. "Gentle when strok'd/Fierce when provoked," the wolfhound is, in the definitive words of the American Kennel Club, "a remarkable combination of power, swiftness, and keen sight." Granted, Clinton defender Paul Begala looks more like a Wallace and Gromit character, and his *Crossfire* costar James Carville is a furless wonder, but their TV appearances course with wolfhound spirit, as do the Democratic-tilting blogs of Al Giordano (bigleftoutside.com), Atrios (atrios.blogspot.com), Kos (dailykos.com), Steve Gilliard (stevegilliard.blogspot.com), Kevin Drum (resident blogger at washingtonmonthly.com), the anti–attack poodles at gadflyer.com, and satirical cut–ups such as Tom Bogg (tbogg.blogspot.com) and Roger Ailes (not to be confused with the cigar-chomping chief of Fox News—rogerailes.blogspot.com), all of whom now set the tempo and frame the debate in the blogosphere after the brief reign of the right-wing warbloggers. What differentiates wolfhounds from poodles is that wolfhounds embrace difference, practice inclusivity, and refuse to stoop to demonizing entire groups, countries, and beliefs. However supercharged their rhetoric, however raunchy their humor, they're more conscientious with the facts, more cognizant of social injustice and global repercussions, yet more fun to be around. Bookmark their sites; post in their comments sections; donate money to their tip jars. They are today's Tom Paines.

Fewer wolfhounds have achieved black-belt mastery in the moronic inferno of talk radio, where niceties go over like wilted lettuce. One valiant effort to raise the IQ level of talk radio above double digits and give liberal-progressive pinkos their own romper room on the dial is the new Air America network, with stations in New York, Chicago, Los Angeles, San Francisco, and other sinful metropolises. It's a cheekily named enterprise, "Air America" being the name of the CIA-run airline based in Laos (and the subject of a slapstick satire starring Mel Gibson and Robert Downey, Jr., as pilots doing everything from pig running to drug smuggling). Although any stab at nonreactionary radio is inevitably billed in the press as liberalism's belated answer to Rush Limbaugh, Air America isn't trying to duplicate his or anyone else's gunboat bombast. Its talent roster is a lighter, poppier, less ideological blend of comics and performers such as Marc Maron, Al Franken, Janeane Garofalo, rapper Chuck D., and Lizz Winstead, cocreator of Comedy Central's *Daily Show*, which, under host Jon Stewart, practices the art of the put-on to prick holes in hot-air buffoons. For younger viewers, *The Daily Show* isn't just satire, it's also a useful news source (like Jay Leno's monologues), another indicator of the surrealism of everyday life. Accenting humor is a smart strategy by the architects of Air America. "Denunciation is well enough," wrote the critic and agitator John Jay Chapman in 1900, "but laughter is the true ratsbane for hypocrites…for nature's revenge has given them masks for faces. You may see a whole room of them crack with pain because they cannot laugh." Especially at themselves. Richard Perle, Dick Cheney, George Bush; their masks would shatter like vases.

Even if Air America carves out a modest niche, it will be contending with the corporatization of broadcast opinion, which brings us to the next imperative.

Oust Michael Powell as chairman of the FCC. Son of Colin Powell, Michael Powell, chairman of the Federal Communications

Commission under Bush, is the grand pooh-bah of media consolidation. Under the guise of giving viewers "choice," he has swung his considerable rotundity behind every attempt for big media companies to become even bigger and concentrate the public airwaves in a few greedy private hands. It's probably not an accident that the press went gunning with extra zeal for Howard Dean after he began "bashing big media" (*Variety*) and advocating the breakup of media conglomerates, representing a dangerous challenge to the status quo. Big media has no better bud than Powell, who has seldom met a merger he couldn't sanctify with holy water. He also has been at the opportunistic forefront of the crackdown on "indecent broadcasting," the FCC exploiting the Janet Jackson brouhaha to levy fines against stations and owners culpable of gross vulgarity. It's a short hop from regulating smut to straitjacketing political expression, as Lenny Bruce found to his misfortune, and politicians have been falling all over themselves pushing bills in the Congress that would fine not only stations and owners but "nonlicensees"—i.e., talk show hosts, artists, comics, even callers. The butch-sounding Broadcast Decency Enforcement Act (Senate bill 2056), reported the *New York Daily News*, not only raises the ceiling for fines against individuals, but "would remove provisions for a warning and a hearing," eliminating any recourse for appeal.

This plays into the paws of the attack poodles. The Michael Savages, Rush Limbaughs, and Dr. Lauras will never be fined, no matter how odious their utterances. Their free speech will be protected, as it should be. It will be the free speech of those on the cultural and political left that will be arbitrarily policed. An ignoramus like "Bubba the Love Sponge" today, Howard Stern tomorrow, and—if he keeps grinding Dick Cheney into sausage, who knows?—Imus may find himself the next to find fines hanging over his curly head for some off-color remark from Lou or Bernie in the control room. Some optimists believe that the cleanup crusade will relent after the presidential election, when gutless politicans and bureaucrats are no longer quaking before public pressure. But punitive measures, once in place, are just begging to be abused, and a posturing panderer such as Michael Powell is just the man to take advantage. He's an attack poodle backed by the authority of the state.

Unleash the Wolfhound Within. Important as the news and opinion media are, they aren't all-important, and as vital as it is to support those doing battle with the attack poodles, letting others do the arguing remains a surrogate activity, a passive partic-

ipation, Homer Simpsonism. We must be our own wolfhounds. We must summon from within our own combination
of power, swiftness, and keen sight. *You Are the Message* was the
finger-jabbing title of the best-selling communications guide
by Fox News chairman Roger Ailes. Conservatives heeded that
rallying call. They became the individual missiles of their message. Liberals didn't. Ever since the likes of Rush Limbaugh
and Newt Gingrich started banging their washtubs in the
nineties against every full head of hair calling himself a Democrat, too many liberals have become meek and apologetic
about who they are, what they believe, what liberalism has
accomplished, what government can do, and who their heroes
are; they've lived down to the cliché that a liberal is someone
too wishy-washy to take his own side in an argument, some of
them sounding like NPR listeners on a slow train to Loserville.
Elected Democrats contracted this inner cringe. Few Democrats apart from a carom ball like Dennis Kucinich even dare
suggest that the mountainous defense budget be cut; they
accepted the premise that America is in a "war against terrorism," disputing only how best to wage it; they tiptoed around
affirmative action as if afraid it might wake up and start bawling;
they caved on civil liberties, helping pass the Patriot Act and
then assailing its worst infringements; they deplored the lies

that led us into Iraq and the lack of postwar planning, but shirked—still shirk—the responsibility of demanding the resignations of Powell, Rice, Rumsfeld, Wolfowitz, and the censures of Bush and Cheney. Until recently, congressional Democrats let themselves be regularly trounced by the Republicans like the dorky losers fielded to play against the Harlem Globetrotters, allowed to score a few dignity-saving points interspersed between flailing their arms and playing hapless defense.

Elected Democrats didn't suit up for offense until they felt the floorboards beneath their feet rock with the anger and frustration of Democrat voters, tired of hearing Tom Daschle and other Senate leaders using guidance-counselor language to lace-trim their defeatism. Again and again Daschle was "disappointed" in the president's actions or the Republicans' latest humiliation of a Democrat caucus, and when he wasn't "disappointed," he was "deeply disappointed," not to mention "concerned," "troubled," and, yes, "saddened." His face sagged like the doleful countenance of a Dust Bowl farmer. It wasn't until Mary Landrieu scored a surprise upset in the 2002 Louisiana Senate runoff, winning reelection to the Senate by running *against* Bush policies, and Howard Dean's campaign sizzled, that the Beltway brainos realized that, unlike them, registered Democrats weren't disappointed, concerned, troubled, both-ered, saddened, and sunken in malaise, they were truly, madly, deeply, mightily, righteously, scalp-huntingly pissed off. The Dems heeded the howl of the wolfhound and began acting like an opposition party again, filibustering some of the ideological dregs Bush insisted on trying to shovel onto the higher courts. Senator Ted Kennedy, the attack poodle's favorite poster boy of incontinent liberalism, a walking editorial cartoon, with his red bulbous nose and gut snowballing over his low-slung belt, lost weight and regained stature, sounding like his old magnificent self again. Those who ignored the cry of the wolfhound, like presidential candidate Joe Lieberman, found themselves discarded by the side of the road like a tin can.

Under George W. Bush, the United States has never been both more assertive and independent abroad, more cowering and dependent at home. Four more years of Bush's ignorance and arrogance, and Americans won't be able to touch down on foreign soil without feeling like the pariahs of the planet. If the United States reelects an unrepentant Bush, it will deserve pariahhood. We can't cop a second plea of innocence. George Bush forthrightly calls himself a war president, and as long as he is commander in chief the country will have a war mentality and be on a war footing. His reelection campaign will be a sustained fear-based initiative, his massive ad buys serving as his "Shock and Awe" bombardment, the attack poodles amplifying their alarmist messages. For attack poodles are the straw dogs of fear and loathing—four-legged scarecrows crouched at the cross-roads. Only when enough of us are tired of being afraid will the attack poodles and their masters be routed, and that will entail lighting a torch to each and every bundle of lies. I think that day is due. Too much anger is in the air, and the dead of 9/11 can no longer be yoked around the necks of those demanding answers. If Bush buys reelection, it will be a Pyrrhic victory, his second term as ravaged as Nixon's; he will not survive, and he will go down in history reviled. Let the bonfires burn. In the uncompromising words of John Jay Chapman, "It is necessary to destroy reputations when they are lies. Peace be to their ashes. But war and fire until they be ashes. This is positive and constructive work."

And don't let anyone tell you different.

ACKNOWLEDGMENTS

N O WRITER COULD WISH for a more generous support
system than the team of editors, copy editors, and
researchers at *Vanity Fair*, in particular my editor, the brilliant,
dynamic, and unstintingly-devoted-to-her-authors Aimee Bell;
her super assistant Abby Field; and Jennifer Massoni, who
compiled voluminous files for the chapters on Peggy Noonan
and Dennis Miller. Immense thanks to the editor of *Attack Poodles*, Chris Knutsen, who hopped aboard this speeding bullet
and calmly, deftly, encouragingly kept it from veering astray.
The credit for the title of this book belongs to my agent and
fearless champion Elyse Cheney. Lastly, this book couldn't
have been written without the inspiration and heroic example
of two writers to whom enough homage can never be paid,
Norman Mailer and Gore Vidal.

—J.W.